NON-STATE ACTOR DYNAMICS IN INTERNATIONAL LAW

Non-State Actors in International Law, Politics and Governance Series

Series Editors
Professor Dr Math Noortmann, Oxford Brookes University, UK
Dr Bob Reinalda, Radboud University Nijmegen, The Netherlands
Professor Dr Bas Arts, Radboud Wageningen University and Research Centre (WUR), The Netherlands

The proliferation of non-state actors in the international system over the last three decades has increased the need for a broader theoretical analysis and empirical validation. The series explores the capabilities and impact of non-state actors, such as privately-based transnational corporations, non-governmental organizations (NGOs), international criminal organizations, and liberation movements, as well as intergovernmental organizations (in which NGO's often participate). The series seeks to address this need and to deepen the knowledge and understanding of non-state actors by scholars, practitioners and students in the fields of international law, politics and governance. By emphasizing legal, political and governance aspects of non-state actors' activities at the international (global or regional) level, the series intends to transcend traditional disciplinary and organizational boundaries.

Also in the series

Making Corporate Social Responsibility a Global Concern
Norm Construction in a Globalizing World
Lisbeth Segerlund
ISBN 978 0 7546 7707 9

Partners in Peace
Discourses and Practices of Civil-Society Peacebuilding
Mathijs van Leeuwen
ISBN 978 0 7546 7743 7

Closing or Widening the Gap?
Legitimacy and Democracy in Regional Integration Organizations
Edited by Andrea Ribeiro Hoffmann and Anna van der Vleuten
ISBN 978 0 7546 4968 7

Choosing the Lesser Evil
Understanding Decision Making in Humanitarian Aid NGOs
Liesbet Heyse
ISBN 978 0 7546 4612 9

Non-State Actor Dynamics in International Law

From Law-Takers to Law-Makers

Edited by

MATH NOORTMANN
Oxford Brookes University, UK

and

CEDRIC RYNGAERT
Leuven University and Utrecht University

ASHGATE

Published by
Ashgate Publishing Limited
Wey Court East
Union Road
Farnham
Surrey, GU9 7PT
England

Ashgate Publishing Company
Suite 420
101 Cherry Street
Burlington
VT 05401-4405
USA

www.ashgate.com

British Library Cataloguing in Publication Data
Non-state actor dynamics in international law : from law-takers to law-makers. -- (Non-state actors in international law, politics and governance series)
1. Non-state actors (International relations)
2. Non-governmental organizations.
I. Series II. Noortmann, Math. III. Ryngaert, Cedric.
346'.064-dc22

ISBN-13: 9781409403166

Library of Congress Cataloging-in-Publication Data
Non-state actor dynamics in international law : from law-takers to law-makers / by Math Noortmann and Cedric Ryngaert.
p. cm. -- (Non-state actors in international law, politics and governance series)
Includes bibliographical references and index.
ISBN 978-1-4094-0316-6 (hardback) -- ISBN 978-1-4094-0317-3 (ebook)
1. Non-state actors (International relations) 2. Non-governmental organizations. I. Noortmann, Math. II. Ryngaert, Cedric.
KZ3925.N66 2010
346'.064--dc22

2010014678

ISBN 9781409403166 (hbk)
ISBN 9781409403173 (ebk)

Mixed Sources
Product group from well-managed forests and other controlled sources
www.fsc.org Cert no. SA-COC-1565
© 1996 Forest Stewardship Council
FSC

Printed and bound in Great Britain by
MPG Books Group, UK

Contents

PART THREE

List of Contributors

Jean d'Aspremont is associate professor and senior research fellow of the Amsterdam Center for International Law (ACIL) at the University of Amsterdam. He also is guest professor of international humanitarian law at the University of Louvain in Belgium. He is a senior editor of the *Leiden Journal of International Law* and has acted as counsel in proceedings before the International Court of Justice.

Leyla Davarnejad is a doctoral candidate at the Department of Public Law at the University of Bochum, Germany, where she specializes in European law, public international law and international economic law. She is also a teaching and research assistant at the same department. Previously she has worked at the Law Schools of the Universities of Munich, Giessen and Frankfurt.

Noemi Gal-Or is director of the Institute for Transborder Studies (ITS) and professor at the Department of Political Science at the Kwantlen Polytechnic University, Canada. She has published extensively in security and strategic studies, international law, dispute resolution and regional integration. A licensed sole practitioner in British Columbia, she is an active member of the Law Society of British Columbia and the Canadian Bar Association and other legal professional and academic associations, where she served in various positions.

Peter Muchlinski is professor in international commercial law at the School of Oriental and African Studies (SOAS) of the University of London. He specializes in international and European business law, development and commercial regulation, and has authored numerous papers and articles within these fields. His more recent work concentrates on the social dimension of the regulation of international business, with emphasis on human rights and multinational enterprises. He acts as a principal adviser to the United Nations Conference on Trade and Development (UNCTAD) on their major issues papers series concerning international investment agreements.

Janne E. Nijman is a senior lecturer and researcher at the International Law Department and research fellow at the Amsterdam Center for International Law (ACIL), University of Amsterdam. Here she participates in the international rule of law research program. Nijman is also a member of the ILA International Committee on Non-State Actors, editor of the *Netherlands Yearbook of International Law* (NYIL) and features on the editorial board of *Grotiana Journal*.

Math Noortmann is professor in international relations and public international law at the School of Social Sciences and Law of the Oxford Brookes University. He holds a Ph.D. in International Law and a M.Sc. in Political Science. He lectured and published on a variety of subjects including the relationship between international law and politics, sanctions, international responsibility, conflict resolution, non-state actors and international legal and political theory. He is the initiator of Ashgate's series titled *Non-State Actors in International Law, Politics and Governance* and chairs the ILA Committee on Non-State Actors.

Cedric Ryngaert is lecturer in public international law at Leuven University and Utrecht University. He is a co-rapporteur of the Non-State Actor Committee of the International Law Association and holder of a Dutch research grant on non-state actors (VENI NWO).

List of Abbreviations

ACIL	Amsterdam Center for International Law
ACP	African, Caribbean and Pacific Group of States
ATCA	Alien Tort Claims Act
BCSD	Business Council for Sustainable Development
BIAC	Business and Industry Advisory Committee
BIT	bilateral investment treaties
CEP	Committee for Environmental Protection
CFC	chlorofluorocarbon
CNPC	China National Petroleum Corporation
COC	Code of Conduct
COP	Communication on Progress
CSR	corporate social responsibility
DNA	Deoxyribonucleic Acid
ECAFE	United Nations Economic Commission for Asia and the Far East
ECOSOC	United Nations Economic and Social Council
EU	European Union
FCN	Friendship, Commerce and Navigation Treaties
FDI	foreign direct investment
FLO	Fairtrade Labelling Organization International
FTA	free trade agreement
GAL	global administrative law
GDP	Gross Domestic Product
IC	investment committee
ICC	International Chamber of Commerce
ICJ	International Court of Justice
ICRC	International Committee of the Red Cross
ICSID	Convention on the Settlement on Investment Disputes between States and Nationals of Other States
ICTY	International Criminal Tribunal for the Former Yugoslavia
IGO	intergovernmental organization
IIA	international investment agreement
IL	international law
ILA	International Law Association
ILC	International Law Commission
ILO	International Labour Organization
ILP	international legal personality

IMO	International Maritime Organization
IR	international relations
IRoL	international rule of law
ITA	international trade agreement
KP	Kimberley Process
MAI	Multilateral Agreement on Investment
MEA	Multilateral Environmental Agreement
MNC	multinational corporation
MNE	multinational enterprise
NAFTA	North American Free Trade Agreement
NCP	national contact point
NGO	non-governmental organization
NIEO	new international economic order
NIOC	National Iranian Oil Company
NSA	non-state actor
OAU	Organization of African Unity
OECD	Organization for Economic Co-operation and Development
OEEC	Organization for European Economic Co-operation
PDVSA	Petróleos de Venezuela, S.A. [Petroleums of Venezuela]
RoL	rule of law
RSA	Republic of South Africa
SG	Secretary-General of the United Nations
SRSG	Special Representative of the Secretary-General [of the United Nations]
TNC	transnational corporations
TUAC	Trade Union Advisory Committee
UN	United Nations
UNCED	United Nations Conference on Environment and Development
UNCLOS	United Nations Convention on the Law of the Sea
UNCTAD	United Nations Conference on Trade and Development
UNCTC	United Nations Centre for Transnational Corporations
UNDP	United Nations Development Programme
UNGA	United Nations General Assembly
UNRISD	United Nations Research Institute for Social Development
UNSC	United Nations Security Council
US	United States of America
WSSD	World Summit on Sustainable Development
WTO	World Trade Organization
WWII	World War II

Foreword

This volume, edited by Math Noortmann (Oxford Brookes University, UK) and Cedric Ryngaert (Leuven University, Belgium), deals with non-state actor dynamics in international law. The state has lost its exclusive position as law-taker as fragmented sets of international rights and obligations have been attributed to various non-state actors. The idea to investigate non-state actors in a shift from law-takers to law-makers came from the Non-State Actor Committee of the International Law Association in 2008. This international law volume, the first in our series, deals with topics such as transnational corporations, corporate social responsibility, the imposition of international duties, international legal status, contemporary world society and international law-making. In it, the editors reflect on the changes of the discourse on non-state actors in international law and the present world community. More specifically, they question whether non-state actors matter in international law-making to: who matters when, where and how?

Bob Reinalda
Radboud University Nijmegen, The Netherlands

Preface and Acknowledgements

During and after the meeting of the Non-State Actor Committee of the International Law Association, the notion grew that we should address the possibility that non-state actors are no longer merely indirectly affecting international law-making, through such political processes as advocacy and lobbying, but that they could also be perceived as elements in the law-making process in their own right.

Once the Committee's co-rapporteur, Cedric Ryngaert, had obtained a grant from the Flemish Fund for Scientific Research to establish an international 'Research Community' on Non-State Actors, 16 experts in the field were invited to submit chapters for this edited volume and come to the University of Leuven (Belgium) to discuss the contents of this publication.

Seven chapters which found their way into this publication benefitted greatly from the comments and remarks of Michèle Olivier, Tarcisio Gazzini, Malgosia Fitzmaurice, Eric De Brabandere, Aristotelis Constantinides, Veronika Bilkova, Beate Rudolf and Idesbald Goddeeris, who themselves contributed their views to a Special Issue of *Human Rights & International Legal Discourse*. Geert Van Calster and Wouter Vandenhole also participated as discussants. Peter Muchlinski is to be credited for the second part of the title, which constituted the title of his own contribution.

Our editing work was wonderfully supported by Dilan Khoshnaw – a student assistant at the Institute for International Law of Peace and Armed Conflict of the Ruhr-University of Bochum. Dilan 'translated' each individual paper into Ashgate's required format and corrected obvious mistakes while he was 'formatting'. Within Ashgate we had Natalja Mortensen, who reminded us of each deadline and allowed us to break some of them.

Last, but not least, there are those that were not directly involved in the publication of this edited volume, but whose spirit and ideas are inherently linked to the discourses on, and concepts of non-state actors. Similarly we thank those who have actively encouraged research in the field of non-state actors, such as Christine Chinkin, the Director of Studies at the International Law Association. Christine's engagement and support for the establishment of the ILA Committee on Non-State Actors has contributed to this opportunity to take 'non-state actors' to another level of empirical and theoretical significance.

Math Noortmann and Cedric Ryngaert
Oxford and Leuven

Chapter 1
Introduction:
Non-State Actors: International Law's Problematic Case

Math Noortmann and Cedric Ryngaert

The difference between those who 'make' the law, those who determine and enforce the law and those who 'take' the law is generally considered to be a formal distinction, which is exclusively determined by the constitutional characteristics of the legal system in question. As a rule, law-takers outnumber law-makers. The international legal system has been the traditional exception to that rule: states were at the same time the exclusive law-makers and law-takers in an exact ratio of 1:1.

With the definitive and recognized breakthrough of entities, which are not nation-states at the international plane, the state has lost its exclusive position as law-taker. Fragmented sets of international rights and obligations have been attributed to a most diverse cluster of non-state actors (NSAs). The label 'non-state actor' can hardly be considered to constitute a term of art because it includes such wide range of identifiable organizations as non-governmental organizations (NGOs) (Weiss 1999, Charnovitz 2006), multinational enterprises (MNEs) (Kokkini-Iatridou 1983, Muchlinski 1999), national liberation armies (Wilson 1988) and intergovernmental organizations (IGOs) (Huntington 1973), as well as more amorphous groupings such as armed NSAs (Zegveld 2002, Chesterman 2006), indigenous peoples (Howitt 1996), criminal and terrorist organizations (Alexander 2001) and social movements (Keck 1989). The list of NSAs is in contrast to the list of states simple inexhaustible. What is more, each typography of non-state actor contains a specific sub-categorization, which makes it even more difficult to understand and explain every single NSA under one single heading, be it from a legal, political or social disciplinary perspective (Noortmann 2001, Reinalda 2001, Schneckener 2006).

That fragmentation, however, does not undermine the observation that NSAs have, as a category, acquired enforceable and less enforceable international legal entitlements and – what is perhaps more important – it does not determine the general consensus, that NSAs (of whatever nature) should be subjected to regimes of global responsibility and accountability. The International Law Commission's (ILC) conclusion that 'the topic "responsibility of international organizations" was appropriate for inclusion in its long-term programme of work'[1] in 2000 was due ever since the International Court of Justice (ICJ) observed in 1948 that 'the progressive increase in the collective action of States, has already given rise to instances of action upon the international plane by certain entities, which are not States.'[2] That the ILC's work on the responsibility of international organizations is only the beginning of a long set of reports on the responsibility of different kind of NSAs is evidenced by the recent appointment of Prof. John Ruggie as the UN Secretary General's Special Representative on Business and Human Rights.

The mushrooming of non-state actors has not only triggered question as to the diversification of international responsibilities and rights, but also with respect to the question as to the role and position of non-state actors in the international law-making and decision-making process. Notwithstanding the political dimension of that question, it is clear that it transcends the concepts of political power and influence. Unfortunately, the impact and influence of non-state actors and more in particular NGOs and MNEs is rather uncritically assumed then that it is critically investigated in most studies.

The role and position of non-governmental organizations in global humanitarian, human rights and environmental issues has been the subject of an increasing number of legal, political and sociological studies (Arts, Noortmann and Reinalda 2001, Boli 1999). However, as these studies focus on a limited number of specific NGOs, they fail to grasp the complexity and diversity of normative multi actor frameworks such as the small arms complex, investment regimes and diverse forms of corporate social responsibility (CSR) initiatives. The question whether, and if so to which extent, NSAs effect international law with respect to the idea of corporate social responsibility, and whether and to which extent these actors are affected by international law, has been the subject of significant and longstanding interdisciplinary and societal debates. The Late European Middle Ages and the birth of the modern company is often taken as the starting point of the public debates on the enterprise as a socio-economic and political phenomenon, but one could equally take the pre-medieval times or the 'rise of big business' as the focal point for the start of enterprise critical discourses (Micklethwait and Woolridge 2003).

However that may be, there is little doubt that corporate responsibility has become a major issue in both society and in the disciplinary debates of public international law; the question on controlling and regulating MNEs is a thriving subject. Multinational enterprises or transnational corporations have undoubtedly become one of the most discussed and targeted non-state actors in the international system. Since the normative quality of governmental codes of conduct has not been clarified in detail, the CSR debate has been intensified by the increasing

1 See Official Records of the General Assembly, Fifty-fifth Session, Supplement No. 10 (A/55/10), paras 726–728 and 729 (1).

2 Reparation for Injuries suffered in the service of the United Nations, Advisory Opinion: ICJ Reports 1949, p. 174 at 180.

number of private initiatives in recent years. These exclusively non-governmental initiatives, in practice and the public and academic debate seem to eclipse the soft law initiatives in the CSR field. The contributions of Leyla Davarnejad and Peter Muchlinski analyse the particular role and influence of the legal epistemic community, NGOs and corporate actors in the legal CSR debate. Their papers describe and analyse one of the (most important) empirical domains in the NSA discourse in international law.

Leyla Davarnejad in particular, argues that the combination of economic and political power of MNEs, the unclear international legal status, their debated impact on human rights, labour or environmental standards has been ameliorated by the actuality intergovernmental organizations (IGOs), NGOs and MNEs themselves have issued an innumerable amount including (CSR) codes. The new concept of CSR has started to depart the usual boundaries between state and market and entails a complete new division of accountability between public and private actors. What is the impact of these codes? Do they change the law or do they change the actors … or both? Are they considered adequate from a legal perspective? In the end Leyla Davarnejad seems to argue that because governmental codes of conduct set themselves apart from private initiatives due to their public authority and their ability to reconcile and to balance the conflicting interests that characterize the CSR debate, the normative difference between law and non-law is of continued relevance.

Peter Muchlinski shares Davarnejad's socio-political assessment that, given the technological, financial and managerial advantages of MNEs, which are organized and operate across national borders, these actors have significant power and influence in the development of national and international economic and social policy. In the international legal domain, however, Muchlinski observes a process of law-making, which undermines the traditional notion of law-making processes as state or governmental processes. The conceptual separation between (1) the power of MNEs to substantially interact with national policymakers and intergovernmental organizations to develop policy and to exact legal regulation and (2) the constitutional notion of law-making is too formalistic. The question whether MNEs and other NSAs can be considered to act as 'law-makers' in the international legal process is the subject of this edited volume. MNEs set the empirical stage to our contribution to the general NSA discourse. Muchlinski's examination aims to develop a model of the process of international law-making, which takes account of corporate power, and the power of other non-state actors to influence the content of the law.

Part Two of this volume promotes a more particular (re)consideration of such typical legal topics as 'legal personality' (Janne Nijman and Noemi Gal-Or) and 'legitimacy' (Cedric Ryngaert). Janne Nijman's investigation appreciates non-state actors in the context of the notion of the 'rule of law' and discusses the revival of a realist theory of international law. She does so on the basis of a critique on the traditional approach to international legal personality as the conceptual lens through which the position of non-state actors in international law is generally questioned. Her contribution in particular explores a more 'internally' pushed and inter-subjectively created international legal personality of the non-state actor.

Noemi Gal-Or discusses whether, from an international legal perspective, which presumes some legal status for some NSAs, it is desirable to enhance the legal status of the NSA. Hence, the question is not whether a specific NSA should or should not be recognized as a subject of international law, but rather, whether the NSA should be recognized as a general category of an actor to which a basic set of rights and obligations in international law applies and if so which rules and procedures apply to determining who is and who is not entitled to legal personality. These questions will be addressed from two angles. First, stock will be taken of the current state of the art regarding the status of the NSA in international law. Second, a legal theoretical discussion will follow to assess the desirability of any further changes to the present condition of the law measured against the role and nature of international law.

The link between the legitimacy of international law and the participation of non-state actors in the law-making and -implementation process is the topic of the argument of Cedric Ryngaert. He investigates the relevance of (1) liberal internationalism, constructivism and the transnational legal process theory, (2) political (input legitimacy) theories, in particular deliberative democracy/theory of communicative action (Habermas), and (3) law and economics theories (tying regulatory design to expected norm-compliance and social effectiveness; these are utilitarian theories focused on output legitimacy). It will be ascertained how these theories could provide building blocks for the regulation of a global society constituted by a variety of international actors, including non-state actors. The said theories have originally been conceived as applying to states or state regulation. International relations theories typically take the *state* as the chief actor at the international level, and both democracy and economic theories are primarily developed with a view to their application at the domestic (intra-state) level. It is the aim of this article to (1) examine how leading international relations theories could nonetheless be used, or as the case may be, amended with a view to accommodating the role of non-state actors; (2) analyse whether, and to what extent, domestic democracy and law and economic theories could be extrapolated to the international level.

Finally, in Part Three, Math Noortmann and Jean d'Aspremont critically reflect on the added value of a wider non-state actors perspective in the efforts to understand and explain international law. Math Noortmann does so by raising the question whether the notion of 'participants' as advocated by the New Haven School should be reintroduced or whether we should stick to the conceptually poor notion of non-state actors.

The notions of transnational law and international law as an authoritative decision-making process (the policy-orientated approach or New Haven School) were the first to conceptualize the idea of a legal space beyond the classic international legal system of states, in which both states and non-state actors would participate in a constitutive manner. Elaborated in the 1950s, both concepts had lost much of its attraction by the late 1970s to be revived again in the 1990s in response to the unbridled increase of actors which are not states in the global realm. Both notions transcend the confinements of the international legal discipline either because the concept has a corollary in socio-political sciences (trans-nationalism) or because the concept was set up as a trans-disciplinary approach to world order in the first place. The paper scrutinizes both approaches and critically assesses their value for contemporary debates on the role of non-state actors in the law-making process.

Last but not least, Jean d'Aspremont raises the ultimate question: is the notion of non-state actors in international law a scholarly invention? He argues that the contemporary assertion that the law-making role of non-state actors in international law is less the result of an actual practice and empirical evidence than it is the outcome of an inclination of international law scholars to expand their field and subjects of study. While the aspiration for the import of new legal materials into the ambit of international legal scholarship can provide a rational explanation of the proneness of international scholars to depict international law-making processes as diverse and heterogeneous, it is not sufficient to explain all the underlying motives of such a leaning. It is submitted here that, in a few circumstances, the tendency to play down the state-centrism of international law-making processes and the magnification of their heterogeneity can also be traced back to a more general and fundamental endeavour of international legal scholars to convey a cosmopolitan vision of international law with a view to fostering the legitimacy of their object of study. This chapter also explains the attraction of scholars to these heterogeneous representations of international law-making as an attempt by international legal scholars to preserve the importance of their expertise and that of their discipline in areas where they have been subject to the competition of other social sciences.

References

Alexander, Y., Swetnam, M.S. and Levine, H.M. 2001. *ETA: Profile of a Terrorist Group.* Ardsley, NY: Transnational Publishers.

Arts, B., Noortmann, M. and Reinalda, B. (eds). 2001. *Non-State Actors in International Law, Politics and Governance.* Aldershot: Ashgate Publishing Company.

Boli, J. and Thomas, G.M. 1999. INGOs and the Organization of World Culture, in *Constructing World Culture: International Nongovernmental Organizations since 1875*, edited by J. Boli and G.M. Thomas. Stanford, CA: Stanford University Press.

Charnovitz, S. 2006. Non-Governmental Organizations and International Law. *American Journal of International Law*, 100, 348–372.

Howitt, R., Connell, J. and Hirsch, P. 1996. *Resources, Nations, and Indigenous Peoples: Case Studies from Australasia, Melanesia, and Southeast Asia.* Melbourne and New York: Oxford University Press.

Huntington, S.P. 1973. Transnational Organizations in World Politics. *World Politics*, 25, 333–368.

Keck, M.E. and Sikkink, K. 1998. *Activists beyond Borders – Advocacy Networks in International Politics*. London: Cornell University Press.

Kokkini-Iatridou, D. and de Waart, P. 1983. Foreign Investments in Developing Countries; Legal Personality of Multinationals in International Law. *Netherlands Yearbook of International Law*, 14, 87–131.

Micklethwait, J. and Wooldridge, A. 2005. *The Company: A Short History of a Revolutionary Idea*. London: Phoenix.

Muchlinski, P.T. 1999. *Multinational Enterprises and the Law.* Malden: Blackwell Publishing.

Noortmann, M. 2001. Non-State Actors in International Law, in *Non-State Actors in International Relations*, edited by B. Arts, M. Noortmann and B. Reinalda. Aldershot: Ashgate Publishing Company.

PART ONE

Chapter 2
Multinational Enterprises as Actors in International Law: Creating 'Soft Law' Obligations and 'Hard Law' Rights

Peter Muchlinski

> More than any other single institution, the transnational corporation has come to be seen as the primary shaper of the contemporary global economy and a major threat to the economic autonomy of the nation-state.
>
> (Dicken 2007: 106)

Multinational enterprises (MNEs) are among the most prominent non-state actors in the international system. Their size and number, and their location in the major markets and sectors of industry, has given them significant power and influence (for details see further Dicken 2007: chs 1–5, Dunning and Lundan 2008: chs 1–2, United Nations 2008: Part I). This has led to a long standing debate about how such entities should be regulated. The fear of MNEs as unaccountable actors, able to disregard state policies, and to play states off in a global 'race to the bottom' in regulatory standards is not new. It is a fear as old as the modern large corporation.[1] On the other hand, MNEs can also be seen as beneficial to development, as they bring much needed investment and technology to the host countries in which they operate. The question is how to attract and benefit from foreign direct investment (FDI) by MNEs, while avoiding possible adverse economic and social effects. It is in this balancing process that the issue of regulation exists.

In relation to international law this balancing process can be seen in the contrasting norms of investor protection and investor accountability. The former, being located mainly in binding international investment agreements (IIAs), create a regime of protective rules by which host countries should treat foreign investors, thereby reducing investment risk. The latter are located mainly in 'soft law' instruments of a non-binding nature and create a 'best efforts' guide to good corporate practice. It is arguable that this is not a balanced regime as it favours binding investor protection without reciprocal binding norms. That this should

1 For example at the end of the nineteenth century United States federal incorporation for firms was mooted as a means of controlling their power to avoid state regulation by reason of migration to 'regulatory haven' states such as New Jersey (see Urofsky 1982).

be so arises out of the very process of international law-making in the field of corporations and foreign investment. It is the purpose of this paper to analyse that process from the perspective of MNEs as non-state actors.

The starting point is the positivist assertion that corporations are not subjects of international law and so no international law relating to them can exist. International law can only exist in relation to states. And yet there is a growing body of international norms that do deal with corporations and their investments. As noted, some of these norms seek to impose standards of good behaviour on corporations. In this respect, corporations, including MNEs, can be seen as 'law-takers' in that international law is seeking to develop regulatory standards below which corporate behaviour should not fall. That these standards are mainly non-binding comes not from the fact that corporations are not subjects of international law but from the role that corporate interests play in the evolution of this system. How firms lobby home and host states and intergovernmental organizations (IGOs) is a key element here. Equally the binding nature of norms relating to investor protection also arises out of this process. Thus in this regard MNEs can be seen as 'law-makers' even though the traditional law-making process of international law does not formally accord any status to such entities in that process. However, it is on the process of influencing state policy and state practice, and the agendas of intergovernmental organizations, in relation to corporate interests that the law-making function of firms is to be seen.

This chapter begins, in Section I, with a discussion of the effect of the absence of full legal personality for corporations. It goes on to show, in Section II, how this is in practice irrelevant to the ability of states to develop regulatory norms but that the main obstacle to doing so is the influence that corporate interests themselves exert upon the development of international law by states and IGOs. The conclusions drawn from the first two sections on the extent to which MNEs are 'law-takers' or 'law-makers' will be illustrated, in Section III, by reference to the debate on whether MNEs and other business enterprises should be subjected to international obligations to observe internationally agreed standards of corporate social responsibility which includes the responsibility to observe international human rights standards. Finally Section IV will consider the extent to which MNEs are 'law-makers' by reference to the development of investment protection norms in IIAs.

I. The Positivist Restriction on MNEs as Subjects of International Law

The origin of the restriction on corporate actors and subjects of international law arises from the divide between private international law, dealing with the legal implications of private international transactions for national legal systems, and public international law, which deals only with the legal implications of inter-state interactions (see Claire Cutler 2003: 36, citing Janis 1984: 62). MNEs are assimilated to individuals for the purposes of international personality though not all the rules that apply to an individual will automatically apply to the corporate entity as well.[2] Nonetheless, they too are not subjects of international law on this approach. They are indeed 'invisible' to international law (see Johns 1994).[3] As a result corporations have had to rely on claims for diplomatic protection to protect their rights, with the attendant problems this creates, until the development of modern IIAs with international dispute settlement provisions allowing for investor-state arbitration (for an overview of the customary international law relating to foreign investment claims see further Staker 1990, Muchlinski 2009a).

Notwithstanding the above, it can be argued that MNEs have sufficient presence in international legal activities to gain a measure of international personality. For example the conclusion of state contracts between MNEs and host countries may be assimilated to international law (Johns 1994: 901). Indeed, certain leading jurists have argued for the treatment of corporations as subjects of international law to the extent that they enter into agreements with foreign governments (see Friedmann 1964: 221–231, 1969: 121–124, Jenks 1972: 70, Ijalaye 1978: 221–246). In addition there is some authority in international arbitral jurisprudence for the view that an investment agreement between a state and a foreign corporation is an international contract subject to international law. Thus in the *Texaco* arbitration the arbitrator, Professor Rene-Jean Dupuy, held that an oil concession agreement between a US oil company and the Government of Libya was 'internationalized',

---

2 *Barcelona Traction Case* [1970] ICJ 3: 70: 'In allocating corporate entities to States for purposes of diplomatic protection, international law is based, but only to a limited extent, on an analogy with the rules governing the nationality of individuals. The traditional rule attributes the right of diplomatic protection of a corporate entity to the State under the laws of which it is incorporated and in whose territory it has its registered office. These two criteria have been confirmed by long practice and by numerous international instruments. This notwithstanding, further or different links are at times said to be required in order that a right of diplomatic protection should exist. Indeed, it has been the practice of some States to give a company incorporated under their law diplomatic protection solely when it has its seat (*siège social*) or management or centre of control in their territory, or when a majority or a substantial proportion of the shares has been owned by nationals of the State concerned. Only then, it has been held, does there exist between the corporation and the State in question a genuine connection of the kind familiar from other branches of international law. However, in the particular field of the diplomatic protection of corporate entities, no absolute test of the "genuine connection" has found general acceptance. Such tests as have been applied are of a relative nature, and sometimes links with one State have had to be weighed against those with another. In this connection reference has been made to the *Nottebohm* case. In fact the Parties made frequent reference to it in the course of the proceedings. However, given both the legal and factual aspects of protection in the present case the Court is of the opinion that there can be no analogy with the issues raised or the decision given in that case.'

3 Indeed it can be said that MNEs are invisible in national law too in that subsidiaries appear as locally incorporated entities with a controlling foreign shareholding, while parent companies appear as locally incorporated entities with overseas shareholdings, a form that fails to convey the transnational economic and managerial integration of the MNE.

that is assimilated to international law, on two principal grounds.[4] First, the reference to principles of international law and to general principles of law, in the choice of law clause in the concession agreement, was held to define the extent to which Libyan law could apply.[5] Only if Libyan law was in conformity with international law should it be applied to determine the legality of Libya's expropriation of the US company's assets. Secondly, the fact that the contract was an economic development agreement emphasized the need for internationalization. According to Professor Dupuy, such agreements justified assimilation to international law on the basis of their broad subject-matter, long duration and the magnitude of the investment made by the foreign party. This required a measure of stability by which the investor could be protected against legislative uncertainties and governmental measures that might lead to an abrogation or rescission of the contract. Hence stabilization clauses were inserted which removed all or part of the agreement from the internal law and provided for its correlative submission to *sui generis* rules or to a system which was properly an international law system (Muchlinski 2007: 45). Professor Dupuy's approach was followed in the *Revere Copper* arbitration (17 ILM 1321 (1978)). However, it was not followed in the subsequent oil arbitrations of the early 1980s which did not see the economic development aspect of state contracts as sufficient for them to be assimilated into international law but rather saw international law as constituting part of the law of the host country and so applicable to the contract in that way. From the above it can be concluded that Professor Dupuy's approach, based on internationalization implied from the context of the agreement, does not find uniform support in arbitral awards.[6] The decisive factor appears to be the actual content of the agreement particularly the terms of any express choice of law clause used by the parties (see Muchlinski 2007: 581).

Secondly, it has been argued that MNE participation in consultations over new international rules may give them a measure of international personality. For example, business representatives take part in the trilateral structure of discussions at the International Labour Organization (ILO) alongside trade union and governmental representatives in the delegations of each member state. Equally business experts have served on numerous intergovernmental committees dealing with the reform and development of international law and business representatives have met states in intergovernmental conventions (Johns 1994: 902–903). However

4 *Texaco v Libya* 1978. 17 ILM 1.

5 By Clause 28 of the Deeds of Concession: 'This concession shall be governed by and interpreted in accordance with the principles of the law of Libya in common to the principles of international law and in the absence of such common principles then by and in accordance with general principles of law, including such of those principles as may have been applied by international tribunals.'

6 See too the ICSID award in *Klockner v Cameroon* extracted in Paulsson (1984: 157): 'We do not intend to apply new or exceptional legal principles to turn-key operations only because they concern projects affecting the economic and social development of a given country.' See further, Pogany 1992.

this argument confuses the reality of MNE power and influence with legal capacity and is rather unconvincing (Johns 1994: 902–903).

Thirdly, states can determine to confer rights or obligations on MNEs under international treaties (as for example through IIAs with international dispute settlement provisions especially with access to the International Centre for Settlement of Investment Disputes (ICSID)) and states may themselves be liable for corporate breaches of international law by reason of the horizontal effects or *Drittwirkung* doctrine (see Reinisch 2005: 70–72, Jägers 1999: 261–263). Whether this amounts to a measure of international personality for corporate actors is again open to debate. In particular the fact that states choose to give international legal rights or obligations to non-state actors does not require full international personality for the latter. The scheme of the treaty under which this is done gives a sufficient legal structure for those rights and/or obligations to function effectively. There is no need to extrapolate international personality from this process. Equally the notion of state liability for failure to regulate non-state actors in accordance with international law is a legal rule directed at the state itself not the non-state actor. There is no logic in reading into this situation some recognition of international personality for the non-state actor. To the contrary the existence of such liability is a direct consequence of the latter's lack of international personality and the fact that the state holds the obligation to ensure observance of international law in all cases.

It can be further argued, in the light of these examples, that legal personality is a functional process and so it can be granted as and when required for the vindication of the claims of non-state actors (Higgins 1994: 50). Legal personality is a fluid concept even under international law as Nijman and Gal-Or assert in Chapters 5 and 6 respectively. As noted by the International Court of Justice in the *Reparations for Injuries Case*, '[t]he subjects of law in any legal system are not necessarily identical in the nature or in the extent of their rights, and their nature depends upon the needs of the Community.' (*Reparations Case* [1949] ICJ 174 at 178.) Accordingly, even though the above examples may be dismissed as weak illustrations of corporate international personality, a functional approach can be defended, and a measure of international personality for corporate actors recognized, where this is appropriate to achieve the goals that international law seeks in relation to specific fields of regulation. The real problem may not be so much the conceptual conservatism of international law as regards the admission of corporate actors into the body of recognized international legal persons, but the possibility that those actors' interests can be served without such a change.

II. Interactions Between States and Non-State Actors and the International Law-Making Process

The positivist tradition in international law, in failing to consider law in its wider political economic and social context, ignores the actual influence of various interests and groups upon its content cannot be examined. Thus the fact that MNEs, civil society groups and NGOs, and other non-governmental groups, are contesting the content of international legal agendas is brushed aside as if the only element in the law-making process is inter-state diplomacy and state practice. It is as absurd as suggesting that we can understand national law just by reading statutes and cases. This is the scholarship of the past (see further Salter and Mason 2007: ch. 4). It is also a misrepresentation of how international law actually developed. In practice non-state actors have always been central to the development of international legal regimes and continue to be so. Historically the powerful, territorial, nation-state is a recent creation originating in the nineteenth and twentieth centuries. 'If this is so', argues Fred Halliday, 'then the residual, or supposedly recent "non-state" is in fact a continuation of something that prevailed until this modern state was formed. In pre-modern society much that is today controlled by the state was administered by other entities – the family, the tribe, the religious group, the local lord' (Halliday 2001: 27). Accordingly the nation-state can be seen as a construct formed by non-state actors to further specific group interests.

Indeed one explanation of the rise of the modern nation state is as a facilitator of capital accumulation by the capitalist class by way of the institutionalization of the divide between the private sphere of action, which is unregulated, and the public sphere of action which is regulated. This separation allows for capital accumulation though the operation of an unregulated market, which is institutionalized and made effective through the rise of state regulation aimed at protecting the market or 'private' sphere from control by other competing interest groups (Claire Cutler 2003: 43–45). This can be carried over to the international arena by way of creating a deregulated field within which private commercial actors can function. Historically this may be said to have been the function of the medieval 'law merchant' which was subsequently internalized within the national legal order of states and which now has as its contemporary counterpart the law relating to trade and investment liberalization and investor protection (Claire Cutler 2003: chs 4–6). This aim has also been achieved through the use of extraterritorial regimes which assured the application of home country law to nationals working within the legal territory of the host country, thereby highlighting the artificiality of state sovereignty and territorial control in the face of superior foreign state power motivated by the need to protect foreign commercial interests (see further Bishop 1926, Sayre 1928, Keeton 1926, 1927a, 1927b, Wright 1943).

Furthermore, the existence of regulatory havens in the contemporary international economic system also reinforces the view that state authority is used to protect private interests where it is expedient to do so. It results in the paradox that major market states decry the existence of these havens while at the same time protecting their existence. No country is more illustrative of this approach than Great Britain, which – though a member of the OECD, whose policy is to control tax havens – continues to ensure that tax haven jurisdictions located in British overseas territories, or in the self governing isles of Britain, are secure. This can only be explained by the strength of private interest influence (see further Picciotto 1999: 43).[7]

However, to say that the state is merely the handmaiden of commercial interests is too simplistic. The power of MNEs to set regulatory agendas should not be overestimated. Though they can act as powerful and influential lobbyists, MNEs do not possess anything like the power of states (for a discussion of how MNEs have lobbied for changes in international investment law and policy see further Muchlinski 1997: 90–97). They lack diplomatic and military power, and their economic power, though considerable, is highly contingent.[8] Much depends on the general strength, and competitive conditions, of the market or sector in which firms operate, the overall state of the economy, and the degree of unique competitive advantage possessed by the firm. In effect only the most important firms will have the ability to lobby effectively. This tends to be the most financially powerful firms that can afford to spend the most on lobbying activities (see further Chen, Parsley and Yang (2008) who base their findings on publicly available data on the lobbying expenditures of leading US firms in the period 1998–2005. See too Murphy 2004).

Equally the lobbying power of MNEs will be constrained by the fact that they are dependent to a significant degree on their home state to protect their capacity to do business transnationally. That home states should do so indicates an increasing willingness on their part to use their political and economic power to protect the global interests of their corporations. It is an important feature in the emerging framework of international investment law, which will be considered in Section IV of the chapter. In addition, home states may increasingly adopt policies that seek to strengthen the competitiveness of home based MNEs. This could range from the giving of political and diplomatic support for new investment opportunities by way of improved relations with potential host states, to the monitoring of host state policies that give rise to discrimination against home firms, and to more general matters, such as the improvement of education and infrastructure in the home state, that act as a means of preserving the competitive advantage of home based firms (see Muchlinski 2007: 87, see further Porter 1990. See too, on the power of MNEs to influence the economic policy agenda of home states by way of their 'embeddedness' in the state-finance-industry-labour policy networks of the home state, Sally 1994, 1995).

From the above, it can be concluded that MNEs can have a strong influence upon their home states in seeking to lobby for changes in international law conducive to

---

7 On OECD policy concerning the control of tax havens see *Harmful Tax Competition: An Emerging Global Issue* (Paris, OECD, 1998), available at http://www.oecd.org/dataoecd/33/0/1904176.pdf, accessed: 20 February 2010, in the following Harmful Tax Competition.

8 In this regard the oft-cited idea that the capital output of leading MNEs is greater than the GDP of certain nation states is quite misleading. The bases upon which the profits and losses of MNEs are calculated differ so greatly from the methods by which the GDP of states is calculated as to make such a comparison meaningless.

their interests. However, that lobbying is not always successful in the sense that states still retain a strong independent capacity to develop policies regardless of industry lobbying efforts. In particular home states are unlikely to sacrifice wider foreign policy goals to the protection of the special interests of particular corporations or industries located in the home country (see Dunning and Lundan 2008: 693–694). But where state and corporate interests intersect then business friendly regimes may be sought at the international level.

This leads to the further question of whether the state will be prepared to regulate excesses of corporate conduct abroad. The fact that the US has so far not barred human rights litigation against corporations under the Alien Tort Claims Act (ATCA) may be indicative of a tolerance towards, if not as yet a willingness to support, private claims against corporate actors in this field. Indeed John Ruggie, the UN Secretary-General's Special Representative on Human Rights and Business (SRSG) has indicated that access to remedies for alleged human rights abuses by corporations is a factor in the effective discharge of the state's duty to protect, and the corporation's responsibility to respect, human rights. Thus this may be an area in which the state should be increasingly willing in future to take on the responsibility to regulate corporate conduct by the provision of judicial mechanisms to hear complaints and enforce remedies against corporate actors.[9] If so then corporate lobbying might prove ineffectual to stop this development.

In addition, when considering corporate lobbying power it is important to remember that this will be further counterbalanced by the influence of NGOs that can publicize corporate abuses and seek to lobby states on their own account. Concerned NGOs can, through the use of alternative policy models, shift the debate away from industry specific concerns towards a more socially responsive agenda which can remain a powerful source of opinion even where national and parliamentary sovereignties may be weakened by globalization (Muchlinski 2007: 109, see further Braithwaite and Drahos 2008: ch. 26). For example one of the factors contributing to the failure of the Multilateral Agreement on Investment (MAI) was the well organized and vocal opposition to the MAI by NGOs (on which see further Muchlinski 2000: 1048–1049). Therefore, it would be wrong to say that corporate influence exists in a uniformly favourable environment. States will not always prioritize corporate concerns and other non-state actors with an interest in the content of corporate regulation under international law will also have an input.

9 See Report of the Special Representative of the Secretary-General on the issue of human rights and transnational corporations and other business enterprises, John Ruggie, 'Protect, Respect and Remedy: A Framework for Business and Human Rights', UN Doc. A/HRC/8/5, 7 April 2008, 82–83 and 88–91, available at http://www.business-humanrights.org/SpecialRepPortal/Home/ReportstoUNHumanRightsCouncil/2008, accessed: 20 February 2010, in the following *SRSG 2008*.

III. International Corporate Social Responsibility, Environment and Human Rights

Historically, business groups have been wary of any attempts to extend greater international legal accountability for the social consequences of their activities. Corporate responsibility was seen as little more than the making of profits and the protection of shareholder value (see for a statement of this position Henderson 2001). This approach dominated corporate responses to early attempts, in the 1970s, to extend social responsibility norms for MNEs into international law. Thus, in relation to the ILO Tripartite Declaration of Principles concerning Multinational Enterprises and Social Policy (The Tripartite Declaration) the employers' representatives argued for non-mandatory guidelines and got their way. The Tripartite Declaration would not have been passed had a mandatory code been sought (see further Robinson 1983: 172). Equally the adoption of the voluntary OECD Guidelines on Multinational Enterprises in 1976 was an attempt to pre-empt a more intrusive UN Code on Transnational Corporations, which itself was never adopted (see further Muchlinski 2007: 660–662). However, this attitude of resistance could not last indefinitely. More recently, corporations have come to accept that some kind of accountability for the social consequences of their actions may be inevitable under international law and they have sought to influence the resulting framework (see generally Zerk 2006: 23–25, Muchlinski 2007: 100–104). This change in attitude can be illustrated by reference to the development of international environmental standards for corporations and to the emergence of a sense that firms should respect and observe human rights standards in the course of their operations.

Turning, first, to international environmental protection, this has become an area of contestation and lobbying by both business and civil society groups. Indeed, it is arguable that MNEs have used such influence to help construct a more benign set of standards than might have otherwise been adopted (see generally Rowlands 2001). Initially, business perspectives on environmental issues were opposed to international environmental regulation, seeing it as a barrier to the market. Accordingly, business interests sought to limit the effects of such regulation (see Gleckman 1995: 95–96). That approach changed at the UN Conference on Environment and Development (UNCED) and with it a more controlled set of standards, more agreeable to business interests, emerged, but one that also appeared to show business concern for environmental protection.

Originally, the UN Centre for Transnational Corporations (UNCTC) was to have played a major role in formulating sustainable development standards applicable to MNEs (TNCs in UN parlance) (see Muchlinski 2007: 567, on which this paragraph is based). However, the UNCED Secretariat, led by Maurice Strong, was keen to involve MNEs in the process of evolving standards. A new post of corporate adviser to UNCED was created and was filled by Stefan Schmidtheiny, the founder of the Business Council for Sustainable Development (BCSD) (see Gleckman 1995: 95–97). As a result the UNCTC proposals were not adopted and the resulting conference instrument, the Rio Declaration on Environment and Development (Agenda 21), to date the most influential repository of MNE responsibilities in the environmental field (UNCED Agenda 21: *Programme of Action for Sustainable Development*[10]), contained an approach to sustainable development that reflected closely the concerns of the BCSD (see Gleckman 1995: 95–97, Rowlands 2001: 144, Ford 2005: 310–312). Thus its emphasis is on the application of 'green' technology to environmental issues and upon co-operation between business and governments in the realization of sustainable development goals. In this context, investment is seen as a necessary prerequisite for sustainable development (UNCED Agenda 21 para. 2.23). Governments are urged to encourage higher levels of foreign direct investment through national policies that promote investment and through joint ventures and other modalities (UNCED Agenda 21 para. 33.15). A similar effort to keep the environmental regulation of business off the agenda was made at the follow-up to the Rio Conference, the World Summit on Sustainable Development (WSSD) in Johannesburg in 2002. This resulted in little more than the re-affirmation of the Agenda 21 standards (see Ford 2005).[11]

Indeed it has been said that business is not really interested in genuine change in environmental standards but in 'greenwashing' its image so as to create the appearance of change (see Welford 2002: 143–147, on 'greenwash' see Beder 1997). In this process home states are being lobbied to ensure that international standards remain relatively low and that few if any direct obligations are created for corporate actors (Rowlands 2001: 138–143).[12] That said the lobbying power of corporate interests should not be overestimated. Lobbying at the international level is much harder where the home country chooses not to follow the policy preferences of domestic business groups, or where it supports a position not held by most states (Rowlands 2001: 143–147).[13] Equally the countervailing influence of environmental NGOs should be taken into account. Though it is probable that business interests will have a closer relationship with their home

10 Available at: http://www.un.org/esa/sustdev/documents/agenda21/english/agenda21toc.htm, accessed: 20 February 2010, in the following UNCED Agenda 21.

11 The results of the Summit can be found in United Nations 2002. See especially: Annex: Resolution 2: The Plan of Implementation of the WSSD at Para. 18 at p. 15 (encouragement of corporate environmental and social responsibility); Para. 49 at p. 38 (promotion of corporate responsibility based on the Rio Principles); Para. 84 at p. 51 (encouragement of greater flows of FDI to developing countries to support sustainable development) Para. 105 at p. 58 (promotion of environmentally sound technology transfer as agreed in Chapter 34 of Agenda 21).

12 Recently the British House of Commons Environmental Audit Committee recommended that a new scheme for making environmental advertising claims should be introduced to avoid 'greenwash'. 'Shoppers need clear labels to put a stop to "greenwash"' (*The Guardian* 23 March 2009, 9).

13 Rowlands notes that if business interests were unreservedly successful in resisting international environmental regulation this would be inconsistent with the large number of legally binding multilateral instruments already adopted in this field.

country governments than civil society groups, and will have more resources to sustain lobbying campaigns, their overall influence should not be overstated. Environmental NGOs are also making headway in influencing the content of international instruments. For example, in relation to investment it is fair to say that a major contributory cause to the failure of the MAI was NGO lobbying and campaigning against an agreement that at first contained no provisions on labour or environmental issues and which appeared to be in open conflict with obligations under Multilateral Environmental Agreements (MEAs) (see Mabey 1999: 61, Werksman and Santoro 1998: 59, Verhoosel 1998: 451). However, in most international negotiations NGOs are no more than observers and have little influence as compared to corporations that have greater access to national representatives (see Ford 2005: 320–324).

Thus, while the development of international environmental standards for corporate actors is still in its infancy, and a case can be made that corporate influence has helped to create this situation, it is equally plausible to say that corporate actors have accepted the need to made greater efforts to deal with the environmental impact of their activities and to accept certain general principles of action as outlined in Agenda 21 and in the UN Global Compact.[14] This has resulted in a largely self-regulatory approach that may be backed up by mandatory regulation at the national level based on international standards (Muchlinski 2007: 546–574). It may not satisfy activists but it is a lot further than outright rejection. It shows not only how corporate actors influence the development of the law in this area but that they accept the basic premise that they do have a duty to deal with environmental issues.

Turning to human rights obligations of corporate actors, here too there appears to have been an acceptance of the need to observe certain international standards in corporate operations, but with an emphasis on self-regulatory approaches backed up by enforcement sanctions at national level. The initial position was that corporate actors could not be held responsible for human rights violations, which were exclusively the responsibility of states. Indeed the original version of the OECD Guidelines on Multinational Enterprises is silent on human rights in general (OECD *Guidelines for Multinational Enterprises*, 21 June 1976, 15 ILM 977 (1976)). The only human rights related issues were those found in the Guideline on Employment and Industrial Relations which required only that employers follow national standards in employment relations and encouraged MNEs to respect the freedom of association and non-discrimination in employment. It was not until

---

14 See further www.unglobalcompact.org, accessed 20 February 2010: Environment: Principle 7: businesses should support a precautionary approach to environmental challenges; Principle 8: undertake initiatives to promote greater environmental responsibility; and Principle 9: encourage the development and diffusion of environmentally friendly technologies.

the 2000 revision of the Guidelines than an express reference to human rights was made.[15]

By contrast the Draft UN Code of Conduct for Transnational Corporations contained a provision on human rights:

> Transnational corporations should/shall respect human rights and fundamental freedoms in countries in which they operate. In their social and industrial relations, transnational corporations should/shall not discriminate on the basis of race, colour, sex, religion, language, social, national and ethnic origin or political or other opinion. Transnational corporations should/shall conform to government policies designed to extend equality of opportunity and treatment. (United Nations 1986: para. 13 at 31)

The main disagreement was not upon the need to include such a provision in the UN Draft Code but as to its legal force, as seen by the 'should/shall' options. In this the Draft Code lays down what has since become the most contentious issue in the debate over the extension of human rights obligations to MNEs and other business enterprises, namely, whether a legally binding obligation in this regard is possible under international law. Here again the influence of corporate actors is seen in the vigorous initiatives taken to develop self-regulatory responses and to avoid legally binding obligations. In order to explain this development it is first necessary briefly to trace the more recent discussions of the issue before UN human rights bodies.

During the late 1990s the UN Sub-Commission on Human Rights took an interest in the role of human rights obligations for transnational corporations (TNCs). The approach was one of concern about the possibly deleterious effects of profit-orientated business activities on the observance of human rights especially in the case of developing countries (see further Weissbrot and Kruger 2005: 322–328, Backer 2006: 321–332). The response was to establish a Sessional Working Group whose task was to examine the possibility of drawing up a set of Norms for the human rights responsibilities of TNCs and other business enterprises. In 2003 this process resulted in the adoption, by the Sub-Commission of the UN Norms on the Responsibilities of Transnational Corporations and Other Business Enterprises with Regard to Human Rights (UN Norms).[16] The UN Norms sought

15 OECD *Guidelines for Multinational Enterprises*, 21 June 1976, 15 ILM 977 (1976), revision of 27 June 2000, II General Policies 2 'enterprises should ... Respect the human rights of those affected by their activities consistent with the host government's international obligations and commitments.' Available at http://www.oecd.org/dataoecd/56/36/1922428.pdf, accessed: 20 February 2010, in the following OECD Guidelines.

16 Norms on the Responsibilities of Transnational Corporations and Other Business Enterprises with Regard to Human Rights. (UN Doc. E/CN.4/Sub.2/2003/12/Rev.2(2003) 13 August 2003, available at http://www1.umn.edu/humanrts/links/norms-Aug2003.html, accessed 20 February 2010, in the following UN Norms. See too Commentary on the Norms

to establish a normative 'top-down' approach to the extension of human rights obligations to business actors. They would do so through the use of the corporate 'sphere of influence' to require firms to include observance of the UN Norms as a condition of contracts with suppliers and distributors, and to observe the UN Norms internally in their dealings with employees and with the wider community. This self-regulatory approach would be backed up by monitoring and supervision by civil society groups, intergovernmental organizations and others, while states would be expected to provide legal remedies through which business actors could compensate those who had been exposed to human rights infringements.

Specifically, the UN Norms state, that:

> transnational corporations and other business enterprises shall provide prompt, effective and adequate reparation to those persons, entities, and communities that have been adversely affected by failures to comply with these Norms through, inter alia, reparations, restitution, compensation and rehabilitation for any damage done or property taken. (Amnesty International 2004: Section H para. 18)

The UN Norms introduced some clarification of where such reparation was to be determined. In the words of paragraph 18 of the UN Norms: 'In connection with determining damages, in regard to criminal sanctions, and in all other respects, these Norms shall be applied by national courts and/or international tribunals, pursuant to national and international law.' By taking this approach, the UN Norms envisaged a binding enforcement mechanism, centred on national courts and/or international tribunals, which offered directly effective rights of reparation for the individuals or groups affected as a consequence of a violation of the instrument (Muchlinski 2007: 533).

This is a problematic position that gave rise to strong criticism of the UN Norms. In particular, although the UN Norms contain many binding norms of international human rights law some of the rights that are included may not have such a legal status (see further 'In the Matter of the Draft Norms on the Responsibilities of Transnational Corporations and Other Business Enterprises with regard to Human Rights' Opinion of Professor Emeritus Maurice Mendelson QC (4 April 2004)). Therefore, if the reparation mechanism was to be real and effective it required the adoption of an instrument that had the force of law within the legal orders of the signatory states, and which recognized the legal effectiveness of all the norms that

---

on the Responsibilities of Transnational Corporations and Other Business Enterprises with Regard to Human Rights (hereafter Commentary) (UN Doc.E/CN.4/Sub.2/2003/38. Rev.2(2003) available at http://www1.umn.edu/humanrts/links/commentary-Aug2003.html, accessed 20 February 2010, in the following UN Commentary. See further for a summary and analysis of the principal provisions of the UN Norms Muchlinski 2007: 519–24, Weissbrodt and Kruger 2003, Wallace and Martin-Ortega 2004, Backer 2006: 333–355, Amnesty International 2004.

it contained. Such an instrument will not be forthcoming from the UN Human Rights Council, the successor to the UN Human Rights Commission, or any other UN body, given that the UN Norms have now been overtaken by the work of John Ruggie (the SRSG).

Furthermore, the traditional positivist argument that human rights obligations can only be carried by states was repeated against the UN Norms. Thus the United States argued that, 'human rights obligations apply to states, not non-state actors, and it is incumbent on states when they deem necessary to adopt national laws that address the obligations of private actors.'[17] In addition, as the SRSG asserts, 'preliminary research has not identified the emergence of uniform and consistent State practice establishing corporate responsibilities under customary international law.' (See John Ruggie *Business and Human Rights: Mapping International Standards of Responsibility and Accountability for Corporate Acts* UN Doc. A/HRC/4/35 19 February 2007 at para. 34, citing Zerk (2006) and State Survey in A/HRC/4/35/Add.3.) This reality could not be side-stepped by the use, in the UN Norms, of an allocation of 'primary' responsibility for states and 'secondary' responsibility for business actors.

According to Paragraph 1 of the UN Norms:

> States have the primary responsibility to promote, secure the fulfilment of, respect, ensure respect of and protect human rights recognized in international as well as national law, including ensuring that transnational corporations and other business enterprises respect human rights. Within their respective spheres of activity and influence, transnational corporations and other business enterprises have the obligation to promote, secure the fulfilment of, respect, ensure respect of and protect human rights recognized in international as well as national law, including the rights of indigenous peoples and other vulnerable groups.

This provision places states over TNCs and other business enterprises as the principal regulators of human rights observance. In addition, it recognizes that states and businesses operate in different fields and so each has a specific set of responsibilities in their particular field of operations, thereby obviating the possibility that business enterprises could supplant the state in its obligations to uphold and observe human rights, or that the state could use the Norms as an excuse for not taking action to protect human rights (*UN Commentary* at paragraph 2(b)). In response the SRSG has stated that, '(…) the norms would have extended to companies essentially the entire range of duties that States have, separated only by the undefined concepts of "primary" versus "secondary" obligations and

17 United States Statement on Item 17 of the 61st Session of the UN Human Rights Commission, 20 April 2005 available from www.business-humanrights.org. See too opposition from the UK, Saudi Arabia, Egypt and India 'Company norms must be on UN rights agenda' *Financial Times* (8 April 2004 at 9). The International Chamber of Commerce was the foremost business group opposed to the UN Norms.

"corporate sphere of influence". This formula emphasizes precisely the wrong side of the equation: defining a limited list of rights linked to imprecise and expansive responsibilities, rather than defining the specific responsibilities of companies with regard to all rights' (SRSG 2008: 82–83, 88–91).

This is a direct change in approach form the UN Norms. It takes the establishment of human rights obligations for corporate actors away from a normative, compliance based approach, based on the extension of state obligations to observe human rights to corporate actors, towards the idea of a unique corporate 'responsibility to respect' human rights. This is a distinctive concept that seeks to determine what precise responsibilities companies have in relation to rights. In this connection the SRSG emphasizes that while corporations can be considered 'organs of society', 'they are specialized economic organs, not democratic public interest institutions. As such, their responsibilities cannot and should not simply mirror the duties of States. Accordingly, the Special Representative has focused on identifying the distinctive responsibilities of companies in relation to human rights' (SRSG 2008, at para. 53).[18]

Thus John Ruggie rejects the notion central to the UN Norms, that corporate entities do have human rights responsibilities on the basis of their social existence, and returns to their economic functions as the starting point for the 'responsibility to respect' (on the social perspective of the UN Norms and their challenge to established notions of corporate governance see further Backer 2006: 357–374). This concept is developed by the SRSG to explain the extent of human rights obligations of corporate actors in what he would see as a more realistic framework, avoiding what he terms 'strategic gaming' over who is responsible for what. Central to the 'responsibility to respect' is corporate 'due diligence' a process that is already well known to firms as a method for assessing risks. In relation to human rights obligations this should require the development of a corporate human rights policy, the use of human rights impact assessments, the integration of human rights policies throughout the company and the tracking of performance (SRSG 2008, at paras 59–64). The proper exercise of due diligence would avoid corporate complicity in human rights violations (SRSG 2008, at paras 73–81).

More recently, in the light of discussions with stakeholder groups a number of further questions concerning corporate due diligence have emerged.[19] First, the concept is not used in strictly transactional terms by the SRSG but is a wider concept, which focuses on the entire life cycle of a project or business activity aimed at avoiding and mitigating human rights risks. Secondly, not only the

---

18 The reference to 'organs of society' alludes to the use of this phrase in the UN Norms, which is taken from the Universal Declaration on Human Rights.

19 UN Special Representative of the Secretary General on the Issue of Human Rights and Transnational Corporations and Other Business Enterprises 'Business and Human Rights: Towards Operationalizing the Protect, Respect and Remedy Framework (22 April 2009) UN Doc. A/HRC/11/13 paras 71–84. This summary is taken from Muchlinski 2009b.

primary investor but also the bank or other lender financing the investment would have to undertake due diligence, though how this differs from the due diligence of the primary investor requires further clarification. Thirdly, small- and medium-sized enterprises and members of supply chains will also have to undertake due diligence although the precise scope and extent of this is yet to be determined. A fourth issue is how to integrate human rights concerns into the decision-making processes of the firm: if it is a free-standing procedure the firm may not achieve sufficient connection between corporate decisions and human rights concerns while a fully integrated procedure may devalue the special qualities of human rights risk assessment. Finally, the issue of the relationship between due diligence and liability remains open to concern. Some fear that this process could create the risk of new liabilities by providing otherwise unavailable information against the company. This concern is rejected by the SRSG who feels that, to the contrary, a well managed due diligence assessment could avoid liability as it encourages a robust risk assessment, encourages positive action to mitigate known risks and transparency about the state of the company's knowledge of the risk, avoiding accusations of misrepresentations and cover-ups. This approach appears to go beyond the SRSG's earlier assertion that, given the lack of international legal personality of corporate actors, they cannot be directly bound by international law as such, and that, apart from certain narrowly drawn responsibilities in the field of international criminal law, corporations have no existing international obligations in the field of human rights as most codes are voluntary in nature and are addressed to states (UN Special Representative of the Secretary-General on the Issue of Human Rights and Transnational Corporations and Other Business Enterprises, Interim Report (22 February 2006) UN Doc E/CN.4/2006/97 at paras 60–65). It would appear that some limited general responsibilities along the lines stated above could be admitted, even if corporations are not full legal persons. It is an illustration of the effectiveness approach toward the development of international legal obligations for corporations (see Muchlinski 2009b: 6–8).

The SRSG's approach could be seen as emphasizing corporate self-regulation by use of the 'due diligence' concept over a more regulatory approach. This would be to misread the nature of the SRSG's position. The corporate responsibility to respect human rights must be read in the light of the states continuing duty to protect human rights and the joint duty to remedy human rights abuses. Thus this position is not devoid of mandatory regulation. The self-regulatory approach is backed up by legal enforcement mechanisms at the level of the state, which retains the duty to protect human rights. Indeed the SRSG is positive in his view that national legal remedies should be strengthened and made more accessible to claimants (SRSG 2008 Report, at paras 83–91 and see too SRSG 2009 Report at paras 86–115). Equally the barriers to effective remedies must be identified and removed. Thus in his 2009 Report the SRSG notes:

> 94. With regard to civil claims, a complainant may not be able to obtain an effective remedy from a company through a host State's national courts because

of a range of legal and practical impediments. There may be no available course of action. The courts may lack the capacity to handle complex claims. Costs are frequently prohibitive: even filing a case may be too expensive for poor individuals and communities, and cost allocation provisions like the "loser pays" may preclude many more claimants from bringing a case. In the event of a favourable judgement enforcement may be difficult, especially if the company lacks sufficient assets.

95. Where the company is a subsidiary of an overseas parent, additional factors can compound these barriers. The parent company may use its own leverage with the host Government or mobilize the home Government and international financial institutions. The alternative of filing a suit in the parent company's home State for the subsidiary's actions, or for the parent's own acts or omissions, can raise jurisdictional questions about whether it is the appropriate forum, and may trigger policy objections by both home and host State Governments. Moreover, the standards expected of parent companies with regard to subsidiaries may be unclear or untested in national law. Such transnational claims also raise their own evidentiary, representational, and financial difficulties.

96. As regards criminal proceedings, even where a legal basis exists, if State authorities are unwilling or unable to dedicate the resources to pursue allegations, currently there may be little that victims can do.

97. Legal and practical access barriers are often accentuated for "at risk" or vulnerable groups, whether companies are national or transnational. Such groups may include women, children and indigenous peoples, as well as those marginalized for other reasons in their interactions with companies. Governments have a critical role – and in some cases, a duty – to raise awareness of the risks facing these individuals and communities, and to ensure that their rights are adequately protected, including by providing access to remedy.

98. The Special Representative will continue research and consultations on barriers to judicial remedy, as well as possible options to address them. (SRSG 2009 Report)

Furthermore the SRSG does not rule our international enforcement mechanisms. In particular he advocates the further development of non-judicial international grievance mechanisms (SRSG 2009 Report, paras 106–114). Such mechanisms should become a normal feature of voluntary industry and other codes. Furthermore the SRSG is examining the possibility of a new international institution to improve access to non-judicial remedy:

Proposals include a clearing house to direct those with disputes towards mechanisms that might offer remedy; a capacity-building entity to help

> disputing parties use those mechanisms effectively; an expert body to aggregate and analyse outcomes, enabling more systemic learning and dispute prevention; and a grievance mechanism for when local or national mechanisms fail or are inadequate (…) The first three suggestions hold promise of practical, achievable benefits, if done appropriately. (SRSG 2009 Report at paras. 109–110)

In all of these instances access to information about the existence of such a procedure must be assured (SRSG 2009 Report at paras 107–108).

On the other hand the SRSG is more cautious as to the creation of a single, mandatory, non-judicial but adjudicative mechanism at the international level. He sees the following problems emerging:

> In handling complex disputes that involve diverse and economically unequal parties in remote locations, processes based solely on written submissions are unlikely to meet basic standards of fairness and rigor. The demands of appropriate investigations and/or hearings are likely to raise significant evidentiary, practical, financial and political challenges, while offering only limited prospects of remedies that are timely, enforceable and extend beyond a few complaints a year. (SRSG 2009 Report at para 111)

As an alternative the SRSG is also considering mediation and arbitration by existing bodies:

> 112. An alternative option would be to look to an existing body or network with international standing that could offer mediation of disputes involving human rights issues. If it had capacity to enable mediated processes in the locations where disputes arise, this could avoid many of the challenges noted above. At the same time, the mediation process would have to reflect the grievance mechanism principles set out by the Special Representative. Complainants might need advice and support to engage as equal participants in the process, and a funding model would be needed to avoid their facing prohibitive costs.
>
> 113. Arbitration by such entities might also be an option. In particular, companies operating in conflict affected areas should have a strong incentive to agree ex ante to use such mediation/arbitration bodies in the event of disputes with communities, and their investors and States should have a strong interest in seeing them do so. Arbitration would be subject to the same caveats as above, and should not preclude judicial recourse. (SRSG 2009 Report at para. 111)

The reference to arbitration is particularly interesting. Arguably if a new generation of IIAs includes a mandatory human rights observance provision addressed to investors, and this is made subject to the dispute settlement provisions of the agreement, then the system suggested by the SRSG could be put into place. However it would undoubtedly meet strong corporate resistance on the ground that it would divert IIAs from their primary role as investor and investment protection agreements. In addition, it is open to doubt whether arbitral tribunals dealing with investment issues, as currently constituted, would have the necessary mix of expertise to deal with human rights concerns. The inclusion of a human rights clause in IIAs would require a major change in the kind of experts who sit on such tribunals. That said this would be just one of many reasons why investment tribunals might have to move increasingly away from a commercial model to a more public law model of work, given the very important public interests that such cases raise.

From the two examples given above it is clear that while there are no longer any major doubts that corporate responsibility is a proper issue for international law to consider much still remains uncertain as to how this should be put into operation. In both the environmental and human rights fields there appears to have been an initial opposition to any standards being imposed on non-state actors, followed by an acceptance that some level of international regulation might be needed in view of the complex transnational nature of corporate activities, which in turn gave rise to lobbying processes aimed at controlling the degree to which active regulation would emerge.

In the environmental field such lobbying has been reasonably well noted, with varying measures of success, perhaps because home state and corporate interests are not necessarily at one here – states may require stronger regulation as a matter of effectiveness in environmental policy and feel able to disregard corporate lobbying where necessary. Equally corporations may be more willing to go along with increased regulation in this area as a matter of good business practice, as where they espouse the aims and purposes of bodies such as the BCSD, or where they have developed a comparative advantage in environmentally sound technology and wish to secure that advantage internationally through increased and more harmonized regulation (on which see further Murphy 2004: ch. 4, citing Du Ponts support for the banning of CFCs as a strategy for entrenching its advantage in non CFC based technologies).

By contrast, in the human rights field the major home states of firms affected by proposed developments such as the UN Norms have sought to avoid any strong regulatory system from evolving, preferring to support a self-regulatory approach backed by national enforcement mechanisms. In this the rejection of the UN Norms by the SRSG has been key. Having done so, the SRSG is now engaged in a new departure. It would be too easy to say that his approach firmly lies within the position favoured by international business, which itself is actively developing the kinds of due diligence mechanisms that the SRSG favours.[20] Though the due

20 See further John Ruggie Human rights impact assessments – resolving key methodological questions UN Doc. A/HRC/4/74 5 February 2007. The best example of such a reaction is that of Shell Oil which, in response to alleged complicity in human rights abuses in the Niger Delta region, revised its social responsibility policy and included human rights impact assessment into its business planning. See further Royal Dutch Shell: Shell

diligence concept and its operational implications are undoubtedly self-regulatory, it would be wrong to assume that the SRSG is excluding the future development of more mandatory international enforcement mechanisms. It is evident form the above that this is not the case and that the provision of proper accountability and liability mechanisms in national and international law is part of the policy being developed. This is still a work in progress and the possibility of introducing mandatory international obligations on MNEs to observe human rights standards through, for example, a human rights observance clause in IIAs cannot be ruled out.

IV. The Case of International Investment Law

In the previous section it was seen how corporate influence and home state support of specific positions on corporate responsibility issues has shaped the as yet rather limited regulatory system for this emerging field. In this section the development of a business friendly body of international investment law is briefly considered so as to contrast the difference in normative force between corporate control-orientated areas of international law and corporate facilitation orientated areas. International investment law is based on binding 'hard law' obligations contained in IIAs that were developed as a result of private lobbying efforts in Europe in the 1950s and in the United States in the 1970s. By contrast the corporate responsibility field is based on non-binding 'soft law' instruments which, notwithstanding arguments concerning the normative value and eventual 'hardening' of soft law, are of little practical force or effect in the absence of strong national and international regulation. Indeed attempts to introduce corporate duties into international investment law, such as the Draft UN Code of Conduct for TNCs, have so far failed or resulted in 'soft law' instruments such as the ILO Tripartite Declaration, the OECD Guidelines for Multinational Enterprises or the UN Global Compact (Muchlinski 2007: 103, 119–121, 656–662).

How has international investment law come to this position? (For a general introduction to the history of international investment law see Newcombe and Paradell 2009: ch. 1.) The first phase of private sector lobbying activity occurred during the 1950s when attempts at stimulating interest in a multilateral convention on foreign investment were made mainly by private sector bodies, including the International Chamber of Commerce (ICC) and various pressure groups.[21]

General Business Principles available at http://www-static.shell.com/static/aboutshell/downloads/who_we_are/sgbps/sgbp_english.pdf, accessed 20 February 2010. See too Business Leaders Initiative on Human Rights Human Rights Matrix at http://www.blihr.org/, accessed: 20 February 2010.

21 See International Chamber of Commerce, International Code of Fair Treatment of Foreign Investment, ICC Pub. No. 129 (Paris: Lecraw Press, 1948), reprinted in UNCTAD, *International Investment Instruments: A Compendium*, Vol. 3 (New York and Geneva,

In particular, in 1957, the German Society to Advance the Protection of Foreign Investments published a draft code entitled, 'International Convention for the Mutual Protection of Private Property Rights in Foreign Countries' (for an analysis of this code see Miller 1959). In early 1958, another privately inspired draft convention on foreign investments came from a group of European international lawyers headed by Sir Hartley Shawcross (see Brandon 1959: 12–15). These two initiatives were combined into a single draft convention in 1959 (Abs and Shawcross 1960: 116–118). This convention was taken up by the then OEEC (now OECD) for consideration. It led to the OECD Draft Convention on the Protection of Foreign Property (see OECD Publication No.1563 [6] 7 Dec. 1962 reproduced in 1–2 ILM 241 (1962–1963). The last revision of the draft Convention can be found in OECD Publication No. 232081, Nov. 1967 reproduced in 7 ILM 117 (1968)). Although that convention was never adopted it formed the basis for many of the European model post-entry treatment bilateral investment treaties (BITs).

The US by contrast relied on its network of Friendship, Commerce and Navigation (FCN) Treaties to protect its investors abroad (Newcombe and Paradell 2009: 46–47). These were increasingly irrelevant in giving effective protection where needed. Most FCN Treaties were signed with developed capital exporting states where the legal conditions for the protection of foreign investors and their investments were not in issue.[22] What was needed was a new type of investor protection agreement directed at developing host countries in particular. In the 1970s US business interests including the US International Chamber of Commerce began to lobby the US Government to offer the same protection through BITs as enjoyed by their European counterparts (Newcombe and Paradell 2009: 47, see further Vandevelde 1988: 206–209). In addition, The State Department's Advisory Committee on Transnational Enterprises recommended that the State Department commence a BIT program so as to counter the apparent erosion of investor protection guarantees under instruments such as the Charter of Economic Rights and Duties of States which spearheaded the attempt to assert sovereign control over economic policy under the New International Economic Order.[23]

United Nations, 1996) at 273 available from www.unctad.org/iia, accessed: 20 February 2010, in the following ICC in UNCTAD. Apart from these initiatives certain states also made proposals to international organizations for the adoption of a multilateral convention for the protection of foreign investments. Thus at the 14th Session of the UN Economic Commission for Asia and the Far East (ECAFE) in March 1958, the Prime Minister of Malaya suggested the conclusion of an international investment charter; also in 1958 both the German and Swiss governments submitted draft investment conventions to the OEEC. In 1957 discussions took place under the auspices of the Council of Europe for an investment convention between the Member States of the Council and certain African states.

22 That said the US did invoke its FCN Treaty with Italy to found a case of diplomatic protection arising out of an alleged expropriation of a US investment in Italy. See Elettronica Sicula SpA (ELSI) (*US v Italy*) judgment 20 July 1989, [1989] ICJ Rep 14.

23 The principal UN General Assembly Resolutions on the New International Economic Order are: Res. 3201 (S-VI) of 9 May 1974 The Declaration on the Establishment

A further factor in making international investment law a strong normative order has been the establishment of effective investor-state dispute settlement procedures under the auspices of the World Bank. The Washington Convention on the Settlement of Investment Disputes between States and Nationals of Other States was adopted by resolution of the Executive Directors of the World Bank (575 UNTS 159). This allowed for a reform of BITs to include a revised dispute settlement clause that gave the investor the option of taking the host country to international arbitration before ICSID. The idea for a World Bank forum came from within the staff of the Bank, notably its General Counsel Aaron Broches, following their experience in the provision of good offices in the resolution of investment disputes (Schreuer et al. 2009: 2, Muchlinski 2007: 717. For example the Bank acted in a conciliatory role between shareholders and the Egyptian Government following the latter's nationalization of the Suez Canal Company in 1956). Its aim was to 'depoliticize' investor-state disputes (Shihata 1986).

Whether this is an accurate description is open to argument. In one sense it can be said that the ICSID system does precisely the opposite by enshrining in binding legal obligations the assumption that host country laws and practices cannot be relied upon to offer a just resolution of investor-state disputes and that therefore only international dispute resolution can be treated with confidence by investors. This is little more than an acceptance of a specific prejudice, rooted in the politics of decolonization in the 1960s and the Cold War, that results in the suspicion of nationalist and socialist leaders and the legal systems that they dominated at the time. Arguably, in a world where investment is eagerly sought by host countries such a prejudice should not inform international law.

BIT dispute settlement clauses and ICSID have created a system that has grown far beyond what was envisaged as necessary in the 1960s, when the main type of case likely to concern ICSID would have been a nationalization of foreign owned property by a developing country government, generally a rare event. In the twenty-first century investor-state arbitration has boomed, taking into account many different types of claims of a kind that could be described as ordinary judicial review cases and not the major nationalization claims typical of the 1960s. With this arises the concern that non-state actors are now not only recognized under international treaties as having enforceable rights under international law but that they enjoy unacceptable procedural privileges as well. The possibility of bankrupting a host state by reason of multiple awards made against it under BITs is now real, as the situation of Argentina following the Peso crisis of 2001 shows. Should all the claims against Argentina made under BITs be successful, the liability could be over $80 billion! (see Burke-White and von Staden 2008: 311) Whether this is a politically

of a New International Economic Order; Res.3202 (S-VI) of 16 May 1974 The Programme of Action on the Establishment of a New International Economic Order both reproduced in 13 ILM 715–766 (1974). These were followed by Res. 3281 (XXIX) of 15 January 1975 The Charter of Economic Rights and Duties of States reproduced in 14 ILM 251–265 (1975).

acceptable outcome is in question. Whatever else, investor-state arbitration, far from being 'depoliticized' is now 'hyper-political' and appears to give private non-state actors very significant rights that are in fact independent of the states rights under the relevant BIT. The national state of the investor has no residual interest in these new rights and obligations (see further Douglas 2003: 282; but see, for an argument that investors may acquire a degree of international personality as holders of rights under investment treaties, Spiermann 2007).

Such concerns have led to the questioning of the continued validity of BITs by a number of countries. UNCTAD notes that in 2008 the denunciation of BITs has increased. This entails, 'a unilateral act of withdrawal from an agreement.' According to UNCTAD data:

> 2008 saw the denunciation of 11 BITs. Ecuador denounced nine BITs, mainly with neighbouring Latin American countries. The other denounced BITs are the one between El Salvador and Nicaragua and the one between the Netherlands and the Bolivarian Republic of Venezuela. Among the reasons likely to motivate such a development could be a general reluctance towards BITs, and questions about the effects that BITs have on a country's economic development as well as the objective of ensuring compatibility between IIAs and domestic laws, including – as in the case of the Plurinational State of Bolivia and Ecuador – the country's constitution. (ICC in UNCTAD at 6)

Equally some of the same countries have denounced the ICSID Convention. That said the system remains robust and new agreements based on the classical investor protection model continue to be concluded (see ICC in UNCTAD for details).

However the problems of BITs and the restriction of national policy space have begun to concern even the leading capital exporting states. In particular, in the United States, a major debate over the future of its BIT has arisen in response to President Barack Obama's pre-election pledge to review the effect and content of the US IIAs. During the campaign, President Obama stated:

> I will ensure that foreign investor rights are strictly limited and will fully exempt any law or regulation written to protect public safety or promote the public interest. And I will never agree to granting foreign investors any rights in the US greater than those of Americans. Our judicial system is strong and gives everyone conducting business in the United States recourse in our courts.[24]

24 Pennsylvania Fair Trade Coalition, 2008 Presidential Candidate Questionnaire, answer of Sen. Barack Obama, Question 10, available at http://www.citizenstrade.org/pdf/Questionnaire PennsylvaniaFairTradeCoalition040108FINAL_SenatorObamaResponse.pdf, accessed 20 February 2010; see *also* Barack Obama for President, *A Blueprint for Change*, Strengthening the economy: Trade, 13, available at http://www.barackobama.com/issues/, accessed 20 February 2010, where it is promised to amend the NAFTA. For a full discussion

On entering office the Obama Administration announced in the President's Trade Policy Agenda that it would 'review the implementation of our FTAs and BITs to ensure that they advance the public interest.'[25] This has led to hearings before the House Ways and Means Committee and the State Department respectively in May and July 2009.

The US debate is significant for a number of reasons. First the US is still the most important exporter of foreign direct investment (FDI) and so any changes in its Model BIT will have major international repercussions as regards the nature and extent of foreign investment and investor protection (according to UNCTAD the US maintained its position as the largest source of FDI in 2007: United Nations 2008: 7). Secondly the US is currently negotiating over new BITs with China and India, two of the most important emerging economic superpowers. Any changes to the US Model will therefore have significant effects on the ability of the US to obtain the best deal for its investors in those countries. Thirdly, the US faces, in common with other countries, the policy implications of the global financial crisis. The question arises of how BITs fit into this context and how they might be recalibrated to meet the ensuing challenges to regulation more effectively. Finally the US has experience as a respondent party to claims brought against it by investors under NAFTA.[26] This led directly to the revision of the Model BIT in 2004 which seeks to preserve host country policy space by clarifying the scope of certain substantive provisions and by introducing detailed principles upon which investor-state arbitration and other forms of dispute settlement should be conducted, so as to ensure that the host country is not unduly exposed to such claims. Whether the 2004 Model gets this balance right is at the heart of the continuing debates. In the hearings so far submissions fall into two broad groups. The business lobby argues for no change in the 2004 Model BIT or change that increases investor rights and protections especially in relation to state-owned enterprises (which are of great concern to US investors in China and who want to see any future BIT with that country contain provisions dealing with their economic power), while civil society groups argue for the end to investor-state arbitration, which is seen as an unwarranted privileging of investors over US citizens, and the recalibration of

of the debates over the future of BITs in Norway, South Africa and the United States see further Muchlinski 2010 on which this section draws.

25 Cited in Advisory from the Committee on Ways and Means Subcommittee on Trade: Trade Subcommittee Chairman Levin announces a hearing on investment protections in US trade and investment agreements 7 May 2009 tr-2. http://waysandmeans.house.gov/hearings.asp?formmode=view&id=7743.

26 For a review of the cases against the US see Testimony of Todd Tucker, Research Director Public Citizen's Global Trade Watch Division For Public Meeting of the Administration Review of the US Model Bilateral Investment Treaty Program July 29, 2009 US State Department at 10–12 available at http://www.regulations.gov/search/Regs/home.html#docketDetail?R=USTR-2009-0019, accessed: 20 February 2010.

substantive rights so that they offer no greater protection to foreign investors than would be available under the US Constitution and US laws.[27]

The debate in the US is not unique. Other countries are also undertaking or have recently undertaken a review of their BIT policies. Two countries in particular can be highlighted. Earlier in 2009 Norway decided not to go ahead with a revised Model BIT based on its consultative draft Model Agreement of 2007.[28] This was due to the extensive criticism of the draft from business groups, who felt it gave too little protection to their investments, and civil society groups, who thought it did not give enough protection to the states legitimate regulatory interests particularly in the context of the development policy of developing countries (see Vis-Dunbar 2009).[29] By contrast South Africa is continuing its review of BIT policy. The South African Government has issued a policy paper that is critical of existing BITs signed early on in the post-apartheid era (Republic of South Africa *Bilateral Investment Treaty Policy Framework Review* Government Position Paper, Department of Trade and Industry, Pretoria June 2009).[30] In particular:

> This review was partly necessitated by various arbitral proceedings initiated against the Republic of South Africa (RSA) and the need to conduct a comprehensive risk assessment. Prior to 1994, the RSA had no history of negotiating BITs and the risks posed by such treaties were not fully appreciated at that time. The Executive had not been fully apprised of all the possible consequences of BITs. While it was understood that the democratically elected government of the time had to demonstrate that the RSA was an investment friendly destination, the impact of BITs on future policies were not critically evaluated. As a result the Executive entered into agreements that were heavily stacked in favour of investors without the necessary safeguards to preserve flexibility in a number of critical policy areas. In reviewing the *travaux préparatoires* of the various BITs entered into at the time, it became apparent that the inexperience of negotiators at that time and the lack of knowledge about investment law in general resulted in agreements that were not in the long term interest of the RSA.

---

27 Submissions can be found on the House Ways and Means Committee BIT hearings website http://waysandmeans.house.gov/hearings.asp?formmode=detail&hearing=678, accessed 20 February 2010, and for the submissions to the State Department see http://www.regulations.gov/search/Regs/home.html#docketDetail?R=USTR-2009-0019, accessed 20 February 2010.

28 See Norway Draft Model BIT 2007 at http://ita.law.uvic.ca/documents/NorwayModel2007.doc, accessed 20 February 2010, see too *Norway Proposes Significant Reforms to its Investment Treaty Practices*, by Luke Eric Peterson, Investment Treaty News, 27 March 2008, available at http://www.iisd.org/pdf/2008/itn_mar27_2008.pdf, accessed 20 February 2010.

29 Available at: http://www.investmenttreatynews.org/documents/p/158.aspx, accessed 20 February 2010.

30 Available at: http://www.thedti.gov.za/ads/bi-lateral_policy.pdf, accessed 20 February 2010.

> To a large extent, the review seeks to correct this misalignment and to place before the Executive the true facts inherent to commitments undertaken by the RSA under BITs whilst at the same time updating the RSA's BIT regime as is being contemplated by many developed as well as developing countries whose history and experience of BITs is similar to that of the RSA.[31]

This strong statement of concern is striking as it openly acknowledges the lack of understanding that the South African government had in this process. Given that such an advanced country can think this then it is by no means uncertain that other less developed countries have faced similar issues. Furthermore, the review has been motivated by the considerable disappointment with the impact of first generation BITs, especially in the light of the case of *Foresti and others v the Republic of South Africa* (ICSID Case No ARB(AF)/07/1. The claimants have since withdrawn their claim and South Africa has applied to the tribunal for a default award) brought by Italian mining investors who argued that their investment had been indirectly expropriated as a result of South Africa's post-apartheid equal opportunities and land rights policy.

Thus reviews of first generation investor friendly BITs are taking place. However a new recalibrated and more balanced model agreement, which includes investor obligations as well as rights and, possibly, home country obligations in addition to host country obligations, is yet to emerge. For now the influence of business remains paramount and governments have not yet changed their approach. However the effect of the global economic crisis, and the resulting undermining of the liberal economic policies that led to it, are creating new demands for more accountable business. This may yet lead to the reform of BITs in ways that reflect the need to make MNEs act as 'law-takers' and not only as informal 'law-makers' in the system of international investment law.

V. Concluding Remarks

This chapter has sought to offer a brief overview of the question whether MNEs have a role to play in the development of international law, notwithstanding their lack of formal legal personality. It has been shown that they are in fact highly significant actors in the field and that their interests have been well attended to by states and IGOs, resulting in 'soft law' obligations and 'hard law' rights. Corporate interests have had a record of considerable success in lobbying for such a regime. This does not mean that they will always get their way, or that, in given cases, other counterbalancing interests of states and other non-states actors might affect the development of the law more strongly. That said it would appear misguided to pretend that MNEs are irrelevant and also to pretend that international law is

31 http://www.thedti.gov.za/ads/bi-lateral_policy.pdf, accessed 20 February 2010, at 5.

somehow 'neutral' or 'depoliticized' in its approach to these important non-state actors. To the contrary, international law has always displayed a specific agenda for private property protection and this has helped to protect corporate interests and to allow for the evolution of international investment law. The task now remains to ensure that the international law of corporate social responsibility develops to provide an equal normative basis as a counterweight to this position. The current crisis of capitalism may demand such a recalibration of the law if it is to retain any credibility in an increasingly anti-corporate world.

References

Abs, H. and Shawcross, H. 1960. Draft Convention on Investments Abroad. *J.Pub. L.*, 9, 116–124.

Amnesty International. 2004. *The UN Human Rights Norms for Business: Towards Legal Accountability*. London: Amnesty International.

Backer, L.C. 2006. Multinational Corporations, Transnational Law: The United Nation's Norms on the Responsibilities of Transnational Corporations as Harbinger of Corporate Responsibility in International Law. *Columbia HRLR*, 37, 287–389.

Beder, S. 1997. *Global Spin: The Corporate Assault on Environmentalism*. Melbourne: Scribe Publications.

Bishop, C.M. 1926. American Extraterritorial Jurisdiction in China. *AJIL*, 20(2), 281–299.

Braithwaite, J. and Drahos, P. 2000. *Global Business Regulation*. Cambridge: Cambridge University Press.

Brandon, M. 1959. An International Investment Code: Current Plans. *JBL*, 7, 12–15.

Burke-White, W.W. and von Staden, A. 2008. Investment Protection in Extraordinary Times: The Interpretation and Application of Non-precluded Measures Provisions in Bilateral Investment Treaties. *Va. Jo Int'l l*, 48(2), 307–410.

Chen, H., Parsley, D. and Yang, Y.-W. 2008. *Corporate Lobbying and Financial Performance*. [Online]. Available at: http://papers.ssrn.com/sol3/papers.cfm?abstract_id=1014264 [accessed: 17 September 2009].

Claire Cutler, A. 2003. *Private Power and Global Authority*. Cambridge: Cambridge University Press.

Dicken, P. 2007. *Global Shift: Mapping the Contours of the World Economy*. London: Sage Publications.

Douglas, Z. 2003. The Hybrid Foundations of Investment Treaty Arbitration. *BYIL*, 74, 151–290.

Dunning, J.H. and Lundan, S.M. 2008. *Multinational Enterprises and the Global Economy*. 2nd Edition. Cheltenham: Edward Elgar Publishing Ltd.

Ford, L.H. 2005. Challenging Global Environmental Governance of Toxics: Social Movement Agency and Global Civil Society, in *The Business of Global Environmental Governance*, edited by D.L. Levy and P.J. Newell. Cambridge, Mass.: The MIT Press, 305–328.

Friedmann, W. 1964. *The Changing Structure of International Law*. London: Stevens & Sons.

Friedmann, W. 1969. General Course in Public International Law. *Hague Recueil*, 127(2), 39–246.

Gleckman, H. 1995. Transnational Corporations' Strategic Responses to 'Sustainable Development', in *Green Globe Yearbook*, edited by H.O. Bergesen and G. Parmann, 93–106.

Halliday, F. 2001. The Romance of Non-State Actors, in *Non-State Actors in World Politics*, edited by D. Josselin and W. Wallace. Basingstoke: Palgrave, 21–40.

Henderson, D. 2001. *Misguided Virtue: False Notions of Corporate Social Responsibility*. Wellington, New Zealand: Business Roundtable.

Higgins, R. 1994. *Problems and Process: International Law and How We Use It*. Oxford: Oxford University Press.

Ijalaye, D.A. 1978. *The Extension of Corporate Personality in International Law*. Dobbs Ferry, NY: Oceana.

Jägers, N. 1999. The Legal Status of the Multinational Corporation under International Law, in *Human Rights Standards and the Responsibility of Transnational Corporations*, edited by M. Addo. The Hague: Kluwer Law International, 259–272.

Janis, M. 1984. Individuals as Subjects of International Law. *Cornell Jo Int'l L*, 17, 61–78.

Jenks, W. 1972. Multinational Entities and the Law of Nations, in *Transnational Law in a Changing Society*, edited by W. Friedmann, L. Henkin and O. Lissitzyn. New York: Columbia University Press, 70–83.

Johns, F. 1994. The Invisibility of the Transnational Corporation: An Analysis of International Law and Legal Theory. *Melbourne University LR*, 19, 893–923.

Keeton, G.W. 1926. The Growth and Scope of Extraterritoriality in China (Part I). *LQR*, 42, 481–501.

Keeton, G.W. 1927a. The Growth and Scope of Extraterritoriality in China (Part II). *LQR*, 43, 238–261.

Keeton, G.W. 1927b. The Growth and Scope of Extraterritoriality in China (Part III). *LQR*, 43, 515ff.

Mabey, N. 1999. Defending the Legacy of Rio: The Civil Society Campaign against the MAI, in *Regulating International Business: Beyond Liberalization*, edited by S. Picciotto and R. Mayne. London: MacMillan/Oxfam, 60–81.

Miller, A.S. 1959. Protection of Private Foreign Investment by Multilateral Convention. *AJIL*, 53, 371–378.

Muchlinski, P.T. 1997. 'Global Bukowina' Examined: Viewing the Multinational Enterprise as a Transnational Law-making Community, in *Global Law Without a State*, edited by G. Teubner. Aldershot: Dartmouth Publishing, 79–108.

Muchlinski, P.T. 2000. The Rise and Fall of the Multilateral Agreement on Investment: Where Now? *Int'L.Law*, 34, 1,033–1,054.
Muchlinski, P.T. 2007. Multinational Enterprises and the Law. 2nd Edition. Oxford: Oxford University Press.
Muchlinski, P.T. 2009a. The Diplomatic Protection of Foreign Investors: A Tale of Judicial Caution, in *International Investment Law for the 21st Century: Essays in Honour of Christoph Schreuer*, edited by C. Binder et al. Oxford: Oxford University Press, 341–362.
Muchlinski, P.T. 2009b. Corporations in International Law, in *Max Planck Encyclopaedia of International Law*, revised edition, edited by R. Wolfrum. Oxford: Oxford University Press. Available at: http://www.mpepil.com/ [accessed: 18 February 2010].
Muchlinski, P.T. 2010. Trends in International Investment Agreements: Calls for Reforms of Model Bilateral Investment Treaties in Norway, South Africa and the United States, in *Yearbook on International Investment Law and Policy 2009–2010*, edited by Karl P. Sauvant. New York: Oxford University Press (forthcoming).
Murphy, D.D. 2004. *The Structure of Regulatory Competition: Corporations and Public Policies in a Global Economy*. Oxford: Oxford University Press.
Newcombe, A. and Paradell, L. 2009. *Law and Practice of Investment Treaties*. The Hague: Kluwer Law International.
Paulsson, J. 1984. The ICSID Klockner v Cameroon Award: The Duties of Partners in North-South Economic Development Agreements. *Jo. Int'l. Arb.*, 1, 145ff.
Picciotto, S. 1999. Offshore: The State as Legal Fiction, in *Offshore Financial Centres and Tax Havens: The Rise of Global Capital*, edited by M.P. Hampton and J.P. Abbott. London: MacMillan, 43–79.
Pogany, I. 1992. Economic Development Agreements. *ICSID Rev-FILJ*, 7(1), 1–20.
Porter, M. 1990. *The Competitive Advantage of Nations*. London: Macmillan.
Reinisch, A. 2005. The Changing International Legal. Framework for Dealing with Non-States Actors, in *Non-State Actors and Human Rights*, edited by P. Alston. Oxford: Oxford University Press, 37–89.
Robinson, J. 1983. *Multinationals and Political Control*. Aldershot: Gower.
Rowlands, I.H. 2001. Transnational Corporations and Global Environmental Politics, in *Non-State Actors in World Politics*, edited by D. Josselin and W. Wallace. London: Palgrave, 133–149.
Sally, R. 1994. Multinational Enterprises, Political Economy and Institutional Theory: Domestic Embeddedness in the Context of Internationalisation, in *Review of International Political Economy*, 1, 161–194.
Sally, R. 1995. *States and Firms*. London: Routledge.
Salter, M. and Mason, J. 2007. *Writing Law Dissertations: An Introduction and Guide to the Conduct of Legal Research*. Harlow: Pearson Longman.
Sayre, F.W. 1928. The Passing of Extraterritoriality in Siam. *AJIL*, 22(1), 70–88.

Schreuer, C. et al. 2009. *ICSID: A Commentary*. 2nd Edition. Cambridge: Cambridge University Press.

Shihata, I.F.I. 1986. Towards a Greater Depoliticization of Investment Disputes: The Roles of ICSID and MIGA. *ICSID Rev*, 1, 1–32.

Spiermann, O. 2007. Twentieth Century Internationalism in Law. *European Journal of International Law*, 18(5), 785–814.

Staker, C. 1990. Diplomatic Protection of Private Business Companies: Determining Corporate Personality for International Law Purposes. *BYIL*, 61, 155–174.

United Nations. 1986. *The United Nations Code of Conduct on Transnational Corporations*. UNCTC Current Studies Series A No. 4. New York: United Nations Publications.

United Nations. 2002. *Report on the World Summit on Sustainable Development*. Johannesburg, South Africa, 26 August–4 September 2002, UN Doc. A/CONF.199/20. New York: United Nations Publications.

United Nations. 2008. *UNCTAD World Investment Report 2008*. New York and Geneva: United Nations Publications.

Urofsky, M.I. 1982. Proposed Federal Incorporation in the Progressive Era. *Am. J. Legal Hist.*, 26, 160–183.

Vandevelde, K.J. 1988. The Bilateral Investment Treaty Program of the United States. *Cornell Int'l L.J.*, 21, 201–276.

Verhoosel, G. 1998. Foreign Direct Investment and Legal Constraints on Domestic Environmental Policies: Striking a 'Reasonable' Balance Between Stability and Change. *Law and Pol. in Int'l Bus.*, 29, 451–479.

Vis-Dunbar, D. 2009. *Norway Shelves its Draft Model Bilateral Investment Treaty*. Investment Treaty News, 8 June. Available at: http://www.investmenttreatynews.org/documents/p/158.aspx [accessed: 18 February 2010].

Wallace, R.M.M. and Martin-Ortega, O. 2004. The UN Norms: A First Step to Universal Regulation of Transnational Corporations' Responsibilities for Human Rights? *Dublin Univ. L.J.*, 26, 304–319.

Weissbrodt, D. and Kruger, M. 2003. Norms on the Responsibilities of Transnational Corporations and Other Business Enterprises with Regard to Human Rights. *AJIL*, 97, 901–922.

Weissbrodt, D. and Kruger, M. 2005. Human Rights Responsibilities of Business as Non-State Actors, in *Non-State Actors and Human Rights*, edited by P. Alston. New York: Oxford University Press, 315–350.

Welford, R. 2002. Disturbing Development: Conflicts Between Corporate Environmentalism, the International Economic order and Sustainability, in *The Greening of Business in Developing Countries*, edited by P. Utting. London: Zed Books/UNRISD, 135–158.

Werksman, J. and Santoro, C. 1998. Investing in Sustainable Development: the Potential Interaction Between the Kyoto Protocol and the Multilateral Agreement on Investment, in *Global Climate Governance: Inter-linkages between the Kyoto Protocol and other Multilateral Regimes*, edited by W.B. Chambers. Tokyo: United Nations University, 59–74.

Wright, Q. 1943. The End of Extraterritoriality in China. *AJIL*, 37, 286–289.
Zerk, J. 2006. *Multinationals and Corporate Social Responsibility*. Cambridge: Cambridge University Press.

Chapter 3
The Impact of Non-State Actors on the International Law Regime of Corporate Social Responsibility: Blessing or Curse?

Leyla Davarnejad

I. Introduction

The control and regulation of multinational enterprises (MNEs)[1] by international law is both an old and a new topic. The current importance of this issue is due to the increasing activities of MNEs. There is no uniform definition available for MNEs. However, according to the OECD *Guidelines for Multinational Enterprises* (OECD Guidelines), they can be described as 'companies or other entities established in more than one country and so linked that they may co-ordinate their operations in various ways.'[2] World foreign direct investment inflows rose to a record level of $1.8 trillion in 2007 (UNCTAD World Investment Report 2008, p. iii). MNEs are the main providers of investment. Due to their economic and political power they are able to negotiate the legal terms of their investments with host states. As investment has considerable social, political and environmental impacts beside economic growth, which is its main aim, MNEs can play both a negative and a positive role in this context (UNCTAD World Investment Report 2007, at 145). But international investment agreements (IIAs) are the immediate legal framework and mainly protect the interests of investors aimed at a predictable investment environment, and not the interests of the wider communities in which they operate. Many countries conclude IIAs to attract foreign investment and limit, at the same time, their own scope to design national policies. Especially for

---

1 Among experts of public international law the terms 'multinational enterprises' and 'transnational enterprises' are used synonymously. However, there is a difference in the language usage of international organizations: whereas the OECD speaks of multinational enterprises, the UN prefers the notion transnational enterprises or corporations.

2 OECD Guidelines, at 12, I. Concepts and Principles, No. 3. The Guidelines revised version of 27 June 2000. With regard to the difficulties of and controversies over defining multinational enterprises in the 1970s, see in particular Fischer 2000: 921–922.

developing countries it is a challenge to strike a balance between attracting foreign direct investment and maintaining policy autonomy (ibid).

In recent years, concerns about this imbalance in the international investment law regime have grown. A social or societal dimension of IIAs is being increasingly called for, in particular for the inclusion of human rights obligations on MNEs (Ortino 2007: 243, Davarnejad 2008). But, as of yet, only few IIAs provisions are touching on societal aspects in practice (compare the survey of more than 400 IIAs in Gordon 2008). Most are concerned with environmental and labour issues rather than human rights and corruption.

But it is not only the immediate legal framework of international investment law that lacks provisions for the control and regulation of MNEs. As the international legal personality of MNEs is generally not recognized, they are not obliged to respect human rights, labour or environmental standards imposed by international law. Therefore, some international law experts speak of a legal vacuum (Kinley and Tadaki 2004: 933) or an accountability gap (Stephens 2002: 56) with reference to MNEs. The CRS notion encompasses the call for a corporate responsibility to respect human rights, social and environmental standards.

Various codes of conduct, including CSR, have been issued by IGOs, NGOs and MNEs themselves to improve this situation. These approaches of soft law and self-regulation have been conceived to compensate for the lack of hard law regulation of MNEs activities. However, there are doubts concerning the normative quality of soft law and its efficacy in controlling MNEs. The following is a survey of the various CSR instruments. The distinctiveness of their normative quality will be highlighted, paying special attention to the differing role and influence of non-state actors in their creation and implementation (generally on non-state actors see Peters et al. 2009, Arts, Noortmann and Reinalda 2001, Hofmann 1999, Risse-Kappen 1995).

This chapter has, in its main part, three sections. Section II provides a review of the CSR debate and the role of non-state actors in this field. The characteristics of this issue will be assessed from the point of view of public international law in particular. The following section (III) looks at the OECD Guidelines for Multinational Enterprises and also at private initiatives without any state or IGO participation. The participation of non-state actors will be exemplified by the Guidelines, which are regarded as being the most comprehensive and developed initiative of CSR so far, in comparison to the legal relevance of the voluntary means of self-regulation of non-governmental initiatives. The final section (IV) draws together some conclusions from the preceding sections and reflects on how the interplay between state and non-state actors in the CSR framework could be enhanced.

II. The Initial Point: Obstacles to Controlling MNEs

In this section, the two main debates in public international law about the control and regulation of MNEs will be outlined. Following this, the changing nature of the CSR debate on MNEs will be explained. It will hereby be highlighted why CSR is not only a matter of public international law, and not a typical one either. Thirdly, governmental and non-governmental regulation of MNEs will be outlined.

Similarities and Differences Between the Two International Law Debates Concerning MNEs

In public international law, the current CSR debate is one of many in a historical series of discourses on and disputes about the control and regulation of MNEs. If we disregard the historical discourses, which can be traced back to the European Middle Ages (Fischer 1980, 2000), then the first debate can be said to date back to the 1960s/70s when the colonial era was still a recent memory and developing countries tried to fend off the growing economic and political power of MNEs and sometimes also indirectly the interference of their home states. The relationship between developing countries and MNEs was often characterized by political interventionism. In that respect, the involvement of the American ITT Corporation in the 1973 overthrow of Chilean President Salvador Allende is the main example always cited (see Multinational Corporations and United States Foreign Policy: Hearings before the Subcomm. On Multinational Corporations of the Senate Comm. on Foreign Relations, 94th Cong., 1st Sess., p. 381–386 (1975)).

MNE discourses of that time were embedded in the broader debate about a new international economic order (NIEO) (Fischer 2000: 924, Sauvant and Lanier 1980: 349–350). This was meant to be a revision of the international economic system in favour of developing countries, replacing the Bretton Woods system, which had benefitted the leading states that had created it (Cassese 2005: 508–509). The United Nations Conference on Tariffs and Trade (UNCTAD) provided a platform for the developing countries to promote their interests *vis-à-vis* industrialized nations, in particular the improvement of terms of trade, the increase of development aid and the reduction of customs. Today, the significance of those UN resolutions[3] calling for the NIEO is regarded as minor, especially by experts of international law, because of the 'soft' normative quality of resolutions of the United Nations General Assembly (UNGA). However, some effects of those resolutions have been remarkable: while in the 1970s the 'seven sisters'[4] who had dominated oil production, refining and distribution were oil companies domiciled in industrialized countries, the 'new seven sisters' (Hoyos 2007) who dominate

---

3 Compare the initial document: United Nations General Assembly document (A/RES/S-6/3201) of 1 May 1974: Declaration for the Establishment of a New International Economic Order.

4 The term is coined by the Italian entrepeneur Enrico Mattei.

today's oil industry are mainly state-owned national oil and gas companies from countries outside the OECD.[5]

One can identify a paradigm shift from these debates of the 1970s to today's discussions about MNEs. While in this first phase the challenge was to protect the interests of host states against certain forms of conduct by foreign investors, the current controversies revolve around the rights and interests of individuals at risk of corporate abuse. The discussion since the 1990s can be summarized as having been dominated by human rights concerns and as having been spurt by civil society. After the revelation of some scandals of MNEs being involved in human rights violations, compliance of MNEs with human rights as well as minimum labour and environmental standards is now called for. Some place this demand of both legal and political nature under the new label of 'CSR' while others do not because for them, this term has a stricter sense (Zerk 2006).

One of the difficulties of the controversies of today is that the range of legal problems is considerable: while in some situations business actors are directly involved in human rights violations, there are also incidents of business complicity in human rights infringements by states. To assess this last category of cases of indirect but decisive involvement from a legal point of view is even more difficult. The following cases shall serve as examples to illustrate these two categories.

In the case concerning Shell Oil Company and its operations in Nigeria the Movement for the Survival of the Ogoni People, led by the author Ken Saro-Wiwa, protested against environmental damage caused, in particular, by the activities of Royal Dutch Shell. They requested a fairer share of Nigeria's oil wealth to be spent in Ogoniland (compare the set of information about this case on the website of the Business and Human Rights Resource Centre[6], including information about the US claim and finally concluded agreement with Shell). The military regime of Nigeria reacted by burning villages of the Ogoni and committing murders and rapes. In November 1995, Saro-Wiwa and eight other protesters were executed because they were said to have 'interfered' with efforts to revitalize the oil industry. These incidents were accompanied by world-wide protests and, as a result, the United Kingdom excluded Nigeria from the Commonwealth of Nations. Likewise, Royal Dutch Shell were criticized for failing to assume responsibility by not exerting their influence on the military regime, although being important investors and business partners.

Another well-known example for business involvement in human rights violations by states or political/military groups is described by the term 'conflict' or 'blood diamonds' (for general information: UN, Conflict Diamonds – Sanctions

5 The 'new seven sisters' are Saudi Aramco (Saudi Arabia), JSC Gazprom (Russia), CNPC (China), NIOC (Iran), PDVSA (Venezuela), Petrobras (Brazil), Petronas (Malaysia).

6 http://www.business-humanrights.org/, accessed 25 September 2009, in the following Business & Human Rights Resource Centre.

and War[7]; the website of the Kimberley Process[8]). Under this term the diamond industry was and partly is still reproached for fuelling civil wars in Africa by doing business with rebel groups that finance their power struggles and purchase of arms by selling diamonds (compare also the numerous UN resolutions of the Security Council to this subject: UN-Doc. S/RES/1173, UN-Doc. S/RES/1295, UN-Doc. S/RES/1306, UN-Doc. S/RES/1343, UN-Doc. S/RES/1459, UN-Doc. S/RES/1521, UN-Doc. S/RES/1579, UN-Doc. S/RES/1643). The difficulty of conflict diamonds demonstrates that MNEs can aggravate or even provoke armed conflicts by indirectly financing them.

Thus, the challenge of controlling MNEs and the CSR debate is also linked to questions of international security. Many industrial sectors have a direct or indirect impact on international security, for example the arms sector or the private security and army sectors as well as, in a broader context, the exploitation of raw materials (compare information about these sectors in Business & Human Rights Resource Centre). The control of MNEs can therefore also be regarded as a means to prevent conflicts. In this respect, it is remarkable that the only legal initiatives of the European Union (EU) related to CSR are those concerning international security issues. As a member of the *Kimberley Process* (KP) the EU has adopted a Council Regulation for implementing the KP-certification scheme for the international trade in rough diamonds.[9] The KP is an international initiative to stem the flow of conflict diamonds, joined by 75 governments, the diamond industry and civil society (read for more information the website of the Kimberley Process). Beside these initiatives, the EU's CSR commitment is limited to activities of a more political nature (compare the website of the European Commission[10]).

Examples for the other category of problematic cases in which the immediate sphere of business is affected can be found in every industry sector (compare Business & Human Rights Resource Centre). This fact emphasizes the practical relevance of CSR. For instance, MNEs in the apparel and textile industry are criticized for inhumane working conditions including the non-observance of core labour standards as those agreed on within the framework of the International Labour Organization (ILO) concerning for example child labour, forced labour, living wage and the freedom of association.

To summarize, the following can be said: despite the developments of and differences between the two international law debates concerning MNEs, the knowledge about the NIEO debate of the 1970s is still relevant for the current CSR controversies. It is noteworthy that even in the debates of the 1970s,

---

7 http://www.un.org/peace/africa/Diamond.html, accessed 25 September 2009.

8 http://www.kimberleyprocess.com/, accessed 25 September 2009.

9 Compare the Council Regulation (EC) No 2368/2002 of 20 December 2002 implementing the Kimberley Process certification scheme for the international trade in rough diamonds and for the EU Code of Conduct for arms exports: Bull. 5-1998, point 1.3.6; Bull. 6-1998, point 1.4.7.

10 http://ec.europa.eu/enterprise/csr/index_en.htm, accessed 18 September 2009.

dedicated parts of civil society demanded regulation and control of MNEs. But the inclusion of non-state actors is even more prominent in the CSR debates. These have not only influenced the codes of conduct from IGOs and participated in their implementation but have also created their own initiatives.

Thus, the debates about regulating MNEs have been characterized until today by limited governmental impact on the one hand and the growing influence of non-state actors on the other. The latter are, at the same time, as far as MNEs are concerned, the reason and, as regards civil society represented by NGOs in particular, the motivation for discussing the human rights responsibility, accountability or liability of MNEs on the political agenda and in international law debates.

Furthermore, already the NIEO debate marked a growing scepticism with regard to soft law, which is still one of the main controversies in the current CSR debate. A good evidence of this scepticism is to be found in the speech of Sir Robert Jennings at the 1976 conference of the International Law Association when he expressed his concerns that public international law threatened to become submerged beneath 'the rival empires of papers emanating from international assemblies' (see ILA speech of Sir Robert Jennings, ILA Reports, 57, 632). This remark was greatly appreciated by numerous European and US experts of public international law (Schachter 1989: 12–13, dates the beginning of the change of the opinions on soft law to this event) and sums up why the soft law debate is not merely a theoretical discourse but also highly political touching upon substantial law and economic policy interests.

In addition, it is remarkable that also within the Anti-Apartheid Movement of the 1970s there had been soft law approaches in terms of codes of conduct addressing MNEs. The widespread rejection of a legal system based on racial discrimination prompted broad public pressure against US and European MNE activities in South Africa. The Sullivan Principles and the EU's Code of Conduct for South Africa were issued as codes of conduct to prohibit – though as soft law and therefore in a judicially non-enforceable manner – discriminatory practices against black and coloured South Africans in employment, employee housing conditions and job advancement opportunities (compare for the EU Code of Conduct for South Africa: Bull. EG 9-1977, p. 51, from 21 September 1977, McCrudden 1999). For the evaluation of today's CSR codes of conduct and the participation of non-state actors in their promulgation and implementation the experiences with the soft law approaches of the 1970s are relevant and advantageous.

CSR: A Concern of Public International Law?

Although CSR has increasingly been found on the international agenda of the last decades, some date the origin of this concept back to the early eighteenth century, then motivated primarily by religious or ethical convictions (Chahoud 2005: 1). Today's notion encompasses a movement, which started in the 1990s in the US and meanwhile is globally discussed. Its conception is still very vague and has various meanings depending on the context in which it is discussed[11]. In a broader sense, CSR describes the call for corporations to assume responsibility for the impact of their actions on customers, suppliers, employees, shareholders, communities and other stakeholders, as well as the environment[12]. The basic idea of this so-called 'triple bottom line' is that a corporation is not only responsible towards its shareholders, but obliged to show a sustainable commitment to society, the environment and the economy, areas that have traditionally been regarded as falling under the sphere of public responsibility. The 'triple bottom line' encourages corporations to adopt problem-solving approaches in these fields. Therefore CSR departs in many ways from the usual boundaries between state and market and entails a new division of accountability between public and private actors. In other words the CSR concept is a renunciation of Milton Friedman's famous idea that the only social responsibility of business is to increase its profits (Friedman 1962: 133).

The omnipresent CSR debate transgresses the frontiers of several disciplines and its initiatives affect multiple levels: those of law, economics and political sciences, those of public and private law as well as those of national, European and international law. Another distinctive feature of CSR is that it is not only of concern to experts in international law, politics and so forth but also to civil society. Public interest in this debate has led to the active inclusion of a remarkable number of NGOs. The CSR debate has been further developed due to the commitment of this group of non-state actors.

The contentious point at the centre of the CSR debate is the question as to whether its requirements shall have a legally binding nature or not. Answering this in the negative, some regard CSR as being mainly limited to beneficence and charity initiatives of corporations. This paper argues that this answer does not sufficiently take into account the necessary analysis of the legal nature of CSR initiatives. As can be seen by looking at already existing initiatives, their legal nature cannot be clearly assessed. However, although the existing instruments differ widely as regards the basis chosen by IGOs to initiate them, there is a tendency to be observed in the international debate to uniformly classify all initiatives as non-binding and voluntary. In spite of this, it is worth taking a closer look and examine in detail whether an individual initiative is based on a genuinely legal foundation and has thus to be qualified as having a legal nature. To illustrate this approach, the OECD *Guidelines for Multinational Enterprises* will be examined in the following.

11 Synonyms are: corporate responsibility, corporate citizenship, responsible business and corporate social opportunity.

12 Compare for example the definition of the European Commission: KOM (2001) 366, p. 7. 'A concept whereby companies integrate social and environmental concerns in their business operations and in their interaction with their stakeholders on a voluntary basis.'

While the main areas of the CSR debate encompass several subjects beside human rights such as labour rights, environmental issues or corruption, scholars of public international law are primarily concerned with the human rights aspect of CSR. In this regard, the responsibility or accountability of MNEs potentially evoked by acts of international law or extraterritorial jurisdiction is examined (see among the vast literature for example Kamminga and Zia-Zarifi 2000, Zerk 2006, Demirag 2000: 1–15). Beyond public international law, CSR is also an issue for national and international corporation law, transnational and comparative law. In addition, CSR affects for example labour or environmental law, depending on the concrete aspect of its considerable range of subjects (Zumbansen 2006). Despite this complexity the central question of the legal quality of CSR is one of public international law since a number of relevant initiatives are those of IGOs.

Understanding the CSR debate from the point of view of public international law requires revising some of the conventional notions about this law regime and its regulation. This is not only due to the fact that CSR is not immediately concerned with the structure and conduct of states and IGOs but with the conduct and responsibility of MNEs. In addition, it concerns the responsibility of non-state actors in the host states in which they are operating. It could thus be argued that the issue is an internal one and that the question of regulation has to be answered at the national level (De Brabandere 2009). But there are serious difficulties in asking states to control MNEs. On the one hand, as already stated, it would mean asking host states to bite the hand that feeds them. On the other hand, extraterritorial jurisdiction from home states also poses a problem concerning the international law principle of state sovereignty.[13] As CSR and the human rights responsibility of MNEs are in practice dealt with by IGOs – partly in cooperation with non-state actors – CSR has already become a concern of public international law, though one of a new type.

13 Compare Report of the Special Representative of the Secretary-General (SRSG) on the issue of human rights and transnational corporations and other business enterprises 'Business and Human Rights: Mapping International Standards of Responsibility and Accountability for Corporate Acts', UNGA Doc. A/HRC/4/035 p. 6 para 15 and Addendum Corporate responsibility under international law and issues in extraterritorial regulation: summary of legal workshops, UNGA Doc A/HRC/4/35/Add. 2 from 15 February 2007; for an overview of lawsuits look at the corporate legal accountability portal of the Business & Human Rights Ressource Centre which includes concise profiles of lawsuits in which companies are accused of human rights abuses, and expert commentaries: http://www.business-humanrights.org/LegalPortal/; as well as the information of the Castan Centre for Human Rights Law and its documentation of Transnational Human Rights Litigation against Companies: http://law.monash.edu/castancentre/projects/mchr/trans-hr-litigation.html, accessed 12 February 2009.

Governmental and Non-Governmental Initiatives: The Choice between Policy Measures, Self-Regulation and Soft Regulation

Neither on a national, European nor international level is there sufficient political will to make MNEs accountable for human rights abuses. In 2005, the failure of the UN Norms on the Responsibilities of Transnational Corporations and Other Business Enterprises with Regard to Human Rights proved this on the international level (UN Doc. E/CN.4/Sub.2/2003/12/Rev.2). In retrospect, the UN initiatives in particular demonstrate that the control of MNEs has always been problematic. In 1977, the UN Centre on Transnational Corporations was established to regulate MNEs and worked mainly on a Code of Conduct (COC); but as discontent from MNEs and some governments increased, the Centre was disbanded in the early 1990s and the draft code was effectively abandoned in 1983 under pressure from the Reagan Administration (for the text of the draft code see Draft United Nations Code of Conduct on Transnational Corporations, UN Doc. E/1983/17/Rev. 1 (1983). See also Muchlinski 2000).

Instead of legal initiatives, the UN presented the Global Compact as a policy measure in 2000.[14] It is the most explicit UN initiative addressing CSR compared to other instruments, for example the Universal Declaration of Human Rights, which acknowledges corporate entities by using the term 'non-state actors' (see Article 29 of the Universal Declaration of Human Rights, 1948). The Global Compact as a 'value-based platform' is not a legally binding initiative but rather an opportunity for companies to showcase their best practices and learn from others. The Universal Declaration of Human Rights, the Rio Principles on the Environment and Development and the ILO's Fundamental Principles on Rights at Work are all referred to and used as benchmarks for the ten principles of the Compact. In terms of content, the Compact is considered to be a COC and therefore often regarded as being an equivalent of OECD and ILO initiatives. But contrary to the revised OECD Guidelines for Multinational Enterprises[15] and the ILO Tripartite Declaration of Principles concerning Multinational Enterprises and Social Policy[16] the Global Compact has never been accepted by UN members in the form of a resolution of the General Assembly. Therefore the Global Compact should be distinguished from ILO and OECD initiatives not only in formal but also in legal terms. The OECD Guidelines – as will be explained in more detail below – are a component of partly legally binding investment instruments. The ILO Declaration, which draws

14 For detailed information: http://www.unglobalcompact.org/, accessed 12 February 2009.

15 The Guidelines revised version of 27 June 2000 are available at: http://www.oecd.org/about/0,3347,en_2649_34889_1_1_1_1_1,00.html, accessed 16 February 2009.

16 The Tripartite Declaration was adopted by the Governing Body of the ILO at its 204th Session, on 16 November 1977, available at: http://www.ilo.org/public/english/employment/multi/tripartite/declaration.htm, accessed 16 February 2009.

on certain ILO conventions and recommendations that relate to labour and human rights[17] was approved by the Governing Body of the ILO.

Nevertheless, in the words of both IGOs, the OECD Guidelines and the ILO Declaration are both 'voluntary' codes, which aim to encourage positive corporative behaviour.[18] This expression was chosen to avoid the suggestion that MNEs would be held accountable for disregarding these codes of conduct. Still, the term 'voluntary' is misleading as it can only be applied to self-regulating measures such as corporate or industry codes of conduct. The contribution of business representatives to the OECD Guidelines and the ILO Declaration merely demonstrates the acceptance and approval of the codes of conduct by business. These codes of conduct are neither 'voluntary' nor self-regulative as they are governmental instruments.

It can thus be said that, as far as governmental initiatives are concerned, they should be examined based on the question as to whether they are a form of soft law or not. Therefore one needs to understand the normative dimension of the soft law discourse. Perhaps the only point on which there is agreement is the one that soft law cannot be qualified as one of the sources of international law enumerated in Art. 38 (1) ICJ Statute (Kooijmans 1996: 430, Schachter 1977: 300, Hilgenberg 1999: 511, Rotter 1971: 419, Wengler 1976: 194, Ingelse 1993: 77, Münch 1997: 611, Székely 1997: 191–192, Boyle 1999: 902). Compared to so-called hard law, it can be said that soft law is not judicially enforceable. However, that is not the same as stating that soft law is not legally not binding.

The controversy about the normative quality of soft law is one of the most contentious debates in public international law. In addition to codes of conduct, informal international agreements and resolutions are often referred to as manifestations of soft law (Petersmann 1992, Horn 1980, Thürer 2000, Shelton 2000). Many scholars regard soft law only as a kind of *pré-droit* in that it may prove

17 The referred conventions are: Convention 87: Freedom of Association and Protection of the Right to Organize, 1948; Convention 98: The Right to Organize and Collective Bargaining Convention, 1949; Convention 105: Abolition of Forced Labour, 1957; Convention 110: Conditions of Employment of Plantation Workers, 1958; Convention 111: Discrimination in Respect of Employment and Occupation, 1958; Convention 100: Equal Remuneration for Men and Women Workers for Work of Equal Value, 1951; Convention 115: Protection of Workers against Ionizing Radiations, 1960; Convention 119: Guarding of Machinery, 1963; Convention 122: Employment Policy, 1964; Convention 130: Medical Care and Sickness Benefits, 1969; Convention 135: Protection and Facilities to be Afforded to Workers' Representatives in the undertaking, 1971; Convention 136: Protection against Hazards of Poisoning arising from Benzene, 1971; Convention 138 Minimum Age for Admission to Employment, 1973; Convention 139: Prevention and Control of Occupational Hazards caused by Carcinogenic Substances and Agents, 1974; Convention 142: Vocational Guidance and Vocational Training in the Development of Human Resources, 1975; Convention 182: Prohibition and Immediate Action for the Elimination of the Worst Forms of Child Labour, 1999.

18 See OECD Guidelines, at 11, 14, 41, 44 and *ILO Tripartite Declaration* at 8, 16, 19, 22.

helpful in developing, interpreting and clarifying international law. But beyond these functions, many scholars argue that soft law has already acquired the quality of law because of its specific normative values and functions. As a body of norms, however it is considered to produce significant legal effects (Virally 1983: 343–344, Thürer 1985: 433, Wellens and Borchardt 1989: 274, Gruchalla-Wesnierski 1984, Seidl-Hohenveldern 1979: 173–246, Pellett 1989: 33, Aubert 1989: 23). Identifying these legal effects is a difficult task, both in general as well as with regard to specific codes of conduct for MNEs. Codes of conduct – like soft law in general – are always being compared to hard law and therefore regarded with scepticism. Because of the lack of enforcability, their legal quality is contested.

Beside the difficulties involved in defining the concept of soft law, codes of conduct in particular also contain confusing elements as the term 'codes of conduct' is generally used for both governmental and non-governmental initiatives containing principles of corporate conduct. But only the codes of conduct created by IGOs can – if based on a legal basis – be characterized as soft law (von Bogdandy 2008: 299). This expression has established itself in public international law as IGOs issued codes of conduct as early as the 1970s. A particular difficulty in clarifying the normative quality of codes of conduct in relation to soft law in general seems to be the variety of codes of conduct and the – in terms of law – unclear and not easily classifiable impact of non-state actors on the creation and the implementation process. Governmental soft law regulation on the one hand and non-governmental self-regulation on the other hand often seem to be confounded, as the former are declared to be 'voluntary' just as the latter. Moreover, while public international law scholars have recently become interested in non-governmental initiatives, the relevance of those instances for public international law are generally considered to be unimportant, in particular from state-centred point of view as Muchlinski already indicated in Chapter 2 (see for example Keller 2008). Thus, the CSR debate is an ideal basis for the discussion of the potential as well as the limits of the impact of non-state actors on the international law regime. However, discussing the role of non-state actors also requires a reconsideration of the role of state actors. These points will be elaborated on in detail in the following section.

III. Non-State Actors and Codes of Conduct[19]

The differences indicated between soft law and self-regulation will be illustrated by reference to the OECD Guidelines and specific non-governmental initiatives,

19 It is not possible to examine so-called 'voluntary initiatives' pertaining to social and environmental concerns such as reporting, certification, labelling, corporate social investment and improvements in environmental management systems within the framework of this chapter. Neither does the scope of this chapter allow dealing with national laws that have cross-border implications for MNEs like for example the US Alien Torts Claims Act (ATCA). Some US courts have tried to use this act as a basis for adjudicating civil liability

which could be classified as corporate self-regulation, civil regulation and multi-stakeholder initiatives. The labelling of these initiatives as government-driven or top-down and business-driven or bottom-up indicates a fundamental difference in this respect (Chahoud 2005: 2).

The OECD Guidelines: History, Content, Legal Quality and Legal Effects

On 27 June 2000, the revised OECD *Guidelines for Multinational Enterprises* were adopted by the governments of the 30 member countries of the OECD and Argentina, Brazil and Chile. So far, another eight non-OECD countries have signed this document: Egypt, Estonia, Israel, Latvia, Lithuania, Peru, Romania and Slovenia. Since their broad revision in 2000, the OECD Guidelines are regarded as the most comprehensive CSR initiative taken by an intergovernmental organization. In a number of different areas standards of corporate conduct are stipulated, including employment and industrial relations, human rights, environment, information disclosure, competition, taxation, and science and technology.

In legal terms, the OECD Guidelines indeed represent the most developed international CSR instrument. Since the Guidelines are Codes of Conduct and therefore a resolution of an IGO, a legal basis is required to affirm their legal quality. The legal construction of the OECD Guidelines is complex and has to be viewed in context with other legal instruments. Taken together, these instruments constitute a combined 'package of investment measures'. The OECD Guidelines are annexed to the OECD Declaration on International Investment and Multinational Enterprises which, at present, represents one of the three legal instruments of the OECD on international investment and trade in services (OECD Declaration, DAFFE/IME(2000)20)[20]. However, the Declaration is not among the legal acts of the organization enumerated in Article 5 of the OECD Convention[21], which are in detail binding decisions (lit. a), recommendations (lit. b) and agreements (lit. c).

---

for corporate complicity in human rights violations committed by MNEs outside the United States. But so far none of the disputed cases has been closed in confirming this kind of extraterritorial jurisdiction (compare with regard to extraterritorial jurisdiction in public international law Kamminga 2008). However, several claims led to settlements and financial compensation, such as recently in the case *Wiwa v. Shell* in June 2009 (compare the website of the Business & Human Rights Resource Centre for further information). As of today, lawsuits, in which companies are accused of human rights abuses, have been filed in a total of 17 states. But it would go beyond the scope of this paper to pursue the important question of the possibility of making MNEs accountable for human rights violations. In respect of the role of non-state actors in these claims it is worth mentioning that they can also be relevant in these legal actions. NGOs in particular support in numerous cases plaintiffs by offering legal advice or financial help.

20 OECD Declaration, DAFFE/IME (2000)20, available at: http://www.oecd.org/document/34/0,3343,en_2649_34889_1932962_1_1_1_1,00.html, accessed 13 March 2009.

21 Convention on the Organization for Economic Co-operation and Development, Paris 14th December 1960, available at: http://www.oecd.org/document/7/0,3343,en_

This inconsistency can be explained by the mere fact that the Convention is not comprehensive. According to the OECD Council and the Directorate for Legal Affairs, the term 'OECD instruments' is used to define not only OECD acts (decisions or recommendations) but also all other legal instruments, whether internal (for example Council Resolutions) or external (for example declarations), developed by the OECD within its legal framework (OECD Council, *The Concept of the OECD 'Acquis'*, C(2007) 30, from 15 March 2007, at Footnote 1). As 'other legal instruments declarations are also developed within the framework of the Organization' and insofar they are 'solemn texts setting out relatively precise policy commitments (…). They are not formal acts of the Organization and are not intended to be legally binding, but they are taken into account by the OECD Council and their application is generally monitored by the responsible OECD body.' (OECD Council, at 4 and at 2). Moreover, the Declaration on International Investment and Multinational Enterprises is considered to be one of the most important legal instruments of the OECD as it is qualified as a constitutional part of the OECD 'acquis' and is thus non-negotiable and must be accepted by an accession candidate country in the accession process (OECD Council, at 2; compare also the open letter of the Directorate of Legal Affairs, Andrea Bonucci, to the UN Secretary General's Special Representativ for Business and Human Rights, Prof. Ruggie, from 4 October 2006).

With regard to its content, the Declaration constitutes a policy commitment to improve the investment climate, encourage the positive contribution MNEs can make to economic and social progress and minimize and resolve difficulties, which may arise from their operations. Beside the OECD Guidelines, the Declaration consists of three other elements: National Treatment[22], conflicting requirements[23] and international investment incentives and disincentives[24]. Each of these elements has been underpinned by a decision by the OECD Council. According to Art. 5 lit. a of the OECD Convention, decisions are binding on all members (OECD Convention).

Assessing the legal quality of the Guidelines and their corresponding OECD instruments is therefore a complicated task. The legal nature of the Guidelines cannot be considered without examining that of their associated documents as well. The Guidelines are an annex to the Declaration as a so-called legal (though not binding) instrument, which forms part of the OECD 'acquis'. This qualification of an instrument being at the same time 'legal' but 'not legally binding', appears to be contradictory, however, it can be explained as a linguistic impreciseness. Legally speaking, the expression 'legally not binding' means 'judicially not enforceable'.

2649_201185_1915847_1_1_1_1,00.html, accessed 13 March 2009.

22 Adhering countries shall accord to foreign-controlled enterprises on their territories treatment no less favourable than that accorded in like situations to domestic enterprises.

23 Adhering countries shall co-operate so as to avoid or minimize the imposition of conflicting requirements on multinational enterprises.

24 Adhering countries recognize the need to give due weight to the interest of adhering countries affected by laws and practices in this field; they will endeavour to make measures as transparent as possible.

Accordingly, the Guidelines stipulate: 'The Guidelines are recommendations jointly addressed by governments to multinational enterprises. They provide principles and standards of good practice consistent with applicable laws. Observance of the Guidelines by enterprises is voluntary and not legally enforceable' (OECD Guidelines, at 12, Part I).

This formulation also reflects the negotiations about the revised Guidelines, which were characterized in particular by the opposing interests about the legal nature of the Guidelines and which ended up in this compromise of their constituting soft law.

The question as to whether judicial enforceability is a constitutive element of law is one of the contentious points in the soft law debate. To elaborate in detail on this theoretical question would go beyond the scope of this chapter. It is asserted that legal enforceability is not a constitutive element of law, whether national or international. The qualification of not being judicially enforceable is in fact the reason for the softness of legal acts, which are qualified as soft law in the first place. But not every international instrument, which is judicially not enforceable and therefore considered to be soft, can automatically be pigeonholed as soft law. Regrettably, scholars of public international law often categorize international instruments not mentioned in Art. 38 ICJ Statute as soft law, a term, which is then used as a 'collecting pond' for every international instrument and cannot therefore, fulfil any useful function in the public international law regime. To determine the legal quality of initiatives of IGOs in particular, one needs to examine whether the instrument in question has been adopted on a legal basis. If no such legal foundation can be determined, one is facing a mere political declaration.

With regard to the OECD Guidelines the requirement of a legal basis is met: The OECD Council stated that the Declaration on International Investment and Multinational Enterprises – and therefore the Guidelines as an annex to this Declaration – are a legal instrument and, even more, are to be qualified as a part of the OECD 'acquis'. The legal quality of the Guidelines is furthermore underpinned by a legally binding decision, which obligates the member states to set up National Contact Points to ensure the implementation procedures of the Guidelines (see OECD Guidelines, at 29, Part II). Such combinations of hard law and soft law acts, which have to be regarded as combined are sometimes called 'zebra codes'; a vivid expression that was already used in the 1970s (Baade 1980: 14–15). Hence, due to their legal basis the Guidelines have a legal quality and are thus legally binding. The Guidelines constitute soft law in the strict sense as explained above: they are an international instrument, which is soft as it is not judicially enforceable but law as, due to its legal basis, it is nevertheless legally binding.

Compared to a political declaration, the way the Guidelines are presented in the ministerial booklet is different. According to this official document, the Guidelines are the central part of the 'investment package', 'accompanied' by the Declaration and the decision about National Contact Points. This is reflected in, and strengthened by, the title of the booklet, namely 'OECD Guidelines for Multinational Enterprises'.

Corporate social responsibility is often misjudged as standing outside the realm of international law. In reality, however, it has already become a part of the international legal system, as the analysis of the OECD Guidelines undertaken above has shown. In other words, the Guidelines establish normative CSR standards for MNEs (different view: Muchlinski 2000: 1038, compare also Muchlinski 2007: 474). The comprehensive revision of the Guidelines turned MNEs into addressees of these CSR standards, which gave the Guidelines their legal significance. Thus, the legal effects of the Guidelines are remarkable as they transform the political CSR concept into a legal one. By crossing the policy threshold and turning to law-making, the participating members states declare that they not only share the same values as laid down in the CSR standards established by the Guidelines, but that they furthermore agree to help ensure compliance with the OECD standards. The Declaration and the Guidelines are more than a declaration of intent. They display a qualitative difference that is unique in the framework of CSR. Despite their softness, they have a legally binding nature, even though they cannot be enforced.

The addressees of the Guidelines are both the participating states and MNEs. According to the 'stronger' legal quality of the decision establishing the implementation procedure, the participating states are primarily addressed and obliged. This is just insofar as CSR is a subject of public interest. States and IGOs, with their legitimate public authority (von Bogdandy et al. 2009), should therefore fulfil their obligations as principal actors of the international legal system, of which CSR has already become a part.

The Role of Non-State Actors in the Review of the Guidelines

The OECD has co-operated with civil society since its creation. Principally this co-operation has taken place through the Business and Industry Advisory Committee to the OECD (BIAC) and the Trade Union Advisory Committee to the OECD (TUAC). The BIAC consists of the industrial and employer's associations of the OECD member states and is therefore representative of business and industry in the industrialized world. The TUAC is composed of national trade unions from OECD countries. In the past decade, the OECD has extended these activities to a broader range of stakeholders, notably other international civil society organizations. With regard to the Guidelines, BIAC and TUAC have become associated with this work since the 1976 Declaration. Their support and efforts to promote the Guidelines are regarded as 'fundamental' to their ultimate effectiveness.[25]

In addition, the participation of civil society has noticeably increased in the revision process of the Guidelines. This must be seen in the light of the failed Multilateral Agreement on Investment (MAI) in 1998 which represented a 'fortunate coincidence' for NGOs, unions and MNEs to have a stronger impact on the reviewed Guidelines (compare Muchlinski 2000b). Beside its rather

25 According to the official website of the OECD.

unbalanced relation of investor rights and duties, the negotiating atmosphere with its initial ignorance towards public opinion and civil society prevented the success of the MAI (compare Muchlinski 2000b). The participation of civil society in the negotiations of the Guidelines can be reconstructed in detail using proceedings which have not only been published but also made available on the internet.[26] Insofar it is remarkable that out of the 118 participants of the decisive conference on the Guidelines which was held in Budapest in November 1998 21 participants came from the business sector, 12 from trade unions, and six from NGOs; in other words, about one third of all participants, beside those representatives from governments (including 69 from OECD-Members and three from non-OECD members) and from IGOs (a total of 10 including 6 from the OECD).

The Role of Non-State Actors in the Implementation of the Guidelines

The governments of the countries adhering to the Guidelines are obliged to promote their respect by enterprises operating in or from their territory. The institutional set-up for promoting respect of the Guidelines consists mainly of the following three elements: (1) the National Contact Points (NCPs), (2) the OECD Investment Committee (OECD-IC) and the advisory committees of business and labour federations, BIAC and TUAC respectively, and (3) NGOs represented by OECD Watch.

Implementation is primarily a governmental task, though it depends on the input of non-state actors. An NCP is a government office responsible for encouraging observance of the Guidelines in a national context and for ensuring that the Guidelines are known and understood by the national business community and by other interested parties. The NCP collects information on national experiences with the Guidelines and discusses matters related to them. The NCPs meet annually to share their experience and to report to the OECD-IC (OECD Guidelines, at 30). Their central work and duty according to the OECD Council Decision of June 2000 is to handle complaints, called specific instances. Each NCP is expected to offer a forum for discussion and to assist the business community, employee organizations and other parties concerned in dealing with the issues raised. When problems arise concerning the implementation of the Guidelines in relation to specific instances of business conduct, the NCP is expected to help resolve them. Any person or organization may approach an NCP to enquire about a matter related to the Guidelines. Since 2000, some 160 complaints have been considered; half of them have been resolved.

The effectiveness of the NCP is a crucial factor in determining how influential the Guidelines are in each national context. While it is acknowledged that

26 A summary of the proceedings from the Conference on the OECD Guidelines for Multinational Enterprises from November 1998 in Budapest is available on: http://www.olis.oecd.org/olis/1998doc.nsf/LinkTo/NT00000C32/$FILE/11E88731.pdf., last visited 20 February 2009.

governments should be accorded flexibility in the way they organize NCPs, it is nevertheless expected that all NCPs function in a visible, accessible, transparent and accountable manner (OECD Guidelines, at 56 para. 8). These four criteria should guide NCPs in carrying out their activities. As has often been stated, the significance and effectiveness of the Guidelines mainly depend on the functioning of the specific instances they deal with. This is true not only because their particular implementation procedures distinguish the Guidelines from other CSR instruments but also because the Guidelines are soft law and – given the lack of enforcement mechanisms – depend on the consideration and acceptance on the part of their addressees. At present, there is some inconsistency to be observed in dealing with specific instances by the NCPs, a fact that has often been criticized.

In Contrast: The Role of Non-State Actors in Private Initiatives

The following overview of a great number of activities can only give an impression of the variety of the commitment of non-state actors. Their activities range from corporate Codes of Conduct, mostly initiated by MNEs, industry or trade associations[27], multi-stakeholder initiatives (in the form of partnerships of stakeholders such as NGOs and unions)[28] to civil society ones. Although the heyday of private codes of conduct was in the 1990s, they are the forerunners of the codes of conduct of IGOs. As long ago as 1931, the International Chamber of Commerce (ICC) issued a Code of Standards of Advertising Practice (ILO: Codes of Conduct and Multinational Enterprises, CD-Rom, Geneva 2001). While the scope of regulation of this code was limited to marketing, the regulations in the 1970s were representative of the political issues of the day, for example the Sullivan Principles, which stipulated anti-apartheid standards for companies operating in South Africa.[29] In 1999, these Principles were extended to the Global Sullivan Principles of Social Responsibility as a global framework for CSR[30]. Hence, even though the 1970s mark the decisive period for intergovernmental codes, private initiatives displayed time and again progressive approaches. From the late 1980s, various industrial organizations began to draft guidelines for their

27 Compare amongst others: Compa and Hinchliffe-Darricarrère 1995, OECD Doc., Codes of Corporate Conduct: Expanded Review of their Contents, Working Papers on International Investment, Number 2001/6).

28 Compare the comprehensive study of multi-stakeholder initiatives of: Utting 2002, Keller 2008: 235.

29 The *Sullivan Principles* established an elaborate audit mechanism administered by an independent accounting and consulting firm to ensure compliance. Their importance diminished as they were later superseded by congressional passage of comprehensive economic sanctions against South Africa: Anti-Apartheid Act of 1986, 22 USC. §§ 5,001–5,116 (1988).

30 Available at: http://www.thesullivanfoundation.org/gsp/default.asp, accessed 27 February 2009.

member companies to follow. But many reports labelled corporate – in particular environmental – self-regulation as 'greenwash' rather than a genuine attempt at improving not only the environmental but also the social performance of business. While companies such as Chevron and Royal Dutch Shell attempted to pacify activists and public opinion by adopting certain environmentally sustainable business practices, they were also denounced for aggressively lobbying against certain international environmental agreements.

The 1990s mark a period when proactive initiative of civil society to foster higher social and environmental standards for corporate activities achieved their climax (compare for a list of the enumeration of corporate and civil society initiatives for example: ILO: Codes of Conduct and Multinational Enterprises (CD-Rom, Geneva 2001). Disappointment with ineffective governmental regulations towards MNEs led to a number of multi-stakeholder approaches. Some influential NGOs even changed their roles 'from confrontation to cooperation' as they not only worked with governments but in partnership with business as well (Abrahams 2004: 3). In particular, several Northern NGOs became influential in shaping the CSR agenda. The content of that agenda partly reflected their perceptions and priorities, which were not always those of stakeholders in developing countries. And although 'civil regulation' attempted to go beyond corporate self-regulation by drafting codes, which were more comprehensive and prioritized transparency, stakeholder participation and monitoring, this form of regulation has been limited with regard to its acceptance and compliance by MNEs. Inasmuch as this kind of decision-making and norm-setting power is not limited but effective, a problem arises with regard to its legitimacy that is understood by some not only in the classical sense of democratic legitimacy, but also in the sense of international, procedural and substantive legitimacy.[31]

The relevance of these non-governmental initiatives – whether in comparison to governmental codes of conduct or as such – is unclear. As a substitute for insufficient legal standards, these private initiatives are regarded by some as a 'transnational normative regime' (Keller 2008: 222). They are considered 'informal instruments', because they have not been issued by a national legislator. However, they are considered to have a public function because they aim to protect or enhance social or ecological values. In that respect, they could be called 'hybrid' as well (Keller 2008: 222).

31 Compare with regard to Fairtrade Labelling Organization International (FLO) exercises through standard setting and certification: van den Berghe (2006). But compare also Keller (2008) with regard to the legitimacy of private codes of conduct and von Bogdandy (2008: 299) who addresses the legitimacy of international law in the light of its lacunae: 'At issue is whether a legitimate COC can justify a gap in international law and the relevant omission by the international community. A gap by the broad meaning of this contribution exists either because the relevant international law doesn't apply, or because existing international law is not respected, or because there is no adequate regulation in international law.'

The normative classification of these private initiatives is indeed difficult. When evaluating them, attention should be paid to the distinction between normative and non- or pre-normative rules (compare also Weil 1983: 417); this may already be familiar from the soft law debate. But in that case, the challenge is rather to analyse the individual case with regard to its normative quality. Soft law is generally regarded sceptically because its range is considered to be too extensive since some perceive non-normative acts like the resolutions of the UN General Assembly as soft law as well. However, this paper argues that only those interstate agreements and resolutions of IGOs with a legally binding though not judicially enforceable character should be qualified as soft law. By contrast, analysing each case of private initiatives is not necessary as they are not issued by a public authority and cannot therefore qualify as law (at least not in the framework of public international law). This does not mean that these initiatives have no relevance. On the contrary, the CSR commitment of civil society has an essential significance in stimulating the political debate of CSR, which could lead to normative acts. The role of civil society in this international issue is the same as in any domestic issue: a serious participant in a discussion but not the legislator.

IV. Conclusion

Answering the question formulated in the title of this paper has required presenting an overview of the CSR initiatives, which are, at present, such of self and soft regulation. Evaluating whether the influence of non-state actors on these instruments is positive or negative entails an assessment of the respective normative value and the potential of commitment and compliance that is inherent to both types of regulation.

The active contribution of non-state actors to the making and implementation of various codes of conduct appears to be positive and desirable at first sight. But the problem is that the numerous initiatives, which are devoid of any kind of governmental participation, could raise unrealisable expectations or be simply paper tigers. Their popularity, expressed in their inflationary number, could detract from governmental initiatives. Those, in contrast, are often evaluated in an equalizing and too sceptical way. In principle, both forms of initiatives can hardly fulfil the expectations usually associated with law in the sense of hard law. But contrary to self-regulation, soft law, understood strictly in the sense embodied by the OECD Guidelines, is a legally binding though not enforceable form of law and possesses public authority. This authority is given because the Guidelines are mainly a governmental initiative, however with significant participation of non-state actors. This public authority is essential with regard to the abidance by soft law as this kind of law lacks the possibility to be enforced. General scepticism towards soft law has to be questioned taking into consideration the advanced design of the Guidelines as regards their contents and implementation. The amplitude of obligations and their richness in detail as well as the highly structured implementation procedure make the Guidelines codes of conduct 'of a second generation' and demand the qualification as soft law.

In comparison, self-regulation mechanisms lack such inherent authority that demands compliance, especially when there is no possibility of independent control. Furthermore, the myriad quantities of different kinds of self-regulation initiatives are disadvantageous as they have the potential to be fragmenting and thus aggravate legal uncertainty.

The Role of Non-State Actors in Making Arrangements for CSR

As demonstrated above, the ideas of codes of conduct and self-regulation derive from corporate initiatives. Some IGOs picked up this approach in the 1970s by simply copying and transforming it into soft, that is to say, judicially not enforceable regulations. In doing so, they turned codes of conduct into formal instruments. But the authority of governmental organizations alone without any provisions with regard to the implementations of these instruments could not give them sufficient effectiveness. This defect had two consequences: a proliferation of private initiatives in the 1990s and the further development of governmental codes, for example the OECD Guidelines. Both developments are due to the significant contribution of non-state actors.

Considering these developments, the questions are: which of these approaches is more promising with regard to fulfilling the aims of CSR as well as with regard to the efforts of non-state actors? What can be learned from the various forms of impact of non-state actors in the international law regime of CSR? Are they more than initiators of CSR regulation and are they capable of fulfilling the task of a CSR legislator?

Non-state actors such as representatives from civil society as well as MNEs are invaluable participants in the creation and implementation of CSR regulations. But since they promote particular interests and might therefore be biased their contribution should primarily be regarded as policy-making and not as law. This is the case in particular with regard to MNEs, as their action is intended to regulate and control their own conduct. In comparison to groups of civil society, MNEs are the leading, 'number one' non-state actors as far as their impact on the international law regime of CSR is concerned. They exercise 'private power', which, at present, provides the foundation for CSR initiatives.

In comparison to MNEs the influence of parts of civil society is still limited. Admittedly, as Wilfred Bolewski put it, 'state and government structures are not the only ones promoting transformative social change' and 'in transnational civil societies with their associational networks social change movements foster a continuous process of transboundary interactions' (Bolewski 2007: 85, who speaks also of a 'private authority in transnational relations'). But the influence of this 'transnational civil society' on social, political and economic developments is limited, as its new regulatory norms are not accepted as authoritative. They have constructed their own transboundary networks and their positions are taken heed of by governments and by business. But their capacity to bring about change in the policies and practices of governments and IGOs is limited.

In summary, pure corporate initiatives can be regarded as a marketing strategy and a promise, which can be 'picked up' as a basis for a confrontation in case of disregard. On the other hand, multi-stakeholder initiatives are valuable forums for discussions if equipped with an independent monitoring mechanism. It should be avoided to regard purely civil society codes of conduct as law; they are neither national, transnational nor international law. If private actors are willing to bind themselves legally, such agreements represent contracts or one-sided assurances and are, thus, a private legal act even if the contents of the obligations concern public issues. Without the participation of states and IGOs non-state actors cannot therefore fulfil the task of a CSR legislator.

From the point of view of civil society as represented especially by NGOs, the crucial question could be: which input is more promising? Having a say in a governmental context or acting in a self-contained way? This question cannot be answered unequivocally as, on the one hand, the efficiency of governmental and non-governmental initiatives differs a great deal and as, on the other hand, the desired outcome can be manifold. Whether soft or self-regulations really improve the CSR standards is difficult to assess: functioning monitoring procedures and compliance review mechanisms are necessary. Private activities have made valuable contribution and, by starting their own activities, non-state actors have catapulted the CSR debate into a new era. In the elaboration of governmental codes of conduct such as the OECD Guidelines, they should be regarded by participating states as equal contributors in comparison to MNEs. Especially with regard to specific instances, their concerns should be taken more seriously. For the functioning of soft law an implementation system, which would truly ensure compliance, is crucial.

Implications for the Role of State and Non-State Actors in Public International Law

Finally, what conclusion can be drawn from the variety of CSR instruments and the varied participation of non-state actors for their consideration in public international law? And what is the appropriate and meaningful role of civil society and MNEs in public international law next to that of states and IGOs? I agree with Philip Alston that the world is a much more 'poly-centric place than it was in 1945' and anyone who contemplates 'the world essentially through the prism of the "State" will be seeing a rather distorted image' (Alston 2005: 4). The rights and obligations of non-state actors in the international law regime should be regulated in relation to their impact, which is nowadays significant. As demonstrated, this is true in particular with regard to CSR. Non-state actors are important participants of CSR initiatives but the significance of self-regulation and thus their contribution in this respect should not be overestimated. Instead, governmental initiatives should provide for the participation of non-state actors in an equal and balanced way.

The active engagement of non-state actors in the CSR debate should not result in losing sight of the role and responsibility of states in this context. While generally representing the principal actors in the international legal system, their role in the CSR debate is ambivalent and restrained. Many states even decide to ask MNEs to regulate themselves instead of issuing their own governmental regulations. Taking CSR seriously requires clear governmental commitment. States should furthermore invite non-state actors to participate in governmental CSR initiatives, but refrain from shifting their responsibility for this public concern to non-state actors.

These results of the CSR debate could be reconsidered in principle for the role of non-state actors in the broader framework of public international law in general. State and non-state actors are both invaluable for the realization of CSR standards, but each actor has its own contribution to make; these roles are not interchangeable. Civil society is an important initiator and a partner, which should be taken seriously in the CSR debate. MNEs are at the same time subject and object of the CSR issue and must be involved in the debate to increase the prospects of success of any initiative. States and IGOs are still the legitimate public authority and should fulfil their obligations as principal actors in the international legal system.

References

Abrahams, D. 2004. *Regulating Corporations – A Resource Guide*, [Online]. Available at: http://www.unrisd.org/unrisd/website/document.nsf/(httpPublications)/81A67BDFE6D6E4A9C1256EED005041F8?OpenDocument [accessed: 15 March 2009].

Alston, P. 2005. The 'Not-a-Cat' Syndrome: Can the International Human Rights Regime Accommodate Non-State Actors?, in *Non-State Actors and Human Rights*, edited by P. Alston. New York: Oxford University Press, 3–36.

Arts, B., Noortmann, M. and Reinalda, B. (eds). 2001. *Non-State Actors in International Relations*. Aldershot: Ashgate.

Aubert, J.-F. 1989. Observations d'un Constitutionaliste sur l'Evolution des Sources du Droit International. *Schweizer Jahrbuch für Internationales Recht*, 46, 13–38.

Baade, H.W. 1980. The Legal Effects of Codes of Conduct for MNEs, in *Legal Problems of Codes of Conduct for Multinational Enterprises*, edited by N. Horn. Deventer: Kluwer, 3–43.

Bolewski, W. 2007. *Diplomacy and International Law in Globalized Relations*. Berlin: Springer.

Boyle, A.E. 1999. Some Reflections on the Relationship of Treaties and Soft Law. *International and Comparative Law Quarterly*, 48, 901–913.

Cassese, A. 2005. *International Law*. 2nd Edition. Oxford: Oxford University Press.

Chahoud, T. 2005. *International Instruments for Promoting Corporate Social Responsibility (CSR)*, Briefing Paper, 2, 1–4. Bonn: German Development Institute.

Compa, L. and Hinchliffe-Darricarrère, T. 1995. Enforcing International Labor Rights through Corporate Codes of Conduct. *Comp. J. Transnational L.*, 33, 663–689.

Davarnejad, L. 2008. *Strengthening the Social Dimension of International Investment Agreements by Integrating Codes of Conduct for Multinational Enterprises*. [Online]. Available at: http://www.oecd.org/dataoecd/10/5/40352144.pdf [accessed: 12 September 2009].

De Brabandere, E. 2009. *State-Centrism and Human Rights Obligations Challenging 'Stateless' Approaches towards Direct Corporate Responsibility*. [Online]. Available at: http://www.ggs.kuleuven.be/non_state_actors/publications.html [accessed: 12 September 2009].

Demirag, I. (ed.) 2005. *Corporate Social Responsibility, Accountability and Governance, Global Perspectives*. Sheffield: Greenleaf Publishing.

Fischer, P. 1980. Das Transnationale Unternehmen als Phänomen in der Völkerrechtsgeschichte, in *Völkerrecht und Rechtsphilosophie – Internationale Festschrift für Stephan Verosta*, edited by P. Fischer et al. Berlin: Duncker und Humblot, 345–370.

Fischer, P. 2000. Transnational Enterprises. *Encyclopedia of Public International Law, IV*, edited by R. Bernhardt. Amsterdam, 921–926.

Friedman, M. 1962. *Capitalism and Freedom*. Chicago: Chicago University Press.

Gordon, K. 2008. International Investment Agreements: A Survey of Environmental, Labour and Anti-corruption Issues, in *International Investment Law. Understanding Concepts and Tracking Innovations*, edited by OECD. Paris: OECD Publishing, 135–240.

Gruchalla-Wesnierski, T. 1984. A Framework for Understanding Soft Law. *McGill L.J.*, 30, 37–88.

Hilgenberg, H. 1999. A Fresh Look at Soft Law. *EJIL*, 10(3), 499–515.

Hofmann, R. (ed.) 1999. *Non-State Actors as New Subjects of International Law. International Law – From the Traditional State Order Towards the Law of the Global Community. Proceedings of an International Symposium of the Kiel Walther-Schücking-Institute of International Law, March 25 to 28, 1998*. Berlin: Duncker & Humblot.

Horn, N. (ed.) 1980. *Legal Problems of Code of Conduct for Multinational Enterprises*. Deventer, The Netherlands: Kluwer.

Hoyos, C. 2007. The New Seven Sisters: Oil and Gas Giants Dwarf Western Rivals. *The Financial Times*, 12 March 2007.

Ingelse, C. 1993. *Soft Law? Pol. Yb. I.L.*, 20, 75–90.

Kamminga, M.T. and Zia-Zarifi, S. (eds). 2000. *Liability of Multinational Corporations under International Law*. The Hague: Martinus Nijhoff.

Kamminga, M.T. 2008. Extraterritoriality, in *Max Planck Encyclopedia of Public International Law*, edited by R. Wolfrum. Oxford: Oxford University Press.

Keller, H. 2008. Codes of Conduct and their Implementation: The Question of Legitimacy, in *Legitimacy in International Law*, edited by R. Wolfrum and V. Röben. Berlin: Springer, 219–298.

Kinley, D. and Tadaki, J. 2004. From Talk to Walk: The Emergence of Human Rights Responsibilities for Corporations at International Law. *Virginia Journal of International Law*, 44(4), 931–1,023.

Kooijmans, P.H. 1996. Some Thoughts on the Relation between Extra-Legal Agreements and the Law-Creating Process, in *Theory of International Law at the Threshold of the 21st Century, Essays in Honour of Krzystof Skubisziewsk*. The Hague: Kluwer Law International, 425–437.

McCrudden, C. 1999. Human Rights Codes for Transnational Corporations: What can the Sullivan and Mac Bride Principles tell us? *Oxford Journal of Legal Studies*, 19, 167–201.

McLean, A. 1999. The European Union Code of Conduct on Arms Exports, in *Human Rights Standards and the Responsibility of Transnational Corporations*, edited by M.K. Addo. The Hague: Kluwer Law International, 115–122.

Muchlinski, P. 2000a. Attempts To Extend the Accountability of Transnational Corporations: The Role of UNCTAD, in *Liability of Multinational Corporations under International Law*, edited by M.T. Kamminga and S. Zia-Zarifi. The Hague: Martinus Nijhoff, 97–117.

Muchlinski, P. 2000b. The Rise and Fall of the Multilateral Agreement on Investment: Where Now? *Int'l Law*, 34, 1,033–1,054.

Muchlinski, P. 2007. *Multinational Enterprises and the Law*. Oxford: Oxford University Press.

Münch, F. 1997. Non-Binding Agreements. *Encyclopedia of Public International Law, III*, edited by R. Bernhardt. Amsterdam: North-Holland Publishing, 606–661.

Ortino, F. 2007. The Social Dimension of International Investment Agreements: Drafting a New BIT/MIT Model? *International Law FORUM du droit international*, 7, 243–250.

Pellet, A. 1989. The Normative Dilemma: Will and Consent in International Law-making. *The Australian Yearbook of International Law*, 12, 22–53.

Peters, A. et al. (eds). *Non-State Actors as Standard Setters*. Cambridge: Cambridge University Press.

Petersmann, E.-U. 1992. Codes of Conduct, *Encyclopedia of Public International Law, I*, edited by R. Bernhardt. Amsterdam: North-Holland Publishing, 627–632.

Risse-Kappen, T. (ed). 1995. *Bringing Transnational Relations Back in. Non-State Actors, Domestic Structures and International Institutions*. Cambridge: Cambridge University Press.

Rotter, M. 1971. Die Abgrenzung zwischen völkerrechtlichem Vertrag und außerrechtlicher zwischenstaatlicher Abmachung, in *Internationale Festschrift für Alfred Verdross*, edited by M. René et al. Munich and Salzburg: Fink, 413–434.

Sauvant, K.P. and Lanier, E.R. 1980. Host – Country Councils: Concept and Legal Aspects, in *Legal Problems of Codes of Conduct for Multinational Enterprises*, edited by N. Horn. Denveter: Kluwer, 341–405.

Schachter, O. 1977. The Twilight Existence of Nonbinding International Agreements. *American Journal of International Law*, 71, 296–304.

Schachter, O. 1989. Recent Trends in International Law-making. *Austr. Yb. I.L.*, 12, 1–15.

Seidl-Hohenveldern, I. 1979. International Economic 'Soft Law'. *Recueil des Cours de l'Académie de Droit Internationale de la Haye*, 163(2), 165–246.

Shelton, D. (ed.) 2000. *Commitment and Compliance. The Role of Non-Binding Norms in the International Legal System*. New York: Oxford University Press.

Stephens, B. 2002. The Amorality of Profit: Transnational Corporations and Human Rights. *Berkeley Journal of International Law*, 20(1), 45–90.

Székely, A. 1997. Non-binding Commitments: A Commentary on the Softening of International Law Evidenced in the Environmental Field, in *International Law on the Eve of the Twenty-First Century – Views from the International Law Commission*. New York: United Nations Publications, 173–200.

Thürer, D. 1985. 'Soft Law' – eine neue Form von Völkerrecht? *Zeitschrift für Schweizerisches Recht*, 104(1), 429–453.

Thürer, D. 2000. Soft Law, *Encyclopedia of Public International Law, IV*, edited by R. Bernhardt, Amsterdam: North-Holland Publishing, 452–460.

Utting, P. 2002. Regulating Business via Multistakeholder Initiatives: A Preliminary Assessment, in *Voluntary Approaches to Corporate Responsibility: Readings and Resource Guide*. Geneva: UN – NGLS Publications, 61–130.

van den Berghe, F. 2006. Good Coffee, Bad Governance? The Legitimacy of FLO. *CHRGJ*, Working Paper No. 12.

Virally, M. 1983. La Distinction entre Textes Internationaux de portée Juridique et Textes Internationaux dépourvus de portée Juridique (à L'exception des Textes émanant des Organizations Internationales). *Annuaire de l'Institute de Droit International*, 60(I), 166–257.

von Bogdandy, A. 2008. Codes of Conduct and the Legitimacy of International Law, in *Legitimacy in International Law*, edited by R. Wolfrum and V. Röben. Berlin: Springer, 299–308.

von Bogdandy, A. et al. (eds). 2009. *The Exercise of Public Authority by International Institutions. Advancing International Institutional Law*. Berlin: Springer.

Weil, P. 1983. Towards Relative Normativity in International Law? *American Journal of International Law*, 77, 413–442.

Wellens, K.C. and Borchardt, G.M. 1989. Soft Law in European Community Law. *European Law Review*, 14(5), 267–321.

PART TWO

Chapter 4
Imposing International Duties on Non-State Actors and the Legitimacy of International Law

Cedric Ryngaert

> The prevailing rules for who may play the game of war and who may not are self-interested rules, drawn up by national governments and in no case I am aware of placed before the citizenry for approval. In effect they define diplomacy, including the use of military force as the ultimate diplomatic measure, as a matter solely between governments.
>
> (Coetzee 2008: 21)

International legal personality in essence means that a person is bearer of (certain) rights and duties under international law. In the classic conception of international law as a consensual system, actors – traditionally states – only incur rights and duties to the extent that they have given their consent to be bound by those duties or to enjoy those rights. The question now arises whether the international community of states could encumber other legal persons in the international sphere with international legal duties, possibly *without their consent* (we will only tangentially touch upon the enjoyment of rights, as persons will ordinarily not oppose benefits that accrue to them, see Section I). Put differently, can an already constituted subject of international law, in practice the state, as the original subject of international law, or an intergovernmental organization (of which the international personality, being directly derived from the international personality of states as their founders, is hardly contested), create duties under international law for non-state actors (as opposed to domestic law, where the creation of duties for non-state actors is self-evident)?

The *Leitmotiv* of the analysis will be the legitimacy of rules: can rules be legitimate, in the sense of being justified and able to command widespread support, if they are imposed on actors without their consent (Section II) (Thürer 1999: 54)? The general answer in this contribution will be in the negative (Section IV). It will be argued, in line with discursive democracy and legitimacy theories, that international rules forfeit their legitimacy if those who are governed by them had no opportunity of participating in their making. Procedural rules of inclusive or participatory governance are of the essence if the substantive rules are to be considered legitimate. Demanding direct compliance of non-state actors with international obligations can therefore only be justified if those actors have been represented in the adoption process of the rules giving rise to the obligations, or to put it more succinctly, if they are considered as genuine *subjects* of international law.

This contribution mainly emphasizes the necessity of an enhanced legal position of non-state actors in international decision-making processes. This will allow them to influence the making of the law and to secure their consent, and may thus safeguard the legitimacy of imposing obligations on them. At the same time, this argument will be nuanced somewhat. When it comes to protecting the most basic values of the international community, one may arguably loosen the requirement of consent, along the lines of the theory of *jus cogens* (Section III). Consent is in fact a function of the substantive values protected by the rules. The more basic the values are, the more relaxed the formal consent requirement might become. After all, the basic rules of the game should not be held hostage by actors who refuse to give their consent and, moreover, if they are to be considered as so central, one could presume *implicit* consent. Ideally of course, because the definition of what constitute 'the basic rules' remains elusive, and appears to be based on moral *a priori*, it appears wise to invite all those affected in the process of giving these rules shape to have their say, and thus to enhance the *procedural* legitimacy of international law. The general consent deficit of *jus cogens* rules nevertheless exceeds the scope of this contribution – which focuses on non-state actors – so that the argument of substantive legitimacy is in the end only touched upon briefly here.

I. The Creation of Rights for Non-State Actors

Let us first shed some light on the issue of the creation of rights for non-state actors. In the post-World War II period, states have signed and ratified a vast number of human rights treaties which do not appear to create reciprocal (state-to-state) rights and duties, but confer rights on individuals – who are of course non-state actors – within their jurisdiction, rights that have to be guaranteed by the state. It could be argued that states thus established (limited) international legal personality for the individual. However, in another reading of this process of rights-creation, international human rights treaties do not create rights under international law for individuals, but merely create the obligation of states parties to respect, protect and promote the human rights of individuals within their jurisdiction, with the other states parties, as it were, at the international rights-enjoying side of the bargain. In this view, states establish reciprocal human rights duties, and states can take each other to task when another state violates human rights, since human rights obligations can be seen as *erga omnes* obligations. In this reading, human rights are only domestic entitlements of citizens, which all states parties to the relevant human rights conventions nonetheless undertake to protect. However, this restricted view of human rights is challenged by the procedural rights that the conventions accord to individuals, in particular the right to petition an international human rights supervisory body (whether a committee or a full-blown court) in case of human rights violations. The very granting of procedural rights to non-state actors testifies to an understanding of states parties that the reciprocal system would not work for human rights violations, since states ordinarily have no incentive to take other states to task for violations which do not directly threaten state interests. Thus, it could be submitted, rather convincingly, that by granting those procedural rights, states have created international rights for, and international legal personality of, non-state actors.

II. Duties and the Legitimacy of the Law

The creation of international rights, such as human rights, for non-state actors, is not very problematic, however. Non-state actors, as any actors for that matter, will normally greet any rights that may be accorded to them with enthusiasm.[1] When a subject is not problematic, ordinarily it does not lend itself to an interesting study. Problems do arise, however, in respect of *duties* imposed on non-state actors, all the more so if those duties are created without their consent to be bound. If states create international legal duties for non-state actors without the latter's consent, the legitimacy of the international legal system may potentially come under strain. And indeed, a system that is strained is a subject fit for academic contemplation.

The legitimacy of the law, that is to say, the justification of the binding force of the law, has been studied for centuries by both political philosophers and legal theorists. It would lead us too far to revisit this debate in its entirety. For our purposes, it suffices to identify the two main strands of thought in legal-political thinking on legitimacy. The first strand has it that law is legitimate if its process of creation is just (that is to say, input-legitimacy or procedural legitimacy). Pursuant to the second one, law is legitimate because the substance of the law itself is just or the law proves effective (that is to say, output legitimacy or substantive legitimacy). In order to ground the binding character of international law for non-state actors, one thus has to prove that either the process of creation of the international legal norm is just, which implies that the non-state actor has at least to some extent participated in the creation of the norm (democratic participation/participatory governance), or that the legal norm or its implementation has in itself an important substantive value.

Substantive Legitimacy

Let us first turn to the second strand of legitimating the binding character of international law for non-state actors, the strand pursuant to which international law

1 Compare Article 34 (1) of the Vienna Convention on the Law of Treaties, pursuant to which the assent of a third state for which a right arises from a treaty shall be presumed so long as the contrary is not indicated (unless the treaty otherwise provides).

is legitimate because it protects important values. It is understood that, precisely because of the (expected) output of the norm's implementation, the legitimacy of the process of creation of the norm is of lesser relevance. This means that consent of the non-state actor as addressee of the norm need not be secured, or at least to a lesser extent.

It is useful to recall that in international law there exists a category of norms, norms of *jus cogens*, which are considered to be binding on all addressees irrespective of whether or not they have given their consent to be bound. However, *jus cogens* is also addressed at states, and not only at non-state actors. As the issue is therefore not peculiar to non-state actors, we refer to general discussions of *jus cogens*, and the legitimacy and consent problems, which it elicits.

The characterization of norms as *jus cogens* norms is nonetheless germane to our discussion to the extent that some of those norms attract individual – that is to say, non-state actor – criminal responsibility under both treaty and customary international law. It is currently indeed uncontested that individuals could be held liable under international law for such *jus cogens* violations as crimes against humanity, war crimes and genocide (even if they are not liable under domestic law). International law – in practice states, as states ratify treaties, and only state practice is taken into account in order to ascertain the existence of customary international law – thus creates limited duties for non-state actors without their consent.

It is noted that the international criminalization of the said transgressions, and the possibility of being brought to justice before an international court (or a national court acting as agent of the international community, for example, a court exercising universal jurisdiction), is justified because of the heinous character of the violations. The transgressors are considered to be enemies of mankind (*hostes humani generis*), and their punishment to be a moral imperative and contributing to societal reconciliation and a lasting peace. Casting this discussion in terms of theories of legitimacy, it may be submitted that, precisely because criminal accountability for, and punishment of heinous crimes are important substantive values of the international community, imposing duties of international criminal liability on non-state actors appears as legitimate; in other words, the norms that create those duties are legitimate because they effectively contribute to an internationally desirable state of affairs (output legitimacy). To the extent that certain norms could be considered as the most basic values of the international community, similar to the paradigms of international crimes, they could be imposed on non-state actors, without their explicit consent.

Almost in passing, it is observed that, as far as those paradigms are concerned, consent is *in fact* implicit: it is indeed almost inconceivable that a non-state actor would *a priori* oppose accountability for crimes so grave as to shock the conscience of mankind. If all actors are rational – which is the premise of natural law theories ultimately underlying the international criminalization of heinous acts – they cannot but give their assent to be bound by international accountability norms. In that sense, those norms are imbued with a certain measure of input legitimacy.

Procedural Legitimacy

To the extent that transgressions of international norms by non-state actors do not rise to the level of heinousness comparable to the said paradigms – these are, as we write, practically all norm violations – will the international law norms be in need of input or procedural legitimacy. Their legitimacy will then hinge on the fairness of the procedure rather than the substantive values, which the norms protect. Of course, the more the norm approaches the paradigms, the more relaxed the requirement of procedural fairness might become. Substantive justness and procedural fairness may therefore be conceived as communicating vessels. Ideally, however, a norm is both legitimate because it is substantively just and because its procedure of will-formation is fair and inclusive. International law should therefore strive for the full realization of both substantive justice and proper procedural rights for participants in law-creation.

III. Non-State Actors and International Law's Procedural Legitimacy Deficit

Let us now focus more intensely on the input or procedural legitimacy of the binding character of international norms in respect of non-state actors. In line with Jürgen Habermas' well-known legitimacy theory of deliberative democracy and communication, which we will use as our theoretical point of departure, the legitimacy of a norm is derived from the quality of the process of will-formation accompanying the creation of the norm (Habermas 1992: 666).[2] This process is characterized by the participation in the formative process of all actors affected by the norm. Legitimacy then is a function of granting adequate participatory rights, or allocating legal personality in the process of law-creation, not only to states, but all relevant actors, including non-state actors.

An international law norm will only be legitimate provided that the actors affected by the norm are involved in its creation, preferably by having a legally guaranteed position, which enables them to influence the content of the norm. Thus, international norms that affect non-state actors, are in need of the latter's participation in order to be legitimate. This implies that the legitimacy of norms that bind non-state actors but that are only adopted by states without the former's involvement, is open to doubt (Franck 1995: 484).[3]

2 The author agrees with Miller (2008) that this theory, which may admittedly have originally been conceived to apply in a state-like context to relations between individuals, could also be applied to relations between collective entities, such as non-state actors, states, and international organizations.

3 Franck's concept of 'fairness' might in fact be a close analogy to the concept of 'legitimacy' used in this article: '[F]airness discourse requires fairness in the selection of participants. At present, the term 'global discourse' suggests a conversation between nations.

To be true, it may be argued that this legitimacy deficit is more apparent than real: after all, is the legitimacy question regarding the imposition of direct international obligations on non-state actors not wholly answered at the domestic level? Are *states* not the representatives of non-state actors? Pursuant to this argument, there are no such things as 'non-state actors' at the international level: that level only consists of states, which *indirectly* represent citizens, civil society, and non-state actors in general. In order for non-state actors to effectively weigh on the international policy agenda, they should not claim participatory rights in international forums, but rather maximize their international impact through state governments. This will mainly occur by electing, or having elected, those governments that truly represent their will, and by lobbying with state delegations to include particular non-state perspectives in their negotiation strategy. According to Thomas Franck [the] 'textbook solution' to [the international democratic deficit] would be world governance through directly elected representatives. Since this is not about to happen, a second best approach is to ensure that those who speak in global discourse [states] themselves represent democratically elected governments (Franck 1999: 261).

On both counts, this argument is misconceived, as it confounds *Sollen* with *Sein*, and presents too rosy a picture. First, although the advancement of democracy in the world has ensured more representation of the genuine popular – in effect 'non-state actor' – will,[4] nation-state democracy is definitely not fully acquired yet, leaving the legitimate interests of a sizable proportion of the world's non-state actors possibly unaccounted for (Boyle and Chinkin 2007: 61). Moreover, the tendencies of nation-state democracies to decide by majority may silence minority views that are widely shared across national boundaries (for example, the interests of diasporas, religious groups, environmental groups, and so forth) (Wedgewood 1999).[5] Secondly, as far as the argument of lobbying is concerned, it might indeed be true that this is the way non-state actors currently weigh on the international agenda, but whether this is normatively desirable is an entirely different matter. Lobbying almost necessarily involves backroom dealings where power often trumps rational arguments made in the public interest, and where the non-state actor always remains at the mercy of the government. The accountability, transparency

---

That limited view, however, is wrong. Not only is it inaccurate, overlooking the many actors – multinational corporations, churches, service organizations, gender- and ethno-culturally specific groups, scientific networks, and a myriad others – who are already part of this discourse. In addition, and centrally, the mental model's wrongness lies in its unfairness' (Franck 1995).

4 Boyle and Chinkin (2007) raise the issue, without necessarily concluding that enhanced non-state participation at the international level could be dispensed with. See also (Wouters 2004).

5 In this respect, Alkoby (2003: 63) interestingly observed that the fact that the largest number of non-state actors 'acting in the international realm come from liberal democratic states', 'suggests that a legitimacy deficit exists' even in a community of democratic states.

and predictability of international law-making are hardly served by such dealings. Besides, if the issue at hand is essentially transnational in character, for example, climate change, it may not be very effective for transnational organized non-state actors, for example, organized under an umbrella group, to lobby each single government. Instead, it makes more sense for them to raise their voices, preferably publicly, in international forums where the assembled governments cannot simply ignore non-state actor demands. The publicity accompanying those statements may ensure that a toll is exacted on a gathering of states that neglects non-state actor input and pushes through a policy agenda without any consent or agreement of non-state actors.

The problematic character of imposing obligations on legal subjects under international law without their consent is not only based on policy considerations. It is in fact already recognized within the structure of international law itself. Article 35 of the Vienna Convention on the Law Treaties provides that '[a]n obligation [only] arises for a third state from a provision of a treaty if the parties to the treaty intend the provision to be the means of establishing the obligation and the third state expressly accepts that obligation in writing.' Without the consent of a third party, either at the stage of the creation of the norm or at a later stage, the norm lacks legitimacy, and, under the law of treaties, at least in respect of states, cannot possibly impose binding obligations on the third party. Article 35 of the Vienna Convention could be interpreted *per analogiam* and be applied to agreements that create obligations for other legal persons, such as non-state actors. This is at least the manner in which Antonio Cassese has attempted to justify the binding character of Additional Protocol II to the Geneva Conventions (1977) relating to the Protection of Victims of Non-International Armed Conflicts – which sets out rules for non-international armed conflicts – for (non-state) insurgent groups as opposed to being only applicable to the *state* parties. Cassese has based his argument on Article 35 of the Vienna Convention – which he apparently considered as a general principle of law, applicable to treaties that create obligations for any third international actor (and not only to treaties that create obligation for third states)[6] – and submitted that Additional Protocol II was binding for insurgent groups to the extent that the state parties intended to establish the obligatory force for those groups of the norms contained therein (which is actually open to doubt, given the contradictory statements of states in the *travaux préparatoires* in this respect),[7] *and* that the insurgent group also accepted the obligation (Cassese 1981).

---

6 It could not be argued that such treaties are not within the scope of the Vienna Convention on the Law of Treaties, since the Convention only 'does not apply to international agreements concluded between states and other subjects of international law or between such other subjects of international law or to international agreements not in written form.' On the terms of the Convention, treaties between states that create obligations for other subjects of international law remain subject to the Convention.

7 There is less doubt regarding the intentions of the states parties to the 1949 Geneva Conventions, Common Article 3 of which obliges *each party to the conflict*, without that

The acceptance by a non-state actor, such as an insurgent group, of obligations under a treaty, in the case Additional Protocol II, is not *a priori* given. Non-state actors will only accept obligations if they have something to gain from this acceptance, such as the recognition of their legitimacy as international players. The legitimacy of international norms binding non-state actors is then dependent on those actors' striving for international political legitimacy. This dynamic explains how international norms could become binding for non-state actors after the norms' adoption by states. It does not, however, fully explain how non-state actors participate in norm-creation. Obviously, non-state actors will only participate when participation yields benefits for them. Yet the participation of non-state actors in norm-creation is not just the result of their own preferences, but also critically depends on the other actors in norm-creation. For a process of will-formation to adequately work, indeed, all participants need to accept each other's legal position in that process.

Why would the other actors, states in the first place (and established non-state actors in the second place), accept a legal role and position of non-state actors in the process? Part of the answer is that involvement of non-state actors in norm-creation increases the likelihood of norm-compliance. 'Ownership' of rules indeed furthers the effectiveness of the rules, because non-state actors, having made the law (or at least having been involved in the making of the law), can be considered to have internalized that law.[8] In normal circumstances, they would not have consented to the rule during its formative process (assuming, of course, that this process is largely power-free) if the rule was not in line with their interests and if they had no desire to live up to it. Therefore, when non-state actors are granted

party needing to be a state party, to apply a number of minimum standards in the case of an armed conflict not of an international character occurring in the territory of one of the High Contracting parties. According to Pictet, 'The words "each party" mark the great progress, which the passage of a few years has sufficed to bring about in international law. For until recently it would have been considered impossible in law for an international Convention to bind a non-signatory party – a party, moreover, which was not yet in existence and which was not even required to represent a legal entity capable of undertaking international obligations … At the Diplomatic Conference doubt was expressed as to whether insurgents could be legally bound by a Convention which they had not themselves signed. But if the responsible authority at their head exercises effective sovereignty, it is bound by the very fact that it claims to represent the country, or part of the country' (Pictet 1960).

8 Compare Koh's opinion (1997: 2643). 'Nations [CR: and one could say non-state actors as well] thus obey international rules not just because of sophisticated calculations about how compliance or non-compliance will affect their interests, but because a repeated habit of compliance remakes their interests so that they come to value rule compliance' with his opinion that 'if transnational actors obey international law as a result of repeated interaction with other actors in the transnational legal process, a first step is to empower more actors to participate. It is here that expanding the role of intergovernmental organizations, nongovernmental organizations, private business entities, and "transnational moral entrepreneurs" deserves careful study' (Koh: 2656).

a legal position that enables them to contribute to the formation of international law, and when, in fact, they contribute to that formation, the law that is created is imbued with sufficient legitimacy to bring non-state actors to book for norm violations. After all, having adopted the law and, at the same, having consented to be bound by that very adoption (as indeed, law-maker and law-taker are synonymous in the horizontal international legal order between states), non-state actors cannot convincingly justify their non-compliance on grounds of lack of legitimacy of the norm.

Bearing in mind the necessity of involvement of non-state actors in the process of international law creation given the enhanced legitimacy of that law, states are well-advised not to impose duties on non-state actors through treaty or customary international law without having involved non-state actors.

Treaties Imposing Duties on Non-State Actors

Very few treaties in fact impose duties on non-state actors. An older example is Article 4 of the Convention on the Prevention and Punishment of Genocide (1948), which provides for the punishment of persons committing genocide, irrespective of their status as constitutionally responsible rulers, public officials or private individuals. There is scant evidence of the involvement of non-state actors in the preparation of those conventions. As noted above, however, this is not necessarily fatal to the legitimacy of the duties, which the said conventions impose on non-state actors. Given the substantive aims of the conventions – the safeguarding of the foundational values of the international community, values which non-state actors are presumed to consent to – their formative process could well do without substantial involvement of non-state actors. It remains no less true, however, that the very definition of what values precisely constitute international foundational values should not be the reserved domain of states. Non-state actors could also act as agents of the international community, and should therefore, as far as possible, be granted a legal position to both define values and endow them with an international normative qualification.

In this respect, it could also be argued that non-state actors should also have their role to play in the law-making process leading to the adoption of international human rights and international humanitarian law conventions. After all, do these conventions not require that states impose obligations on non-state actors, typically by demanding that those states parties undertake to respect and to ensure respect to individuals within their jurisdiction?[9] However, the obligations laid down in those conventions are not really of an international character, as the relevant conventions only impose international duties on states. States, rather than non-state actors themselves, should see to it that the latter are adequately regulated (they often incur due diligence obligations in this respect). This regulation should

9 For example, Article 2 (1) ICCPR and Common Article 1 of the Geneva Conventions (1949).

occur at the domestic rather than at the international level. The upshot is that the conventions only indirectly impose obligations on non-state actors, and lay the ultimate regulatory responsibility with states. Non-state actor involvement in the conventions is therefore not required for the conventional norms to be legitimate. By contrast, non-state actor involvement in domestic norm-setting processes aimed at complying with international standards resting on the state within whose jurisdiction the non-state actor falls, is highly desirable, as it is at the domestic level that the internationally mandated state intervention has its impact on the non-state actor, and at the domestic level that the legitimacy question is brought into stark relief.

Securing Non-State Actor Consent through Participatory Rights

When treaty obligations are imposed on non-state actors, pursuant to the procedural legitimacy theory posited here, it is crucial that these actors are involved in the process resulting in the creation of the obligations. Involvement is desirable, not only because of the inherent value associated with allotting participatory rights to those who are affected by regulation, but also because it contributes to the effectiveness of the regulation and the accountability of the addressees in cases of norm violations.[10] Indeed, the ability to wield influence, however small perhaps, over the outcome of a process of will-formation typically leads to the internalization of the results adopted by the participants, and to increased effectiveness of the regulation. Nils Rosemann for example discusses the effectiveness of a Code of Conduct regulating the activities of private military contractors:

> a [Code of Conduct, CoC] should take into account the interests of companies, stakeholders and groups in civil society, and combine them in a single political initiative. The higher the number of these various group interests and factors are taken into account, the greater the chances of a CoC to succeed. (Rosemann 2008: 15)

Also, the consent-based character of law-formation weakens the strength of *a posteriori* arguments defending non-compliance with adopted norms on grounds of lack of participation by the norm violator. When the law is considered as legitimate, civil disobedience has only a marginal place;[11] the participatory rights

10 See in this respect also the discussion remarks by T. Stein and J. Delbrück who make accountability and liability of non-state actors dependent on their integration into the international legal order (Hofmann and Geissler 1999).

11 This is of course not to say that norm violations will *in practice* no longer occur. The continuing widespread violations of human rights in many states that have ratified international human rights conventions bear testimony to the difficulties of implementing consensually agreed international norms, which are also partly caused by the absence of a powerful centralized law-enforcement institution at the international level. It is in fact only

of non-state actors in decision-making processes ensure that those actors can be held accountable for any transgressions of the decisions in which they have participated (Alkoby 2003). Math Noortmann would even go so far to argue that 'international accountability can only be required from NGOs in combination with recognized rights under international law' (Noortmann 2001: 72).

Some conventions already provide, albeit tentatively, for non-state actor participation in international decision-making. The Convention on Access to Information, Public Participation in Decision-Making, and Access to Justice in Environmental Matters (1998)[12] is a case in point. While the convention primarily aims to increase public participation in *domestic* decision-making, its Article 3(7) nevertheless provides: 'Each party shall promote the application of the principles [of public participation] of this Convention in international environmental decision-making processes and within the framework of international organizations in matters relating to the environment' (what this means in practice is left open).[13]

In the case of the International Maritime Organization (IMO), in whose midst the 2001 Liability Convention was negotiated and adopted, it is most interesting to note that in the Organization Strategic Plan 2008–2013, under the telling heading 'Enhancing the status and effectiveness of IMO', it is observed:

> An inclusive and comprehensive approach to [technical matters of all kinds affecting international shipping and related legal matters] will be a hallmark of IMO. In order to maintain that primacy, it will [amongst others]: actively engage the various stakeholders, new and existing, in the shipping arena, including non-governmental organizations, industry and the public in general, to ensure a more inclusive approach to decision-making.[14]

International organizations in whose midst are negotiated international conventions that impose burdens on non-state actors, such as the IMO, thus seem to realize the legitimacy and effectiveness deficit caused by the absence of non-state actor

---

to say that the norm violators forfeit, by their very participation in the formation of the norm, any rights of *post factum* criticism of the results reached (assuming of course that the participatory process was in itself sound, and that all procedures were respected).

12 Adopted on 25 June 1998, see 38 *I.L.M.* 517.

13 Article 2 (4) of the Convention defined 'the public' as 'one or more natural or legal persons, and, in accordance with national legislation or practice, their associations, organizations or groups', whilst Article 2 (5) defines 'the public concerned' as 'the public affected or likely to be affected by, or having an interest in, the environmental decision-making; for the purposes of this definition, non-governmental organizations promoting environmental protection and meeting any requirements under national law shall be deemed to have an interest.' See Articles 6–8 of the Convention for the rules on public participation in relation to 'the public' and 'the public concerned'.

14 IMO Assembly, Resolution A. 989(25), adopted on 20 November 2007, (Agenda item 7(a)), available at http://www.imo.org/includes/blastDataOnly.asp/data_id%3D21123/989.pdf, point 3.SD.1.2.

inclusion in the organization's work. The states which negotiate the treaties may come round to realizing that it is both unfair and ineffective to create burdens for non-state actors without at least consultation, and preferably a modicum of consent. In this respect, Grainne De Burca (2008) has referred to the 'intrinsic value of democracy' and the 'instrumental reasons' to develop democracy. It is unfair or basically undemocratic because states may not represent the rich variety of non-state actor interests, interests which may thus not be given a fair hearing. For instance, states' collective agendas may be hijacked by narrowly defined state security interests or even the interests of one particularly powerful non-state actor; for example the business community. It is ineffective because states may squander the opportunity to receive useful, technical information on desirable regulation. As a result, they may 'throw pearls to the pigs', adopting regulation which can hardly be implemented in the real world. While from an effectiveness perspective, non-state actor involvement in law-making appears desirable, one ought nevertheless to caution for exaggerated non-state actor involvement in this respect: the effectiveness of international regulation is hardly served if this regulation was merely adopted as a result of non-state actor campaigning and lobbying, thereby bypassing the strategic interests of the great state powers.[15] The limited success, in terms of great power ratification, of the 1997 Mine Ban Treaty and the 1998 Rome Statute of the International Criminal Court, instruments that were mainly adopted at the behest of non-governmental organizations may be cited as a useful reminder here.

Elaborating on the *de facto* influence of non-state actors in international affairs and in particular on the bearing this has on their participatory rights and the ensuing legitimacy of international law, it may be added that in the real world, opening up international decision-making processes to non-state actors is not simply an enlightened decision of states, the supposed masters of the international game. In practice, non-state actors may bring pressure to bear on states to open up the processes, to such an extent that it may be wondered whether the state still has a genuine choice of its own not to extend an invitation to non-state actors. It would indeed be quite naïve to believe that power relationships are a one-way street of states, possibly assembled in international organizations, wielding extraordinary power over international affairs, and non-state actors being sidelined and at the mercy of a hopefully responsible exercise of power by states/organizations. In fact, states/organizations and non-state actors entertain a dialectical relationship, with non-state actors at times doing the bidding of states/organizations, because they may be funded by states, or because they share the goals of international organizations, such as the United Nations (UN),[16] or because states and international

15 Wedgewood (1999: 175) submits that 'the net effect of a campaign [may be] to propound standards that nation states have no intention of observing'.

16 Wedgewood (1999: 175) at the same time, argues that NGOs are useful for the UN, as they could summon support for UN decisions and warns for the multiplication of state influence through state funding of NGOs.

organizations are doing the bidding of (certain) non-state actors (for example, because the former lack any technical expertise, or because public policy has become subservient to corporate profit maximization). At times, the power of non-state actors may have become so overwhelming that states or intergovernmental organizations have no other choice than granting participatory rights to non-state actors. That might in fact well be the case for the IMO, an organization, which Michael Byers (1999: 76) has typified as epitomizing 'industry capture [of] what appear from the outside to be intergovernmental organizations'.

Devising Non-State Actor Participatory Rights

Stating that non-state actors ought to be consulted, when new regulation is contemplated by the international community is one thing. It is quite another to devise formal rules of non-state actor participation in international law-making, let alone rules that are applicable across the board, across the whole range of international norm-making processes and institutions. As we write, one ought to concede, as Alan Boyle and Christine Chinkin (2007: 57) pointed out, that 'it seems premature to assert that there is a right to access and participation' of non-state actors. Non-state actor participation in international norm-setting processes remains a 'discretionary' decision of relevant bodies and institutions. However, considerations of legitimacy joined with effectiveness, which underpin the successful impact of a legal system on society, militate strongly in favour of enhanced participatory rights of non-state actors in relation to all aspects of international governance.

It is premature and probably even undesirable to lay down general principles of non-state actor participatory governance that all processes and institutions should comply with. Yet for those processes and institutions, it appears as unwise to resist the tide of the democratization of international law-making. Their administrators may harbour doubts over how to give shape to democratic principles, how to allot a formal place to non-state actors, and in particular what selection criteria should be used (Boyle and Chinkin 2007: 58–61).[17] Those doubts, however, should not be used to block any meaningful reform of state-centred international processes. After all, immature inclusive democracy is still better than no democracy at all.

In this vein, in her seminal article 'Developing Democracy beyond the state', Grainne De Burca (2008: 126-136) has advocated a 'democratic-striving/democracy-developing approach'. This approach, or 'concept of a democratic system of transnational governance', is 'one which is incomplete by design, in which full participation by definition cannot be achieved other than in a process of continuous revision, and in which pursuit of the public interest or a public-

17 Concerns over the legitimacy of certain non-state actors indeed remain. Do they really represent 'the popular will'? Are non-governmental organizations truly independent of the financial donors that support them? Are bigger non-state actors not outmanoeuvring smaller actors?

regarding quality can never be assumed within any given set of processes' (De Burca 2008: 132). In practical terms, De Burca (2008: 133) proposes to firstly 'identify all of the relevant stakeholders … and to provide for their participation in the initial process.' It may be noted in this respect that costs could be sunk, and effectiveness and systemic coherence could be enhanced by grafting modes of non-state actor participatory governance onto existing modes of governance at the inter-state or institutional level. Meetings that traditionally include representatives of states or international organizations could then be broadened so as to include representatives of non-state actors (Rosemann 2008: 40).[18] Obviously, logistical problems may at times counsel against liberally granting seats around the table to [a] panoply of non-state actors (Charnovitz 1997: 57; Boyle and Chinkin 2007: 187). Considerations of confidentiality, for example in relation to national or international security, may equally militate against the overly enthusiastic inclusion of non-state actors in deliberative processes, although a better solution would probably be to set basic confidential rules which any participant, including non-state actors, are not allowed to violate (for example, by talking to the media).

At the same time, De Burca (2008: 134) takes the concept of inclusive governance to its logical limits, by recommending that the participatory system always remain provisional and open, 'so as to include any new actors or interests who identify themselves as concerned stakeholders [at the end of a regulatory/normative cycle]'. As international priorities change, those impacted by policies designed to cope with new challenges will also change. A changing or extension of the guard at the level of the norm-setters may then be appropriate, and even required, in order to safeguard the legitimacy, effectiveness, and viability of the process of 'transnational' norm-creation. This is an important insight: participatory rights and interests should not be carved in stone, or become 'vested'. Instead, they should develop organically, in unison with new international challenges and the changing public interest according to De Burca (2008: 134), in such a manner that the procedure and the results should 'reflect the public interest and not only the interests of those who are regulated by the particular process in question.' In this respect, the novelty of democracy at the international or transnational level may provide the opportunity not to repeat the mistakes that have been made in the past at the level of the nation-state, where 'vested interests', of business, trade-union or religious elites, have at times sliced the cake amongst themselves, thereby excluding newcomers. Re-slicing the cake at fixed junctures in the life of

18 Rosemann highlights the institutional support of the EU and the UN Security Council for the multi-stakeholder 'Kimberley' process, a joint governments, industry and civil society initiative to stem the flow of conflict diamonds (http://www.kimberleyprocess.com); the development, under the auspices of the UN and United Nations Development Program of the Global Compact, at strategic policy initiative for businesses that are committed to aligning their operations and strategies with ten universally accepted principles in the areas of human rights, labour, environment and anti-corruption (http://www.unglobalcompact.org/), and the role of the OECD and the ILO in business regulation).

an international process or institution will ensure that it is not captured by special interests. The process or institution will keep its autonomy *vis-à-vis* the 'law-makers', state and non-state actors alike. Its legitimacy indeed hinges on its not becoming a vehicle for the promotion of the narrow interests of the participants in law-making; only then could global public goods genuinely be delivered.[19]

An Example of Non-State Actor Participatory Rights: Regulating Global Business

The theory of procedural legitimacy demands inclusion of all relevant actors in the norm-setting process in order for the adopted norms to command widespread support. In the sphere of soft law regulation of business conduct, which Leyla Davarnejad discussed in her chapter, it has indeed been observed that 'exclusive' initiatives have failed, whereas 'inclusive initiatives' seem to be thriving (Rosemann 2008: 39). Undoubtedly, multi-stakeholder initiatives involving states, intergovernmental organizations and non-state actors (businesses and non-governmental organizations), such as the Global Compact and the Equator Principles[20] have not fared poorly. They have been able to attract a sizable number of businesses and business stakeholders, and to develop benchmarks to assess risk and performance, which have been widely adopted.[21]

19 Compare, in particular the opinion of Na'im (2008: 192) who particularly holds that: 'the legitimacy of the state derives from its deep and organic links with various non-state actors in the political field across society at large. But the state's autonomy will be lost or diminished if one group is allowed to capture any organ of the state, or the state as a whole, for its purposes. To facilitate the realization of this necessary combination of legitimacy and autonomy, it is necessary to secure the public arena where non-state actors can compete on free and fair footing to influence state policy, while ensuring the most inclusive participation by all segments of the population in this arena. The rationale for this proposition is that a greater diversity of groups, freely and fairly competing to secure and advance their interests and concerns, decreases the risk that the state or any of its institutions will be compromised by falling under the control of any one group or small set of groups. The legitimacy and efficacy of the state depend on balancing its connectedness to social/political actors against the need to maintain its autonomy from the undue influences of those actors.' Na'im draws on Gill (2003: 18–19) who submits that 'the state can be seen as an arena within which [non-state] actors can compete for the achievement of their aims, but the very diversity of those actors ensures the state's autonomy.'

20 The Equator Principles are financial industry benchmarks for determining, assessing and managing social and environmental risk in project financing. See http://www.equator-principles.com.

21 For example, when a company joins the UN Global Compact, it commits itself to produce an annual Communication on Progress (COP), which is 'a disclosure to stakeholders (for example, investors, consumers, civil society, governments, and so forth) on progress made in implementing the ten principles of the UN Global Compact, and in supporting broad UN development goals (as expressed in the second objective of the UN Global Compact) (http://www.unglobalcompact.org /COP/index.html). Non-communicating and inactive Global Compact participants are 'blacklisted' on the Global Compact's website.

Initiatives that failed to include all relevant stakeholders have been notably less successful, arguably as a result of their perceived lack of legitimacy. Probably the most telling example in this respect is the fate of the UN Draft Norms on the Responsibility of Transnational Corporations and other Business Enterprises with Regard to Human Rights, adopted by the UN Sub-Commission on the Promotion and Protection of Human Rights in 2003 (the Norms) and which Peter Muchlinski elaborates in his chapter.[22] These norms have famously been described as 'dead' and a 'train wreck' by the UN Secretary General's Special Representative on Business and Human Rights, John Ruggie, for a large part because the business community was insufficiently involved in drawing up the norms, and 'the topic of discussion [had become] the shape of the table in the tribunal chamber where companies would be tried'.[23] The lack of participation of the business community, as opposed to the community of non-governmental organizations (NGOs), throughout the whole process of drawing up the Norms was seen as detracting from their legitimacy (contra Kamminga 2009: 172), if not as binding norms of international law (the wording of the Norms in fact suggests this binding character)[24] then at least as authoritative soft law norms.

In fact, the Norms treated corporations as *objects*, rather than as *genuine* subjects of international law (Miller 2008: 388). Our legitimacy theory, legal subjectivity, which is a feature of international legal personality, requires that the subjects of the law have also participated in the making of the law in an inter-subjective context (involving the different actors holding stakes in regulation). Miller (2008: 389) (original emphasis) argues that competences in norm creation and enforcement are 'central to any assertion of international legal personality and they are fundamental characteristics of a *subject* of international law'. They should not be mere 'objects' of the law, in the sense of addressees of commands made by others, whether states or other non-state actors such as international organizations or NGOs (Alkoby 2003: 97). Because the Norms appeared to treat corporations as objects rather than as subjects, they could not possibly be considered as fully legitimate. Ultimately, this made them also ineffective, although some of the Norms' insights may be recovered

22 UN Doc. E/CN/4/Sub.2/2003/12/Rev.12 (13 August 2003).

23 Remark by John Ruggie delivered at a forum on Corporate Social Responsibility Co-Sponsored by the Fair Labour Association and the German Network of Business Ethics (Bamberg, Germany, 14 June 2006) available at http://www.reports-and-materials.org/Ruggie-remarks-to-Fair-Labor-Association-and-German-Network-of-Business-Ethics-14-June-2006.pdf. See for an overview of the criticism also: Kinley and Nolan (2007: 34).

24 See Article 1: 'Within their respective spheres of activity and influence, transnational corporations and other business enterprises *have the obligation* to respect for, prevent abuses of, and promote human rights recognized in international law as well as national law' (emphasis added). See also the Draft Commentary on the Norms, UN Doc. E/CN.4/Sub.2/2003/XX. E/CN.4/Sub.2/2003/WG.2/WP.1, commentary (b) to Article 1: 'Transnational corporations and other business enterprises *shall have the responsibility* to ensure that their activities do not contribute directly or indirectly to human rights abuses' (emphasis added).

in subsequent processes of international will-formation regarding business and human rights, for example, in the framework of Ruggie's mandate. Of course, it is required that these processes be inclusive. In that respect, Russell Miller, observing that an anti-business bias 'has led to the paradoxical privileging of [NGOs] over [transnational corporations] in the field of international human rights', has proposed to draw on the ancient tripartite structure of the International Labour Organization (ILO), which not only involves states, but also business and labour representatives (Miller 2008: 304–5). As argued above, it may make sense to graft non-state actor participation onto existing regimes and institutions. An overhaul of the ILO may indeed enable it to play a more prominent role in the debate over business and human rights. One may notably contemplate both increasing and diversifying the number of non-state actors involved, for example, adding NGOs and distinguishing between different sorts of corporations (Cooney 1998).

IV. Concluding Observations

Back in 1997, Theo van Boven (2000: 368) observed, rather crudely, that '[t]he responsibility of non-state actors and their duties to respect and to comply with international law, must be regarded as inherently linked with the claim that they qualify as acceptable parties in national and international society.' This statement should not be construed as a blank cheque for the international community, as constituted at a given moment in time, to impose responsibilities and duties on non-state actors. After all, those liabilities depend on the acceptance and acceptability of non-state actors within 'the international community', that amorphous creature from which international law eventually emanates. Van Boven's statement should be construed in a Boston Tea Party sense: no taxation without representation; for no liabilities could ensue when the actors, who are burdened with them are not acknowledged as 'parties' in the community, with the concomitant democratic right to voice opinions and decide on the desirability of any burdens imposed on them. Without a modicum of participation in the law-making process, the democratic consent of those governed by the laws will be lacking, and the legitimacy of international law, not to speak of their effectiveness, may receive a mortal blow. Fleur Johns (Johns 1993: 894) leaves little doubt:

> Ultimately … if international law is to fulfil any or all [of its descriptive or prescriptive] roles and more importantly, if it is to have a continuing and positive impact upon daily human endeavour, its processes must be opened up to all groups … with direct involvement in any field of human affairs with which these legal process purport to deal.

As non-state actors play an increasingly prominent role in international affairs, and international normative decisions are very likely to affect and create burdens for them, the international legal system should be amended in such a way as to reflect the changing reality on the ground. According to Noortmann (2001: 66), [t]he process of law-making at international level has to be reconsidered in the light of the increase in numbers of actors and participants in this process.' Such an amendment should not be seen as states or international organizations conferring, as they see fit, some participatory rights on selected non-state actors. For all too long, the international legal personality of non-state actors, limited as it is, has been taken hostage by the state as the acknowledged 'original subject'.[25] In our Habermasian deliberative or discursive democracy theory, there is no such thing as 'original subjects' who have the prerogative of pulling the strings of participation in international law-making. Pluralist and functionalist approaches reject the formalism of 'original subjects' According to Noortmann (2001: 64) 'it is possible to assess different forms of legal personality for different actors without qualifying legal personality as 'original' or 'derived'. In the same vein, Ruth Wedgewood (1999: 36) submits that the test for the 'privatization' of the international legal order must be a functional one. Legal subjectivity ought to be a function of wielding real power and of 'being affected' by decisions taken, and, accordingly, of being entitled to certain participatory rights in relation to the decisions.[26] Thus, any 'stakeholders' who meet the criteria of wielding power and being affected should be horizontally situated in an 'original position'. They should have *inherent* rights of participation in will-formation processes, which should not be dependent on invitation by already constituted forums or bodies.

Of course, this is not a description of non-state actor participation in international law and organization as we write, rather on the contrary.

---

25 Alkoby (2003: 42) points out that 'state consent – guided by self-interest – is the reason for cooperation of governments with NGOs'. It has been argued that even 'liberal internationalists', for all their openness to non-state actors, still put *states* centre-stage, by providing an account that makes non-state actor participation dependent on decision of states. See for an excellent critique of the liberal international position in respect of non-state actors in international law (Alkoby 2003: 50–72). It is noted that Anne-Marie Slaughter (1995: 508), one of the leading liberal internationalists, has observed that the 'first assumption' of 'a liberal theory of international law' is that the primary actors in the international system are individuals and groups acting in domestic and transnational civil society. Nonetheless, she may indeed advocate better representation of non-state actors by states rather than full-fledged participation of non-state actors in international relations in parallel with states. She agrees that '[l]iberal theory accepts that NGOs can play a very important role in affecting international outcomes, but assumes that NGOs will be most effective when they convince national governments to change their preferences – either through adversarial or enabling tactics' (Slaughter 2000: 142).

26 Compare Clapham (2006: 68–69) who concludes that 'we need to admit that international rights and duties depend on the capacity of the entity to enjoy those rights and bear those obligations; such rights and obligations do not depend on the mysteries of subjectivity' and Thürer (1999: 53), who criticizes the sterile legal personality approach, and advocates a functional approach of integrating new entities into the broader concept of the international community.

Ad hoc-ism is still the order of the day: selected institutions confer selected participatory rights on selected non-state actors (it would in fact be overoptimistic to state that most institutions confer most participatory rights on most non-state actors). The feasibility of the approach advocated here, may therefore be open to doubt. But bearing in mind that there is nothing as practical as a good theory, any theoretical account, however ideal-typical it may appear, has the potential of opening of the eyes of the gatekeepers of the current system. In our case, this would mean pushing the gates ajar with a view to granting the disenfranchised of the international legal system – non-state actors – their rightful place, thereby ensuring the continuing legitimacy and effectiveness of international law, or as Alkoby (2003: 24) puts it: 'opening up the processes of generation, interpretation and application of international norms to non-state entities would enhance the perceived legitimacy of international law'. In so doing, eventually, a genuine 'international community' could be constituted. The approach advocated here could therefore be described, in line with Daniel Thürer's (1999: 54) writings on the matter, as a *constitutional* one: basic rights of participation of those affected by regulation, including non-state actors, *constitute* the society and guarantee the enduring legitimacy of any international obligations imposed.

References

Alkoby, A. 2003. Non-State Actors and the Legitimacy of International Environmental Law. *Non-State Actors and International Law,* 3, 23–63.

Boyle, A.E. and Chinkin, C.M. 2007. *The Making of International Law*. Oxford and New York: Oxford University Press.

Byers, M. 1999. Comments in *Non-State Actors as New Subjects of International Law – From the Traditional State Order Towards the Law of the Global Community,* edited by R. Hofmann and N. Geissler. Berlin: Duncker & Humblot.

Cassese, A. 1981. The Status of Rebels under the 1977 Geneva Protocol on Non-International Armed Conflicts. *International and Comparative Law Quarterly*, 30, 416–439.

Charnovitz, S. 1997. Two Centuries of Participation: NGOs and International Governance. *Michigan Journal of International Law*, 18, 183–286.

Clapham, A. 2006. *Human Rights Obligations of Non-State Actors.* Oxford and New York: Oxford University Press.

Coetzee, J.M. 2008. *Diary of a Bad Year*. London: Vintage.

Cooney, S. 1998. Testing Times for the ILO: Institutional Reform for the New International Political Economy. *Comparative Labor Law & Policy Journal*, 20, 365–400.

De Burca, G. 2008. Developing Democracy Beyond the State. *Columbia Journal of Transnational Law*, 101, 121–278.

Franck, T.M. 1995. *Fairness in International Law and Institutions*. Oxford and New York: Oxford University Press, Clarendon Press.

Franck, T.M. 1999. *The Empowered Self: Law and Society in the Age of Individualism*. Oxford and New York: Oxford University Press.

Gill, G.J. 2003. *The Nature and Development of the Modern State*. Houndmills, Basingstoke, Hampshire and New York: Palgrave Macmillan.

Habermas, J. 1992. *Faktizität und Geltung: Beiträge zur Diskurstheorie des Rechts und des Demokratischen Rechtsstaats*. Frankfurt am Main: Suhrkamp.

Hofmann, R. and Geissler, N. (eds). 1999. *Non-State Actors as New Subjects of International Law: From the Traditional State Order Towards the Law of the Global Community*. Berlin: Duncker & Humblot.

Johns, F. 1993. The Invisibility of the Transnational Corporation: An Analysis of International Law and Theory. *Melbourne University Law Review*, 19, 893–923.

Kamminga, M.T. 2009. The Next Frontier: Prosecution of Extraterritorial Corporate Misconduct before Non-US Courts, in *Proceedings of the 2007 Joint Conference on Contemporary Issues in International Law*, edited by W.J.M. van Genugten, M.P. Scharf, S.E. Radin. The Hague: Asser Press, 172–174.

Koh, H. 1997. Why do States Obey International Law? *Yale International Law Journal*, 102, 2,599–2,643.

Miller, R.A. 2008. Paradoxes of Personality: Transnational Corporations, Non-Governmental Organizations and Human Rights, in *International Law. Progress in International Law*, edited by R.A. Miller and R.M. Bratspies. Leiden and Boston: Martinus Nijhof.

Na'im, A.A. 2008. *Islam and the Secular State: Negotiating the Future of Sharia*. Cambridge, Mass.: Harvard University Press.

Noortmann, M. 2001. Non-State Actors in International Law, in *Non-State Actors in International Relations*, edited by B. Arts, M. Noortmann and B. Reinalda. Aldershot: Ashgate Publishing Company, 59–76.

Pictet, J.S. (ed.) 1960. *Commentary II Geneva Convention*. Geneva: ICRC.

Rosemann, N. 2008. *Code of Conduct: Tool for Self-Regulation for Private Military and Security Companies*. Geneva: Geneva Centre for the Democratic Control of Armed Forces.

Slaughter, A.-M. 1995. International Law in a World of Liberal States. *European Journal of International Law*, 6, 503–508.

Slaughter, A.-M. 2000. International Law and International Relations. *Recueil des Cours*, 285(9), 9–249.

Thürer, D. 1999. The Emergence of Non-Governmental Organizations and Transnational Enterprises in International Law and the Changing Role of the state, in *Non-State Actors as New Subjects of International Law – From the Traditional State Order Towards the Law of the Global Community*, edited by R. Hofmann and N. Geissler. Berlin: Duncker & Humblot.

van Boven, T.C. 2000. Non-State Actors: Introductory Comments, in *Human Rights from Exclusion to Inclusion; Principles and Practices: An Anthology from the Work of Theo van Boven,* edited by F. Coomans, C. Flinterman, F. Grunfeld and J. Willems. The Hague: Kluwer, 363–372.

Wedgewood, R. 1999. Legal Personality and the Role of Non-Governmental Organizations and Non-State Political Entities in the United Nations System, in *Non-State Actors as New Subjects of International Law – From the Traditional State Order Towards the Law of the Global Community,* edited by R. Hofmann and N. Geissler. Berlin: Duncker & Humblot.

Wouters, J., De Meester, B. et al. 2004. Democracy and International Law. *Netherlands Yearbook of International Law*, 137–197.

Chapter 5
Non-State Actors and the International Rule of Law: Revisiting the 'Realist Theory' of International Legal Personality[1]

Janne E. Nijman

I. Introduction

In the next ten to twenty years our world will transform dramatically. Globalization, demographic challenges, climate change, and the geopolitics of energy, among other developments, will challenge our current world governance structures. There is a looming global governance deficit as new powers – both state and (notably) non-state[2] – rise and international institutions fail to respond adequately, thus risking to create institutional decay rather than institutional innovation and adaptation. Global Trends 2025: A Transformed World (2008) of the US National Intelligence Council analyses these developments and the way in which these interact as change-driving factors. The report identifies global trends and – depending on how the variables are weighed – calculates four possible scenarios or alternative futures.

In each of these futures, non-state actors (NSAs) play a role and in one of the four scenarios, *Politics is Not Always Local*, NSAs and NSA-networks are assessed as the international agenda setters of the future, who even 'use their clout to elect the UN Secretary-General.' (NIC, *Global Trends 2025: A Transformed World* November 2008)[3] Such clout would in fact be unsurprising to IR/IL scholars. After

---

1 This chapter draws from an Amsterdam Center for International Law Working Paper, which addresses more extensively several points of debate, including the concept and current status of the 'international rule of law' – available at http://papers.ssrn.com. It was prepared for the first seminar of the research project recognized as a 'Research Community' by the Flemish Fund for Scientific Research for the period 2009–2013 and the ILA's Committee on non-state actors. I am grateful to the participants of this seminar for their comments on an earlier draft.

2 Here, 'non-state actors' refers to international actors, which are not a state. I do not include Inter-governmental Organizations as NSAs here. See, for IGOs as NSAs (Brölmann 2007a).

3 Available at http://www.dni.gov/nic/NIC_2025_project.html, accessed 20 February 2010, in the following NIC, *Global Trends 2025*, at 81 and 4. This report is a US National

all, NGOs and NGO-networks have played a significant role in the establishment of international courts and tribunals. Underlying all scenarios is the 'relative certainty' that 'the relative power of various non-state actors – including businesses, tribes, religious organizations, and even criminal networks – will grow as these groups influence decisions on a widening range of social, economic, and political issues.' (NIC, *Global Trends 2025*, at 81). This global trend will bring significant changes to the international system: 'By 2025, nation-states will no longer be the only – and often not the most important – actors on the world stage and the "international system" will have morphed to accommodate the new reality. But the transformation will be incomplete and uneven.' (NIC, *Global Trends 2025,* at 81.) In other words, for the future of the international system one may discern roughly two possible trajectories: either the multiplicity of actors will strengthen the international system for a global public domain to emerge,[4] or this multiplicity will contribute to the further fragmentation of the international system and undermine international cooperation and global governance institutions. The diversification of both state and non-state powers (into multipolarity and into multiplicity) increases the likelihood of the second scenario and complicates working towards realization of the first. 'The need for effective global governance [of the pressing transnational problems such as climate change, regulation of globalized financial markets, migration, failing states, crime networks, etc] will increase faster than existing mechanisms can respond.' (NIC, *Global Trends 2025*, at 81).

Global Trends 2025 is not the first and surely not the only report to identify possible challenges and opportunities of the near future, but the report's explicitness stimulates strategic thinking about (policy) interventions in developments that may cause a growing deficit of accountability/responsibility, a lack of governance at the global level, and the possible weakening of the international legal order. This once again provokes our discipline to deal with the topic of NSAs, their role in shaping international life and their position in a rapidly changing global (institutional) order. At a time in which the international community is committed to strengthening the international rule of law, this contribution also addresses the growing power of NSAs as a potentially undermining factor.

In that context the present chapter argues the inclusion of powerful, international NSAs in the category of 'international legal persons' (ILPs).[5] The argument builds on the generally accepted idea that for the purpose of both the protection and the accountability of entities within the international legal system, these should have

Intelligence Council publication, which is based on the expertise of many both US Government and non-USG experts.

4 John Ruggie goes as far as to argue that 'the newly emerging global public domain' is a public domain which is no longer coterminous with the system of states, the latter is actually becoming increasingly embedded in a 'non-state-based public domain' (Ruggie 2004: 519).

5 Following the general use in international law scholarship, legal personality, legal person, and legal subject are considered to be synonymous here.

the enhanced status of legal 'subject' rather than 'object'. Behind this legal reality lies the normative reality of the international rule of law ideal: powerful entities that operate to some degree independently on the international plane should be controlled by law and held accountable for their actions. In other words: political or economic actors should be visible also in the international *legal* order (Section II). After these preliminary propositions, this chapter examines if and how the international legal personality (ILP) of NSAs may be constructed today. I distinguish three ways in which the ILP of NSAs is construed within the parameters of the conventional conception of ILP: a) 'transnational ILP', b) 'soft ILP', and c) 'regular ILP' (Section III). The chapter proceeds, however, to search for a new grounding of ILP theory. This search is supported by the general dissatisfaction with the formal conception of ILP, which draws on fiction theory. I will suggest to reconsider the 'real personality' theory or 'realist' theory of ILP (Section IV). This theory reconnects to the non-or pre-legal realms – of political and social sciences, ethics, psychology, metaphysics and so forth – that were cut off from the legal concept of international personality in the past. This chapter aims to provoke debate on the possibility of a 'new' realist theory so that we may be better equipped when addressing questions of NSAs and international law. In doing so it also aims to build an argument against the popular conviction that the concept of ILP and its theory has flopped. It defends the view that ILP is relevant and useful in today's international legal reality, provided that a new theoretical grounding is developed.

II. Preliminary Propositions

Based on their Social, Political and Economic Subjectivity, NSAs Should be Legal Subjects, Not Objects

This chapter proceeds from two preliminary claims or propositions. The first is that because NSAs are such important powers in the political and social reality of today's world, it is necessary that they are considered actors in the *legal* reality as well. 'Legal personality' then is the status which 'enables an entity to function in a legal order.' (Cf the treatment of ILP in Brölmann 2007: ch. 3.) Being a 'legal person' or 'subject' of international law better captures today's NSA's role than being an 'object' of international law. This is not an attempt to get back into the prison house (Higgins 1994: 49–50, see also Allott 1990: 373), or to disregard Martti Koskenniemi's fair critique of the object/subject dichotomy (Koskenniemi 1989). It is merely an effort to be clear on the underlying proposition of this chapter: in the confusion about whether to 'relativiz[e] the subjects' or to 'subjectivize the actors' this chapter is inclined to do the latter (Bianchi 2009: xi).

Traditionally, NSAs are not 'subjects' or 'persons' of international law. The conception of the NSA as an object of international law does however not sufficiently explain its present-day position in the international (legal) order. For one thing, it does not explain situations in which NSAs are the driving agents of important treaties (Landmine Ban Treaty) or the establishment of international institutions such as the International Criminal Court, the consultative status of NGOs within the United Nations or the equality of states and MNCs as parties in ICSID procedures. In other words, the power and influence of NSAs in many cases goes far beyond that of entities to which international law has traditionally accorded object-status. The various developments have not caused an (explicit) adjustment of the traditional view on ILP to facilitate *legal* accommodation of these actors. As candidate ILPs, NSAs are living in a conceptual twilight zone.

Indeed, a paradigm shift is required: without the recognition of NSAs as ILPs the gap between 'the *de facto* significance' and 'the *de jure* insignificance' is not resolved and, as Claire Cutler argues with regard to MNCs in particular, a 'crisis of legitimacy' is at hand (Claire Cutler 2001, see also on this point but from a different perspective, Allott 1990: 372) And the inability of theory and practice to deal with the ILP of NSAs in another way than a formalistic way contributes to this crisis (Claire Cutler 2001: 149). Rather than abandoning the conceptual category – possible in theory but hardly feasible in practice – the category of ILPs is now broadened, due to 'a requirement of international life' (ICJ Rep. 1949 *Reparation for Injuries* Case, at 178). When NSAs are not visible – quoting the 1933 Montevideo Convention – 'in the eyes of international law,' (Art. 2 Montevideo Convention on the Rights and Duties of States, signed at Montevideo, 26 December 1933, entered into force on 26 December 1934) there is a disjunction not only between theory and practice, but also between law and state. This ultimately undermines international law's claim to authority (Claire Cutler 2001: 147–149).

As indicated, this chapter defines 'non-state actor' as any entity that is not a state under international law. It thus follows Andrew Clapham in his choice of terms, which means that '[t]he range of possible entities includes: rebel groups, terrorist organizations, religious groups, civil society organizations, corporations, all kinds of businesses, and international organizations. Anything less comprehensive starts to suggest immunity from certain international responsibilities that are being generated and increasingly recognized in international relations' (Clapham 2009: 203).

Thus, the first preliminary claim of this chapter is that in order to clarify the legal position of NSAs, enhance their legal accountability to international society, and defuse a legitimacy crisis, NSAs have to be accommodated as subjects of international law. This leads us to the second proposition.

International Legal Personality (ILP) of NSAs Contributes to the Strengthening of the International Rule of Law

The second preliminary claim of this chapter is that the ILP of NSAs is a prerequisite for the strengthening of the international rule of law (IRoL). In other words, the constructive conception of NSAs as ILPs helps to reinforce the international rule of law, which is a declared need of the international community today, and which has been identified on multiple occasions as a prime objective of the UN. In the words of the UN Legal Counsel Patricia O'Brien: 'the rule of law is today at the centre of the United Nations' concerns' (Address by Legal Counsel of UN on June 15, 2009, *The Rule of Law at the International Level*, at 1.)

In my understanding, an international rule of law cannot but extend international law's power-constraints to *non*-state actors. The exercise of power on the international stage is less and less a state-only privilege, due to the privatization of authority (see for example Chinkin 2007), the privatization of governance (Claire Cutler),[6] deterritorialization (see for example Brölmann 2007b), outsourcing of public tasks (see for example Peters 2007), globalization of corporate power, diversification of actors (among which increased participation of international NGOs), etc. In a vision of an international rule of law NSAs, as powerful governing and governed actors should therefore be conceptualized as ILPs.

The rule of law ***at the international level*** Here, focus is on what is meant by 'the international level' when dealing with the conceptualization of the RoL at this level. In the next paragraph, we will deal with the RoL concept as such.

The conceptualization of the international rule of law (IRoL) – here taken as synonymous with 'the rule of law at the international level' – is going through a revival in practice and theory. In the first decades of the last century as well, the IRoL received much scholarly attention. Back then, between the two world wars in particular, this attention was related to the attack on the late nineteenth century 'idolatry of the state', the reduction of sovereignty, and the attempts to 'rehabilitate' and renew international law (see on these scholarly objectives Nijman 2004). Possibly the current revival rests on similar grounds – another rehabilitation of international law after the weakening of international law during the Bush Administration (see for a complaint about the lack of concern for the rule of law: Sands 2005, 2008); an attempt to strengthen international law in response to its increased fragmentation and diversification (see, ILC Report, *Fragmentation of international law: difficulties arising from the diversification and expansion of international law*, finalized by Martti Koskenniemi, 13 April 2006, UN Doc. A/CN.4/L.682.); another defence of the Kantian project (see for example, Habermas 2006: ch. 8); or a response to the scepticism of Critical Legal Studies scholarship on international law (see for example, Georgiev's response (1993) to Koskenniemi 1990) (like the Realists uttered their critique on international law before). It is also possible the renewed interest has been tinkered by (accountability) questions in relation to failing UN missions (address by Legal Counsel of UN on June 15, 2009, *The Rule of Law at the International Level*, at 5) (such as the one in Srebrenica); questions of transitional justice in conflict and post-conflict societies (Report of the Secretary-General The Rule of Law and Transitional Justice in Conflict and Post-Conflict Societies, UN Doc. S/2004/616

6 See, for example, Claire Cutler's (2002: 32–33) argument that 'firms are basically functioning like governments', reflecting 'deeper processes of globalization at work that are producing a disengagement of law and state' from the arena of global governance.

(23 August 2004)); new international law phenomena, such as the Chapter VII-based International Criminal Tribunals; or it may be called for by an active UN Secretary-General with a view to improving local rule of law programs. This composite and complex background will not be further entered into here.

Over the last decade, many International Relations (IR) and International Law (IL) scholars have become unsatisfied with the traditional state-centric paradigm, and its seemingly limited explanatory power for the contemporary state of global affairs (in 1993, for example, Slaughter proposed a new paradigm, the liberal agenda, to meet *inter alia* the challenge of emerging non-state actors: Slaughter 1993: 227). 'Global governance'[7] has emerged as a viable new paradigm for many IR and IL theorists and practitioners (it was rapidly absorbed by diplomatic and UN jargon) since it recognized the wide range of (non-state) actors now involved in governance at a post-national level. In Slaughter's definition it is 'the formal and informal bundles of rules, roles and relationships that define and regulate the social practices of state and non-state actors in international affairs.' (Slaughter, Tulumello and Wood 1998: 371.) It describes and examines the realities of the changing international (legal) system, while recognizing the increased and variegated participation of sub-state and non-state actors on the global stage (for a succint report of NSAs' involvement in the Copenhagen process see (Spain 2009). In the words of this book's title, NSAs as both law-makers and law-takers. Once the role and impact of NSAs are recognized, the need to adjust accountability and responsibility mechanisms becomes paramount.

A 'global governance' understanding of international life is indeed the context in which the RoL 'at the international level' has to be conceptualized. The challenge then is how to conceive of an IRoL in the absence of a world government and in the reality of global governance, which moreover is not purely inter-statist but involves non-state participants too. This is the international context in which the IRoL has to function and assert meaning. At least two legal approaches to global governance recognize the significant role of NSAs at the international level and the importance of securing RoL values where these actors are involved in global governance practices: global administrative law (GAL) and global constitutionalism (any elaboration on these two very relevant schools of thought has to be left aside here).

7 'At the global level, governance has been viewed primarily as intergovernmental relationships, but it must now be understood as also involving non-governmental organizations (NGOs), citizens' movements, multinational corporations, and the global capital market.' Report of The Commission of Global Governance, *Our Global Neighborhood* (New York: Oxford University Press, 1995), 2–3. See also, Weiss 2000.

***The rule of law** at the international level* To substantiate the claim that the IRoL would benefit more from the reconstitution of NSAs as legal persons it is helpful to briefly look at the RoL concept as such. In spite of its long history (see, for 'the "arrival" of the rule of law argument within the discourse of global order' Kratochwil 2009: 173, see, for the history of the rule of law at the national and international level, also, Chesterman 2008, also, Tamanaha 2004, Palombella 2009), there is no clear definition of the 'international rule of law' (IRoL), neither in customary international law nor in treaty law, nor in pronouncements of the ICJ. Over the past five years, however, the term has come to feature in many UN documents,[8] as the international community through the UN repeatedly expressed its commitment to the 'strengthening of the IRoL.' There is general consensus on such a commitment, yet the precise normative content of the IRoL and the question of whether its definition should be 'thick' or 'thin'[9] remain to be determined. Be that as it may, the history of the IRoL and the fine points of this debate are outside the scope of this chapter, which rather aims to contribute to the conceptualization of 'the international rule of law' by considering the inclusion of NSAs in the international legal system.

I will not discuss the difficulties that come with the transposition to the international level (compare for example, Beaulac 2007, Chesterman 2008) of Albert Dicey's classic definition of the rule of law.[10] At this point I merely want to put in a caveat to avoid a false premise: the IRoL is meant to check states and international organizations, but states are not the beneficiaries of the IRoL. This would go against the essence of the RoL ideal. In the context of this chapter, I would like to try and move behind the more technical considerations to consider the IRoL ideal. To underpin the proposition that the IRoL requires the ILP of international NSAs, I make three claims.

---

8 Three UN documents that are central to UN project on the Rule of Law at this point may be mentioned. The Report of the Secretary-General, *The Rule of Law and Transitional Justice in Conflict and Post-conflict Societies*, 23 August 2004 (UN Doc S/2004/616) famously contains the 'UN definition' of the Rule of Law in § 6. Secondly, the 2006 Secretary-General report, *Uniting our Strengths: Enhancing United Nations Support for the Rule of Law* (UN doc. A/61/636). Thirdly, in August 2009 the UNSG issued the first *Annual Report on United Nations efforts to Strengthen Engagement on the Rule of Law at the National and International Levels*, which focuses on the RoL at the international level, the national level and the internal-institutional level.

9 In this context, an intriguing paragraph of SG Report 2004 is para. 138 'Justice is a vital component of the rule of law.'

10 According to Dicey: [1] the absolute supremacy or predominance of regular law as opposed to the influence of arbitrary power, and excludes the existence of arbitrariness, of prerogative, or even of wide discretionary authority on the part of the government. … [2] equality before the law or the equal subjection of all classes to the ordinary law of the land administered by the ordinary Law Courts; … [and 3] the law of the constitution … are not the source but the consequence of the rights of individuals as defined and enforced by the courts (Dicey 1885: 193–194).

The first is that the RoL is a political ideal, the beneficiaries of which are human individuals also in the international context. From this follows, that *all* international 'governing actors' (that is: actors involved in a form of global governance) are subjected to international law whether state or non-state. This refers to the RoL as an ideal about the relation between the individual, society, politics and law. Applied to the international level, the RoL is an ideal about the relation between (the constitution of) the global political order and international law. With the transposition to the international level, institutional mechanisms and legal arrangements may change, but the objective of the RoL ideal does not. As a political ideal, it is aimed firstly at the protection of individual liberty and human dignity against the arbitrary and unjust use of governing power. Human individuals, not states, are 'the bearers of ultimate value' they are the 'real concerns that underlie the ROL' as Jeremy Waldron points out (2009: 10).

The IRoL may thus be conceived as a model in which states, international institutions, and other NSAs fulfilling global governance functions are obliged to use their power justly and with respect for the liberty and dignity of human individuals. In order to have any significance at all, the IRoL can only mean that *all* international actors participating in global governance are bound by the law. This view on NSAs and the IRoL appears to be supported by the 2004 Transitional Justice report of the UN Secretary-General.[11] The IRoL implies that all governing actors are conceived of as addressees of international law norms and values, or – couched in formal terms – as international 'legal persons'.

My second point is that, while the RoL ideal may be best known for placing governing actors under the law (that is: protecting individuals in a 'vertical' relationship), the RoL equally addresses 'horizontal' relationships. In fact, the RoL first of all stipulates that all actors, *governing and non-governing*, are subject to the law. It presupposes the 'rule by law' – the idea that law governs society. It moreover envisions a legal order, which covers the entire *social* order with its acts and actors. At the international level as well this would mean that international law binds *all* actors, governing and non-governing, state and non-state. In part this is a normative claim inherent to the IRoL ideal: the catalogue of actors subjected to international law is thus expanded to include international NSAs so that their (mostly non-governing) powers, too, are constrained for the protection

11 Report of the Secretary-General *The Rule of Law and Transitional Justice in Conflict and Post-Conflict Societies*, UN Doc. S/2004/616 (23 August 2004), para. 6: 'The rule of law is a concept at the very heart of the Organization's mission. It refers to a principle of governance in which all persons, institutions and entities, public and private, including the State itself, are accountable to laws that are publicly promulgated, equally enforced and independently adjudicated, and which are consistent with international human rights norms and standards. It requires, as well, measures to ensure adherence to the principles of supremacy of law, equality before the law, accountability to the law, fairness in the application of the law, separation of powers, participation in decision-making, legal certainty, avoidance of arbitrariness and procedural and legal transparency.'

of human dignity and individual autonomy.[12] ILP could be instrumental in the reconstitution of global political life and the global public order,[13] so as to further the IRoL and to contribute to the closing of 'the gap between rhetoric and reality' as the UN Secretary-General pleaded in his 2005 report (UNSG Report 2005, *In Larger Freedom*, para 133–4. rule of law section, p. 25).

The third claim is that if the essence of the RoL ideal is protection of the individual against the arbitrary and unjust use of – governing or non-governing – power by any international actor, it follows that the RoL ideal has at least some substantive content, a *minimum level of justice*. In other words, the RoL ideal also has a substantive dimension. Lon Fuller explains that underlying the 'internal morality of law' (his words for the RoL) there is in fact an implicit view of man: human dignity requires the law to be committed to 'man as a responsible agent.'[14] Respect for autonomy and human dignity are moral values that underpin the RoL and set the parameters for the institutional and legal framework created on that basis.

This substantive, and essential, dimension of the RoL is not lost when transposed to the international level. This means that a call for a stronger IRoL entails a moral claim for an international law and international institutional order,

---

12 Compare in this context Weeramantry's (2004: 192) call for a re-assessment of the traditional ILP-doctrine: 'When it is considered that some of the major trading multi nationals have revenues which far [sic] those of over 150 of the nation states, it becomes clear that they have a correspondingly large role to play on the international stage and that any attempt to advance the international rule of law requires reorientation of traditional principles discounting the importance of non state actors [such as the ILP doctrine]. The proliferation of powerful non-governmental organizations, which are often bonded together across national boundaries, is another factor requiring a reconsideration of traditional attitudes. Many of the standard international instrumentalities lack the ability to deal with these entities because of traditional attitudes.'

13 At a 2009 UN Expert Meeting on the Rule of Law, David Kennedy pointed out that 'global governance and the international rule of law are about more than management and problem solving. They concern the structure and ends of our global political life. As a result, in building the global legal order, we must grasp the depth of the injustice of the world today and the urgency of change. ... Revitalizing the international rule of law is to remake the forms and channels of global political life. My own hope is that we carry the revolutionary force of social justice and the democratic promise – of individual rights, of economic self-sufficiency, of citizenship, of community empowerment, and participation in the decisions that affect one's life – to the sites of global and transnational authority, however local they may be.' Opening statement 'The Rule of Law at the International Level', UN, New York, 15 June 2009.

14 Fuller 1969: 162: 'legal morality can be said to be neutral over a wide range of ethical issues. It cannot be neutral in its view of man himself. To embark on the enterprise of subjecting human conduct to the governance of rules involves of necessity a commitment to the view that man is, or can become, a responsible agent, capable of understanding and following rules, and answerable for his defaults. Every departure from the principles of the law's internal morality is an affront to man's dignity as a responsible agent.'

which better respect and protect the autonomy and dignity of the individual. There are in fact signs of support for a normatively 'thicker' conception of the IRoL, such as substantive human rights norms having entered the international RoL discourse, or substantive standards more generally, as expressed in the statements by former UN Secretary-General Kofi Annan: 'Justice is a vital component of the rule of law.' (UNSG Report 2005, *In Larger Freedom*, para. 138.) The commitment to the strengthening of the IRoL includes a commitment to a minimum of substantive justice. [15]

Even from these few points it seems fair to say that the rule of law within international society raises a claim for inclusion of all governing and non-governing powers of the international society in order to prevent any powerful, globally operating actor from being outside or 'above' international law. How else can the IRoL be upheld while a considerable degree of power is shifting away from states to NSAs? The concept of ILP contributes to the IRoL by functioning as a linchpin between the factual and the legal, by bringing actual power under the law (see also, Allott 2002: for example 420–421). The IRoL prescribes international law to rule supremely, and the tool of ILP connects NSAs to international law. Proceeding from here, it is now time to examine *how* to develop the reconstitution of NSAs as international legal persons.

III. Conventional Approaches to ILP[16] – Shortcomings and Opportunities

Unlike most domestic legal systems, international law lacks the rules to stipulate which are the system's legal persons. There is no 'Vienna convention on the law of international legal persons', similar to the *Code Civil Livre Premier: Droit des Personnes* in Civil Law countries. Nor is there an unequivocal, substantive *stare decisis* developed body of law on personality, as in the way of the Common Law tradition. Of course, there are a number of relevant international judgements, most notably the 1949 *Reparation for Injuries* case of the International Court of

15 In Dworkin's (1985: 11–12) reinterpretation, this means that the RoL includes individual rights: 'the second conception of the rule of law [is called] the 'rights' conception. It is in several ways more ambitious than the rule-book conception. It assumes that citizens have moral rights and duties with respect to one another and political rights against the state as a whole. It insists that these moral and political rights be recognizes in positive law, so that they may be enforced upon the demand of individual citizens through courts or other judicial institutions of the familiar type, so far as this is practicable. The rule of law on this conception is the ideal of rule by an accurate public conception of individual rights. It does not distinguish, as the rule-book conception does, between the rule of law and substantive justice; on the contrary it requires, as part of the ideal of law, that the rules in the rule book capture and enforce moral rights.'

16 See, for an extensive examination of twentieth-century ILP scholarship: (Nijman 2004).

Justice. However, no positive international law catalogue of legal persons exists. This may be a shortcoming as well as an opportunity.

In the absence of black letter law, doctrine and practice cover up controversy by quoting from the Court's 1949 Advisory Opinion:

> [Being an international person] does not even imply that all its rights and duties must be upon the international plane, any more than all the rights and duties of a State must be upon that plane. What it does mean is that it is a subject of international law capable of possessing international rights and duties, and that it has capacity to maintain its rights by bringing international claims.

The *dictum* of which this passage is part,[17] has become an incantation for dealing with the controversies of ILP. Being probably the most authoritative judicial statement on ILP, it has come to serve as the basis for the conventional approach to ILP. It defines the ILP as an entity capable of possessing international rights and duties and of bringing international claims when it needs to maintain these rights (see, for example, Brownlie 2003, Cassesse 2005, Dixon 2005, Malanczuk 1997, Shaw 2003, Jennings and Watts 1992). Over the years the *Reparation* definition has also been criticized sharply for being – as Ian Brownlie explains – 'unfortunately circular because the indicia referred to depend on the existence of a legal person.' (Brownlie 1998: 35.) The definition may be circular indeed, but what is relevant is that it provides for ILP *created by* the international legal system (that is to say when this system addresses an actor through an international norm, or when it attributes rights, duties, and/or competences). This implies that inclusion of new, non-state, actors is well possible if international life so requires. The ICJ takes a formal or fictional approach to ILP (as opposed to a 'real personality' approach)[18]: legal personality is created by international law by way of attribution of specific rights and/or duties to an actor (the Court grounds the ILP of the UN on the rights, duties and competences attributed to the United Nations in the Charter, that is to say, international law). This formal concept of ILP has come to dominate mainstream, positivist international law scholarship. In the words of Hans Kelsen, ILP is generally not understood as a '*reality* of positive law or of nature', (Kelsen 1952: 98, emphasis added) but as an epistemological

17 *Advisory Opinion on Reparation for Injuries Suffered in the Service of the United Nations* Case, 1949 *ICJ Rep*., at 178–179; it is preceded by the other famous sentences: '[t]he subjects of law in any legal system are not necessarily identical in their nature or the extent of their rights, and their nature depends upon the needs of the community. Throughout its history, the development of international law has been influenced by the requirements of international life, and the progressive increase in the collective activities of states has already given rise to instances of action upon the international plane by certain entities which are not states.'

18 See below Section IV of this chapter.

fiction and 'thoroughly formal concept.' (Kelsen 1952: 152.) Formal in the sense that not a certain reality causes a legal person to emerge, but merely the law.

One could say that with this inductive line of reasoning the Court provided international law with an – in principle inclusive – open system of ILP. After all, the *Reparation* opinion seemed to suggest that normally NSAs would become international 'legal persons' if international life so required. But, although the 'conventional approach' to ILP is open-textured, in practice it has failed to fulfil an inclusive role. Two related factors may be mentioned by way of explanation.

Firstly, international law never developed a new theory of personality that could have offered a way out of the circularity of the *Reparation* doctrine. Arguably, with an open-textured model the need for a *theory* of international personality increases. If 'legal personality' means '(apparent) capacity of being a subject of rights and duties', there is need for a theory which addresses the question as to '*when* an actor has the capacity of possessing rights and duties?' or 'when an actor *should* possess rights and duties under international law?', or 'to *which social reality* ILP is to be attached,' to name a few. However, according to the conventional approach ILP is a formal concept, that is a legal fiction wielded by the legal order. By consequence scholars have focused on the technical legal aspects, while socio-psychological and ethical dimensions or philosophical underpinnings of the concept were basically left aside (Alston 2005, Nijman 2004: 392). As the prevailing 'fiction theory' ignored all extra-legal considerations, the social reality behind the attribution of ILP was purposely ignored.[19] An alternative theory about the nature of ILP, e.g. grounded on the idea that social circumstances may be a source of ILP, never took hold.

Secondly, how the formal conception of ILP works out, depends on how international law is defined. An actor exists as a legal person in the 'eyes of international law' when international law attributes rights and duties to it and thus grants it legal 'visibility'. Legal personality is merely a legal fiction, collective entities are not 'persons' but in law. In John Dewey's classic words: 'for the purposes of law the conception of "person" is a legal conception; put roughly, "person" signifies what law makes it signify' (Dewey 1926: 655). Only law gives existence to legal personality, the creation of an ILP is a purely formal exercise. This may seem 'politically neutral,' (Friedmann 1967: 557) but international law defined as a law between states 'sees' different subjects than international law defined as 'the universal law of humanity.' In other words, the *conception* of international law plays a vital role in the identification of the international person. The positivist paradigm has famously dominated international law in practice and in theory (Koskenniemi 2002, Nijman 2004). It holds a view of international law that is state-centric and consent-based. Unsurprisingly, the catalogue of ILPs by definition includes states and international organizations established by states.

19 John Dewey (1926): 'There is no general agreement regarding the nature in se of the jural subject; courts and legislators do their work without such agreement, sometimes without any conception or theory at all regarding its nature.'

States are the 'primary' and 'original' persons in international law.[20] Oppenheim's International Law in the third edition captures well the mainstream approach:

> *The conception of International Persons is derived from the conception of the Law of Nations*. As this law is the body of rules, which the civilised States consider legally binding in their intercourse, every State which belongs to the civilised States, and is, therefore, a member of the Family of Nations, is an International Person. And since now the Family of Nations has become an organised community under the name of the League of Nations with distinctive international rights and duties of its own, the League of Nations is an International Person *sui generis* besides the several States. But apart from the League of Nations, sovereign States exclusively are International Persons – *i.e.* subjects of International Law (Oppenheim 1920: 125, emphasis added).[21]

The accommodation of new, non-state, actors into the international legal system is thus hampered by the conventional positivist understanding of international law that is basically defined by the actors it regulates primarily: sovereign states. In other words, together with the formal conception of ILP there is another view on ILP at work, which is determined by the political outlook on international law. When ILP is defined as 'bearing rights and duties under international law', ILP is inferred from the international rights and duties borne by a particular actor. ILP then 'merely is an *ex post* qualification on the basis of apparently performed legal acts.' However, at the same time ILP in relation to some actors is used as 'a threshold – proceeding from an established catalogue of international legal subjects, which keeps actors from being considered as a subject of international law regardless of their actions at the international plane' (Brölmann 2007a: 69–70). If not a priori included in the catalogue, an actor does not have ILP, and neither can it obtain ILP on the basis of actual doings in the international arena. This 'threshold approach' – international law *a priori* stipulating or withholding legal personality for a specific actor – seems to explain the legal practice with regard to *some* NSAs, notably NGOs. Whatever their actual functioning in international law, NGOs are generally excluded from the catalogue of ILPs, according to some in order to prevent further 'empowerment' of these NSAs on the international plane (Brölmann 2007a: 70). This approach, when geared by a mainstream conception of international law, then functions so as to exclude most actors other than states as persons of international law. In addition, both the 'inductive approach' and the 'threshold approach' see

20 Nations-states are the principal subjects of international law the 'normal type' of international legal persons, since 'in spite of the complexities, it is as well to remember the primacy of states as subjects of the law.' (Brownlie 2003: 57).

21 As to the source of ILP, Oppenheim's approach – the international legal person emerges through the explicit or implicit attribution of ILP by international law (to states primarily) – has remained the standard well into the twentieth century.

ILP as attributed by international law. If international law then is defined as inter-state law this will logically mark the choice of actors which qualify for ILP.

Now, when the ILP concept operates in the context of a different view on international law, as in the case of Hans Kelsen's *Pure Theory of Law*, ILP as a legal fiction and a mere point of attribution (*Zurechnungspunkt*), is found to contribute to *inclusion* of the individual – and in principle of all international actors – in the group of international *legal* actors.[22] The same holds true for the views of other progressive scholars of the Interwar and post-WWII years: they supported a truly open and inclusive approach to ILP, but did adhere to the 'fiction theory' on ILP since 'real' personality could only be attached to individuals who therefore counted as the original persons in international law. James Brierly called for 'the broadening [of the] notion of international legal personality' (Brierly 1958: 51–52) and so did sociological school scholars Nicolas Politis (1923) and Georges Scelle (1923a, 1923b). This goes to demonstrate that the formal conception of legal personality, which draws on fiction theory, is *in theory* not an obstruction to the expansion of the catalogue of ILPs.

In short, the formal conception of ILP is not used in a neutral world. ILP may be an epistemological fiction and a purely legal auxiliary device, but its application cannot escape the political agenda or ideological outlook of those who advance fiction theory. Much depends on the general theory of international law that focuses the ILP lens when looking at new, non-state, actors: this may be a conventional, positivist or, for example, an individualistic outlook on international law.[23] Traditional international law creates a legal person by attribution of international rights and duties to an entity, but since it defines international law as the law that is created by states for the regulation of relations between states, other actors are not readily addressed. The term 'non-state actor' is in fact an indication of prevailing exclusivist trends or even fundamental reflection about it.[24] Rather than to include,

22 In 1932, Hans Kelsen (1932: 142–146, 162) argued at the Hague Academy: 'Comme tout droit, le droit international est …, lui aussi, une réglementation de la conduite humaine. C'est à l'homme que s'adressent les normes du droit international, c'est contre l'homme qu'elles dirigent la contrainte, c'est aux hommes qu'elles remettent le soin de créer l'ordre. … La 'personne' en tant que sujet de droits et d'obligations n'est que l'expression personnifié de l'unité d'un système de normes réglementant des actions humaines, de 'unité d'un ordre total (Etat) ou partiel (autres personnes juridiques et 'personnes physiques'). See also, Kelsen's 1926 (243–244) Course at the Hague Academy.

23 Scholarship that firmly upholds this definition of international law and aims to refrain from including non-state actors, the possession of a capacity to create international law is frequently added as a criterion to be fulfilled in order to be an international person. If one has an individualistic take on international law and aims at the inclusion of the individual as legal person in international law, the capacity to make law is not a requirement to be fulfilled.

24 According to Alston: 'Various explanations might be suggested: an intrinsic lack of imagination; a natural affinity with the status quo; a deeply rooted professional commitment to internationalism, albeit one premised on the continuity of the system of sovereign equality; a reluctance to bite the hand that feeds; or simply the conviction that

the mainstream positivist use of ILP excludes new (non-state) actors from the international legal system. This means that the formal conception of ILP leads to an open system in theory, yet a closed system *in practice*.

In light of the growing influence of NSAs in international life and the (related) changing identity of international law, I see three ways in which currently ILP may be, and is, construed for NSAs. In all cases, the notion of legal personality is used in a rather conventional way – as a legal fiction – but it is operationalized by 'new' international law (conceptions). Consequently, 'new' ILPs are created. This is discussed in the following paragraphs a) on 'transnational ILP'; b) on 'soft ILP'; and c) on sufficient 'regular ILP'.

Transnational Legal Personality

Unsurprising for someone standing in the tradition of the Yale School of International Law, Rosalyn Higgins rejects the positivist subject-object dichotomy; it is without 'credible reality' or 'functional purpose'. Higgens argues moreover that '[w]e have erected an intellectual prison of our own choosing and then declared it to be an unalterable constraint' (Higgins 1994: 49–50). The inflexible subject-object dichotomy of the positivist school is 'unhelpful,' both intellectually and operationally, she states, and many have repeated her words since. In her view international law has 'only *participants*'. 'Individuals are participants, along with states, international organizations (…), multinational corporations, and indeed private non-governmental groups' (Higgins 1994: 50). Here too, the definition of 'international law' determines the concept of ILP; when international law appears as a dynamic process of authoritative decision-making aimed at realising certain common values in which many actors interact, only a flexible and holistic notion can serve as a basis for ILP: the participant. A clear-cut legal definition of the 'international legal person' is less important in the 'law as process' approach. Rather, it hinges on a more fluent and inclusive conception which links up with the actor's participatory role in the global decision-making processes. Higgins carries on the line of Myres McDougal who indeed used 'participant' deliberately to include new actors into international law and put an end to the 'blind[ness]' of international law for non-state participants (McDougal 1953: 160–162).

Currently, Harold Koh carries the process approach further with what may be termed the 'transnational legal process' understanding of international law.[25]

---

respect for that system has taken a great deal of time and human suffering to achieve and that it continues to offer a better prospect than any alternative that has so far been put forward' (Alston 2005: 21).

25 According to Koh: 'Transnational legal process describes the theory and practice of how public and private actors – nation-states, international organizations, multinational enterprises, nongovernmental organizations, and private individuals – interact in a variety of public and private, domestic and international fora to make, interpret, enforce, and ultimately, internalize rules of transnational law' (Koh 1996: 183–184).

International law develops into transnational law. National and international law take part in the same system and the same processes. In other words, international law is redefined; a process that Math Noortmann critically engages in Chapter 7. It becomes more dynamic and 'nonstatist: the actors in this process are not just, or even primarily, nation-states, but include non-state actors as well' (Koh 1996: 181). The transnational legal process moreover includes both hard law and soft law instruments. Koh too considers the traditional ILP notion unsuited as a tool for determining which international actors are bound by, and part of, the international *legal* system. In his view, the actual influence of a NSA on policy making and legal decision-making is a yardstick in judging whether that actor is included in the system of transnational law. Anna-Karin Lindblom sums Koh's understanding of ILP well up: 'The New ILP, in Koh's version, requests the lawyer to take the full scope of *societal interaction* into consideration when analysing the process and normativity of transnational law' (Lindblom 2006: 98). If through its interaction – of whatever type – an international actor can be seen to exercise influence on the shaping of transnational law and policy, that actor has ILP in Koh's version of the concept, i.e. 'transnational legal personality'. In this transnationalist version ILP is a more dynamic and more relative concept, defined by a new understanding of international law. It is noteworthy that with this redefinition of international law and ILP, Koh also leaves the 'fiction theory' and opens the door to a 'real theory' of personality, in which social circumstances create 'transnational legal personality'. Legal personality then emerges from *social interaction* and actual *influence* on the transnational decision-making processes in which NSAs participate.

'Soft' International Legal Personality

Outside the 'law as process' school, certainly softness of international law is also an issue. The end of the binary opposition between international law as a system of 'hard' rules on the one hand and 'soft' international law on the other (Chinkin 1989: 850–866), arguably leaves room also for a softer (version of) ILP. The general idea then is that for actors to be addressed by soft international norms, to be involved in the creation of soft law instruments, etc., may not be enough to have full-fledged ILP in international law – yet it stands for something. 'Soft international legal personality' may then express the 'existence' of a particular actor in the eyes of international soft law instruments. In other words, it is not so much a fundamental adaptation of the definition of ILP as it is an implication of the growing 'softness in international law' (d'Aspremont 2008) for the ILP conception. While Jean d'Aspremont is right that the binary nature of law is worth fighting for, I beg to differ on the point of his explanation for the softening of international law. In this case, the introduction of a softer version of ILP for NSAs means a more adequate description of a serious normative development, that is to say, soft law that addresses NSAs (Shelton 2009, also Chinkin 2000). It is not 'an artificial extension of the frontiers of international law' for the sake of mere scholarly pleasure (d'Aspremont 2008). It is worth developing our terminology so as to encompass also softer tones of 'legalness' and recognize that international law can have normative force also for actors which are not formally bound by a particular international norm, yet sometimes willing to comply; or that international normativity can be shaped by international documents which escape the binary structure of law, such as non-binding documents of international organizations, codes of conduct, private governance arrangements. A soft ILP notion would thus accommodate and recognize the new role of NSAs within the international legal system. Otherwise they are left with an unclear, controversial status within a global legal arena that will become only more complex and plural.

Obviously, on the one hand softening ILP is an inclusive exercise. It may serve to rescue ILP from the positivist, binary understanding of international law and contribute to its adaptation to new legal phenomena. On the other hand, softened ILP confirms to some extent the validity of Higgins' critique of how our discipline has 'erected an intellectual prison' that obstructs the adaptation of international law to the social reality. Alston has uttered similar critique with his 'Not-a-Cat' image (Alston 2005: 3–4, 19–20); the use of the term '*non*-state actors' is in itself an intentional technique to exclude these actors from the international legal system. Behind our discipline's terminology functions the exclusive club or 'catalogue' approach to ILP (see also, Alston 2005: 19, Clapham 2006: 70–71: 'doctrinal filters', Brölmann 2007a: 69–70), which stands in the way of inclusion. Against the backdrop of the traditional approach to ILP and the exclusion it builds into international law, the idea of 'soft ILP' is not unappealing. Soft ILP works well for the declaratory as well as constitutive role played by ILP. The idea may suffer from indeterminacy, but it takes hesitations and concerns about the recognition of ILP for NSAs serious as the soft aspect steers clear of the suggestion that NSAs instantly come to possess *rights*, apart from duties and obligations, under general international law. This particular concern regarding the participation of NSAs within the international legal order – of which international human rights law forms an important part – is found neither with Alston nor with Clapham. Both scholars readily accept obligations for NSAs under international law.

Clapman Rescues the Prisoners of Doctrine: Sufficient 'Regular' ILP of NSA.

In order to counter the formal exclusion of NSAs from the international legal system and to rescue them from their doctrinal imprisonment (Clapham 2006: 59), Andrew Clapham calls for 'radical' new thinking with respect to these actors in international law.[26] In his view, '[e]verything [in respect to ILP] turns on the conception that one has of the Law of Nations.' In this sense, Clapham's approach to ILP is rather conventional: only law defines ILP. However, he reconceptualizes international law to be also the law of NSAs and thus renders the 'threshold' or exclusive catalogue approach inoperative. He argues that 'we need to see

26 http://untreaty.un.org/cod/avl/ls/Clapham_IL.html, in the following Clapham: Non-State Actors, accessed 20 February 2010.

international law not only in terms of obligations for governments but also for non-state actors' (Clapham: 2006: 83).

First, Clapham disentangles ILP from 'the misleading concept of 'subjects' of international law and the attendant question of attribution of statehood under international law' (Clapham 2006: 59). This leads to resistance among mainstream scholars, because expansion of the category of ILPs would 'lead to an expansion of the possible authors of international law. [And t]his, of course, is seen to threaten the viable development of a decentralized, state-centred international legal order.' (Clapham 2006: 59. See, for the fears, which prevent MNCs from being recognized as international legal persons: 78–79.) The inclusion of *not-yet*-state actors is seen moreover as another threat to the system: the recognition of their ILP would empower these actors in their quest for statehood. The arguments to include (or exclude) NSAs as an ILP category are – to put it in Koskenniemi's words – 'vulnerable to the charge that such law [or doctrine] is in fact political because apologist or utopian' (Koskenniemi 1990: 8). For that reason, most scholars stick to a functional approach and avoid the question about the formal status of NSAs (Clapham 2006: 60–61). Clapham on the other hand does not dodge the question.

Subsequently, Clapham develops a way around the self-imposed problem of legal formalism by moving from 'personality' to 'capacity'. He draws on the circular description of ILP by the ICJ in the *Reparation for Injuries* opinion (ICJ Rep. 1949 *Reparation for Injuries* opinion, at 179) but only to break out of it. In the view of the ICJ, ILP may be a precondition for the exercise of international rights and duties, but at the same time to have these rights and duties is evidence of an actor's ILP. Clapham focuses on the more general '*capacity to fulfil obligations*,' (Clapham 2006: 65) which was brought in by the Court in 1980: 'subjects of international law …, as such, are bound by any obligations incumbent upon them under general rules of international law …' (Clapham 2006: 65).

Clapham shows how in international relations today, NSAs have acquired direct rights and obligations under positive international law (the prerequisite for ILP) and that under particular circumstances they have a capacity to be party to a claim.[27] From the established capacity to enjoy rights and obligations, it is then 'only a short jump … to imagining that non-state actors may have, not only the capacity to enjoy rights and obligations, but also the capacity to be held accountable for failure to fulfil those obligations to which they have been subjected' (Clapham 2006: 71). From this viewpoint there is no 'conceptual barrier' or formalistic legal problem to preclude recognition of NSAs (including MNCs) as ILPs which are bound by the rights and obligations of general international law (Clapham 2006: 79). Clapham convincingly demonstrates how in recent years positive international law has attributed rights and obligations to NSAs of various types. In particular, developments in international human rights law and international humanitarian law in turn have changed international law radically. NSAs – which have acquired rights and obligations

27 He reminds us however that it is not unusual for actors to have rights and/or duties and yet not to be able to give effect to them.

under international law – may then be conceived of as ILPs (Clapham 2006: 82). In Clapham's view on the ILP of NSAs, the *onus probandi* has turned, since:

> various non-state entities today have enough international legal personality to enjoy directly rights and obligations under general international law as well as under treaties. The burden would now seem to be on those who claim that states are the sole bearers of human rights obligations under international law to explain away the obvious emergence onto the international scene of a variety of actors with sufficient international personality to be the bearers of rights and duties under international law. (Clapham 2006: 82)

In conclusion, all of the abovementioned views in their approach of ILP and NSAs remain within the conventional parameters; based as they are on the understanding that international law creates ILP. Their difference lies primarily in the underlying conceptions of international law. At the same time, all three views show how hard it is in the current international constellation to keep the legal realm and the non-legal or social realm apart. In Koh's approach to international law as transnational legal process, the non-legal reality of 'influence' actually contributes to the emergence of ILP. In the next section, we will try and take it one step further; we will revisit the 'real personality' or 'realist theory' of ILP and explore its possibilities of offering a theoretical framework fitting to contemporary international life.

IV. The Need for Grounding ILP: A New Realist Theory of ILP

Most scholars regard the conventional approach to ILP as useless with respect to questions concerning the position of NSAs. Arguably we have come to a deadlock in ILP doctrine and theory. The idea that legal personality is merely a fiction created by international law through attribution may be flexible and open in theory, in practice *de facto* significant actors are ignored *in jure*. In other words, international law is in need of a theory of personality that can accommodate non-state (collective) entities (see also, Carty 2005). These entities, like the human subject, emerge from 'components'. Elsewhere I have argued for the restoration of the human individual as the original and primary international legal person. Related to this proposition ILP was reconstructed on the basis of anthropology and ethics (Nijman 2007). Here, rather than discussing ILP theory with respect to the collective non-state subject on the basis of the hermeneutics of the collective self, I aim to stir up the debate on the nature of ILP and to revisit 'real personality theory', also called the 'realist theory'. Günther Teubner and Alexander Wendt are already participants in this debate. A revisit of the real personality theory may provide us with leads for a new theory, which can contribute to the grounding of ILP, and can reconnect the emergence of ILP to social facts and moral foundations. Before recapturing three elements of the real personality theory that are relevant here, I will briefly discuss the controversy that surrounded its eclipse.

On the Controversy Over Realist Theory of Personality

Today's conventional use and definition of ILP is formally indifferent to the social reality bearing ILP. As mentioned, it draws on one of the two principal theories on the nature of legal persons, the fiction theory. The real personality or realist theory, which in brief holds that the legal person is not merely a legal fiction created by law but emerges from social facts, disappeared from both the municipal law debate and the international law debate in the early decades of the twentieth century. John Dewey's article *The Historic Background of Corporate Legal Personality* has been critical to the disappearance of the real personality theory in the context of the first debate (Dewey 1926). The international law debate was basically decided around the same time.

Late nineteenth and early twentieth-century mainstream personality discourse focused on the state. For many, the ILP of the state had been firmly connected to a *real* personality of the state or at least to a pre-legal, factual *existence* of a state entity.[28] Gradually, leaving details aside, however, the understanding of both state personality and state 'will' as legal fictions came to dominate mainstream scholarship. Otto von Gierke's realist theory gave way to the fiction theory propagated by, for example, another German voluntarist and legal positivist, Georg Jellinek.[29] International law is then seen as created by the fictitious will of sovereign states to apply a self-imposed order. States were the only subjects of international law (Triepel 1923, Anzilotti 1929, Cavaglieri 1929: 318–319, Heilborn 1925, 1926, Oppenheim 1920: 18–19. See also, for example, Kaufmann 1935: 324–325, Séfériadès 1930: 294–295), safe one or two exceptions. The international rule of law accordingly is weak – international law is law *by* states and not above states (Oppenheim 1920: 19, Triepel 1923: 81, Cavaglieri 1929: 318, Heilborn 1926: 5, Kaufmann: 320–325. The Permanent Court of International Justice confirmed this position in 1927 in the Lotus case, PCIJ Ser. A. 10, at 18 (1927)). As such, it has failed to prevent world war and to constrain state power.

It may be kept in mind that in the nineteenth century, realist theory had emerged in a rather progressive context, and had aimed to contribute to the establishment of the responsibility of corporations. However, developed at that time as part of

28 See, for example, Triepel (1923) who maintained that the state had a *real* personality: '*L'État est une véritable personnalité, il est une personnalité indépendante, distincte de la somme des individus qui le composent.*'

29 Jellinek rejected the idea that legal personality could have its source in factual existence: legal persons come into being *only* by attribution of an entity by the legal order. The law determines which entity has legal personality, the factual existence of an entity, its nature, and properties belong to the world of (social) facts and not to the legal realm. Legal personality is established by the law and is a relation of the law with an entity irrespective of (the nature of) existence. In Jellink's view the state can only be bound by his own sovereign will, international law is created by *Selbst-Verpflichtung*. Hence, international law attaches ILP to sovereign states only. Jellinek conceived of the law of the international society as '*anarchisches Recht*' (Jellinek 1905: 368).

German jurisprudence, it was marked by Hegelian and Neo-Hegelian thinking about the state. This means that the state was personified as a real person, glorified as God marching on Earth. In this version of real theory, the individual as well as all social groups are absorbed by, and merged into, the state collective, thus losing their identity and liberty. The real personality was later perceived to have prepared the way for 'corporative' and fascist states. As Wolfgang Friedmann (1967: 559) points out, it became 'an important stepping-stone towards that merger of the individual in the collective, which is an essential and vital aspect of modern totalitarian government.' (Friedmann 1967: 559.) Realist theory became untenable in the actual political context of growing collectivism and totalitarianism. The individual, its autonomy, dignity and liberty had to be protected. Progressive international law scholars of the *Interbellum* indeed recognized these political dangers intrinsic in the realist legal personality conception and fought against it. Each with their own approach aimed for a renewal of international law and the liberation and emancipation of the individual (Nijman 2004: 126 et seq.). Many – Hans Kelsen was already mentioned – drew on fiction theory, which 'regards the legal personality of entities other than human beings as the result of a fiction. *"Real" personality can only attach to individuals.* States, corporations, institutions, cannot be subjects of rights and duties, but they are treated as if persons' (Friedmann 1967: 556, emphasis added).

Anti-statist liberal IL scholars repudiated collectivist and organic conceptions of the (international) legal personality of the state for having autocratic and anti-democratic tendencies. They noticed the dangers of the state as a 'real corporate personality' – a (mysterious) super-entity with a will and life of its own – and thus adhered to (methodological) individualism.[30] They basically denied the existence of anything like a real collective entity and reduced it to the level of individual actions. Social entities are nothing but the aggregation of individuals. The individual was in their eyes the *true* or *real*, primary and original subject of international law (see, for example, Le Fur 1927: 404. See, more extensively Nijman 2004). Scelle and many more were committed to strengthening the international rule of law[31] and saving individual human responsibility.[32] The ILP of individual human beings makes the individualisation of responsibility conceptually possible.

30 See, for example, Kelsen 1920: 19, Scelle 1932: 118. See also, Politis 1928: 13. Hersch Lauterpacht's theory of law is also carried by methodological individualism. Lauterpacht 1975: 333–337. Also, Brierly 1949: 56, 1958: 51. See, Nijman 2004: 192 et seq. See also, Koskenniemi 2002: 330.

31 In Scelle's words '*le Droit seul est souverain.*' See also, Scelle 1936: 91: '[*l*]*es gouvernants étatique [sont les] principaux sujets du droit des gens*'.

32 The fiction of the (international legal) personality of the state leads to the eclipse of responsibility: '*d'abord, à faire disparaître ensuite la responsabilité. ... on cède à une mystique qui attribue des qualités immanentes à des êtres fictifs, mais qui bénéficie à des personnes réelles devenues irresponsables et toutes puissantes derrière l'écran qui les dissimule*' (Scelle 1932b: 12).

For the abovementioned authors, only individuals have consciousness, will, and personality required to bear the moral obligation to obey (international) law and to further justice through law and institutions. Hence *'[r]eal' personality can only attach to individuals*, not to states nor to any other social actor. If attributed by the legal system to such actor it was a pure fiction.

The realist understanding of ILP has been considered methodologically and epistemologically as well as politically questionable ever since the early twentieth century. Rejection of this old version of realist theory of personality will not be disputed here. The human individual may never be a means to an end, nor merged into a collective subject at the expense of its identity and autonomy. The susceptibility of the 'old' realist theory to absolutist tendencies and the role it allegedly played in the dark history of our continent (Friedmann 1967: 236) are however related particularly to the version of the Hegelian scholar Otto von Gierke. There is another version of the realist theory of personality, which also draws on Gierke, but which is less politically contaminated. In this vision the state is but one of many group personalities rather than the Sovereign Person that absorbs all. This approach was asserted by the so-called Pluralists School (Runciman 1997). For them, the real existence of groups is also the source of their legal personality, but the state does not absorb all legal persons within society, nor does it merge and devour individuals into the divine 'state person'. The state is merely one of many groups, which all have legal personality based on their actual existence. My suggestion to revisit realist theory is not an argument for reviving neither the old version nor the political interpretation given to Gierke's theory. Rather I aim to explore the old idea that legal personality emerges from 'real' existence so as to find leads for the development of a new, modern version of real personality theory.

Revisiting the Realist Theory of (International) Legal Personality

In 1926, John Dewey wrote a firm defence of fiction theory and made a decisive contribution to the end of the debate on legal personality, which had waged heavily since arguably the early 1880s when Gierke attacked fiction theorist (and founder of the historical school) Friedrich Carl von Savigny. With von Savigny, adherent of an individualist theory of personality, the debate had shifted focus from the nature of legal personality to issues of attribution. One reason why Dewey turned against Frederick Maitland was because 'his discussion [of legal personality] depends upon an assumption that there are properties which any unit must antecedently and inherently have in order to be a right-and-duty-bearing unit' (Friedmann 1967: 657). Maitland was indeed a propagator of the realist theory of legal personality. He translated parts of Otto von Gierke's *Das deutsche Genossenschaftsrecht* into English (as *Political Theories of the Middle Age*, 1900) and thereby introduced von Gierke's realist theory into the Anglo-American legal discourse. As the title of the English translation reflects, von Gierke's theory of law and state has German medieval roots. This means that it is a theory that 'starts from the Whole, but ascribes an intrinsic value to every Partial Whole, down to and including the Individual' (Gierke 1900: 7). In a way, this sounds very post-modern.

Von Gierke identified three ways in which the legal person can come into being. Next to explicit attribution (i.e. formal announcement) and implicit attribution of legal personality by the legal order (Gierke 1895: 489–491), he discerned a third option: *Persönlichkeit kraft Daseins* – legal personality which emerges from factual existence.[33] In this case, the basis of legal personality is pre-legal in nature; factual circumstances or particular capacities or properties of an entity determined the emergence of (its) legal personality. ILP is more than a legal relation, it is rooted in factual existence (*Dasein*), the factual existence and characteristics of the entity are the basis of its legal personality. What is this 'pre-juristic being [*vorjuristischen Dasein*],' what are the qualities or capacities of the social reality from which legal personality emerges?

In Gierke's theory, legal personality emerges from social circumstances, which he calls *Genossenschaft* [Fellowship]. This notion refers to the medieval conception of collective unity as 'plurality in unity.'[34] As such, it is a person in its own right. In other words, legal personality is the legal conception of this unity. Maitland explains in his introduction to *Political Theories of the Middle Ages*:

> [W]hatever the Roman *universitas* may have been – and Dr Gierke is for pinning the Roman jurists to Savignianism – our German Fellowship [*Genossenschaft*] is no fiction, no symbol, no piece of the State's machinery, no collective name for individuals, but a living organism and a real person, with body and members and a will of its own. Itself can will, itself can act; it wills and acts by the men who are its organs as a man wills and acts by brain, mouth and hand. It is not a fictitious person; it is a *Gesamtperson*, and its will is a *Gesamtwille*; it is a group-person, and its will is a group-will. (Maitland 2003: xxv–xxvi)

Genossenschaft is used to describe composed, super-individual entities as diverse as companies, cities, churches, unions, and so on. In Gierke's theory of legal personality corporation is declared as '*reale Gesamtperson nicht bloß rechtsfähig, sondern auch willens und handlungsfähig*' (Gierke 1887: 603). The legal person that emerges from the social constellation is thus a real person constituted by, but more than, its members. It has its own capacity to bear rights and obligations, to act and to decide freely. As such, it has 'real' existence without having physical or material existence. Rights and obligations of the Group-persons are inherent to the

---

33 According to Gierke: '*Die Rechtsordnung kann die Anerkennung eines Verbandes als Körperschaft unmittelbar an das Dasein eines geeigneten Thatbestandes knüpfen, so dass die Körperschaften in ähnlicher Weise, wie der einzelne Mensch, durch die Geburt Person wird*' (Gierke 1895: 488).

34 '[A] 'unity-in-plurality' … is, a unity which is prior to, and in some senses determinant of, the individuality of a group's members; the whole comes before the parts' (Runciman 1997: 37).

nature of these persons, they do not lose them being part of the state. They have moral personality (being an organized group that can act and express a will) and legal personality (Maitland 1905). Law applies to *Genossenschaften* as it applies to man, yet law creates neither.

The factual existence of a state is the source of its (international) legal personality. The community of communities from which the legal personality of the state emerges, is an entity with a life and will of its own. In other words, there is ample room for group life within the state; neither individuals nor collective non-state entities are completely subsumed by the state and therewith lose their identity and autonomy. In this view the state *needs* the groups living within it, and without these individuals and collective entities will not be able to take shape. Hence, the real personality of the state (which generates from its community) precedes and gives birth to its (international) legal personality. State or non-state, the legal person is a conscious and willful metaphysical person, a super-individual being with a life, mind, and will of its own (Gierke 1902: 24).

Gierke's and Maitland's challenge to individualism in legal theory was connected to the rise of powerful collective entities such as commercial corporations and labour unions in the context of industrialization. Society was changing rapidly and they felt it should be possible to hold these new powerful actors to account. Others, however, used the realist theory to accomplish the contrary, that is: no regulation of companies by the state. This was one of the reasons for intense debate on corporate personality at the turn of the century (see, for example, Horwitz 1992: 71–72). In short, the realist position conceived of legal personality as rooted in social (-political) and moral life.

In *Moral Personality and Legal Personality* (1905), Maitland shows how legal personality is indeed a theme that resides in 'the borderland where ethical speculation marches with jurisprudence' (Maitland 1905: 62–74). For a realist, moral personality and legal personality cannot be separated, '[f]or the morality of common sense the group is person, is right-and-duty bearing unit.' (Maitland 1905, 2003: 68). Maitland quotes Dicey and explains that when men bind themselves to one another in an association or organized group, 'they create a body, which by no fiction of law, but by the very nature of things, differs from the individuals of whom it is constituted' (Maitland 1905, 2003: 63). Organized groups or collective entities then are 'persons', that is to say, right-and-duty bearing units. To Maitland realist theory is progressive to the extent that it serves responsibility, whereas otherwise the 'responsible right-and-duty-bearing unit' would become an 'irresponsible many.' The law may fail to recognize a collective entity as a person, but 'as a matter of moral sentiment, it does exist' (Maitland 1905, 2003: 68).

Against this background, the present contribution seeks to make a substantiated call for reopening the personality theory debate. Such in particular as we are faced with an imminent crisis of legitimacy due to the situation in which *de facto* international powers live outside international law. Its aim is not to present a completely new theory, but to indicate how a revisit of the realist theory is worthwhile. What then should we take from the revisit of the old realist theory?

First, there should be some reflection on social reality as a source of legal personality, by way of a viable alternative to the current approach to ILP. The old realist theory shows how a non-purely legal foundation of legal personality offers the possibility of social and ethical grounding of the legal person. Let's discuss the possibilities and challenges of a *new* realist theory. Such a theory would be 'new' also because what we consider 'real' today differs greatly from the 'metaphysical realist' and organicist understandings which prevailed at the turn of the previous century. Leaving behind what some have called 'bad metaphysics', the idea that there is something *real* to international legal persons and that internationally operating NSAs fulfil that 'reality' is worth discussing.

Secondly, the 'old' realist theory described above may also be read as an attempt to make powerful actors, which up to then were barely visible to the law, bear responsibility. The realist theory challenged the liberal, individualist theory (in which ILP of a collective was conceived as a fiction) as it could not account well for the newly emerging collective entities. The quest for accountability and responsibility of entities, which dispose of actual power on the international stage remains highly topical in our time.

Thirdly, if legal personality emerges from the 'nature of things', what does this mean? It satisfies the common intuition that *legal* personality implies social, political and/or economic existence. But what underlying social constellation would or should give rise to legal personality? According to the old version of the realist theory, the common nature or essence of all legal persons – whether an individual or collective actor, and whether a state or non-state actor – can be found in the capacity to will and to act. In case of a collective entity, these pre-judicial capacities are born from what Gierke termed 'fellowship' among the group members, they require a group that is well-organized around a purpose and with a 'mind' or 'conscience' of its own. Its 'reality' shows from its actions as one and independent of its members. In these postmodern and post-postmodern days, oneness or unity is a difficult concept. Even man is 'constituted' by fragments. This understanding in a way mirrors Gierke's observation a century ago on the existence of social unities: '*Ein unmittelbarer Beweis für das Dasein von sozialen Lebenseinheiten lässt sich nicht führen. Ist doch auch die individuelle Lebenseinheit nicht unmittelbar erweislich*' (Gierke 1902: 19). Legal personality by virtue of *Dasein* (being, real existence) raises questions with respect to the *Dasein* – from what kind of social existence does legal personality emerge? Which capacities have to exist for legal personality to develop? The emphasis on social existence or on the capacities of a social actor is still relevant and helpful today, be it in a new version which includes the capacity to be held responsible and accountable.

Finally, Gierke's realist theory of personality offers an approach to social actors, which starts neither with the law nor with the state, but with the *reality* of the actor. It doesn't approach legal personality from the outside but from the inside, so to speak. State and non-state actors have legal personality based on their factual existence and the latter actors are neither created by the law nor by the state through the law. This, however, does not mean they are not bound by the law – on the contrary. But it does tell us something about the relationship between law and society, which is worth exploring also at the international level. In the words of John Figgis, one of the British pluralists (who consider it in man's nature to associate and form Group-persons): 'What we actually see in the world is not on the one hand the state, and on the other a mass of unrelated individuals; but a vast complex of gathered unions.' This he described as a '*communitas communitatum*' (Figgis 1913: 47). In this pluralist version of realist theory, the state does not absorb all social actors and communities but it lives among them. This may be an interesting concept to contemplate with respect to the international community, which after all can no longer be modelled as an inter-state community and is in need for new conceptions and theory. In a 'community of communities' each has their own purpose – the international community, as well as the state and non-state actors that are members of the international community – but all also work towards the purpose of the whole, which respects the purpose of the parts. This universal end is no longer God, but may be universal justice. Likewise it is interesting – though outside the scope of this contribution – to explore Gierke's view on the rule of law or Rechtsstaat (see, for example, Runciman 1997: 53), and to examine how it may be useful for the conceptualization of the IRoL.

The Contours of a (Debate on) New Realist ILP Theory

We are in need of a new theory of ILP, which embraces both state and non-state actors. The lack of such a theory hinders international law practice and scholarship from the construction of NSAs as ILPs. A new realist theory on the nature *in se* of the legal person would rely on the existence of a social reality behind both types of collective actors, the social substratum of the ILP. Global developments as described in this chapter's first section arguably reinforce the relevance of real personality theory. An endogenous perspective on ILP, which starts from the idea that there is indeed *something real* to the ILP, is however not very common in IL and IR literature. The mainstream approach is exogenous, that is to say, the international legal system determines which entity has ILP. The (international) legal person has been 'an inert person' around which philosophical, political and economic discussions have subsided (Teubner 1988: 130). A more ontological or essential approach to actors in international relations has long been unpopular and controversial. However, current ontological insights differ significantly from those earlier generation of real personality theory. Today, we have new views on what is 'real', in order to BE one does not need to exist physically or materially.

The progressive *Interbellum* scholars, for whom individuals were the only real persons, worked with a modern ontology of physicalism and firmly rejected any metaphysical realism. This prevented them from being 'realists' about corporate persons. States in particular are social constructions dependent fully on the individual to constitute them. The turn to methodological individualism – so influential for the ILP debate – was part of a more general orientation of pre-WWII liberal international law theory 'to construe international law as a *scientifically* based, operative constraint on the conduct of foreign policy,' as Koskenniemi has put it (Koskenniemi 2002: 411, emphasis added). After the WWII, the metaphysical realist approach was history. The ('fiction theory'-based) reductionist, non-metaphysical approach to legal personality of the (methodological) individualists existed side by side with the mainstream ILP conception which conceived of ILP as a legal fiction attached to states only. In other words, the social and moral grounding of ILP has long been a non-issue in IL scholarship as well. In the work of (only) a few scholars, the non-legal dimensions of legal personality are re-examined on the basis of the latest insights in what is 'real' today. Elsewhere, I have proposed the reconstitution of ILP of the individual and the collective self 'as moral identity constituted in the dialectic relation of Self and Other(nes)s.' (Nijman 2007.) Here the aim is to revive the ILP theory debate and to examine how a new generation realist theory may help us move beyond the state vs non-state dichotomy in relation to legal personality. At this point two different constructivist approaches may be mentioned briefly, which may set the stage for a debate on a new version of realist theory of ILP.

Legal sociologist Günther Teubner moves beyond the old individual – collective opposition by way of a self-referential system theory approach. In Teubner's theory of legal personality, the social substratum of the legal person is conceived of as a 'collectivity,' that is to say, 'the self-description of a (usually formally) organized action system that brings about a cyclical linkage of self-referentially constituted system identity and action.' The internal dynamics of the social substratum is conceived as 'an autonomous communicative process with actual people simply being treated as part of this process' environment.' In Teubner's vocabulary, the substratum of the legal person is an 'autopoietic social system' which is a system of actions/communications that 'reproduces itself by constantly producing from the network of its elements new communications/actions as elements' (Teubner 1988).

Social constructivist Alexander Wendt resumed the discussion on personhood of states in international theory a few years ago (Wendt 2004). Wendt too aimed to move beyond the old metaphysical metaphors and atomizing reduction of the state person, in order to find a conception of personhood that can stand the tests of the latest philosophical, political and social sciences insights. In this exploration of personhood focus is on the state, but this is a matter of choice rather than principle. Wendt's analysis of how states are socially constructed within the international system is an IR disciplinary choice. After all, IR literature and its political realism is a 'states systemic project.' Yet, he notes that a discourse on the social construction of other important (non-state) actors such as MNCs and NGOs might be equally needed to explain contemporary world politics (Wendt 1999: 9, 2004: 292). Social constructivism as a method is not prescribing which actors to study (Wendt 1999: 7–10). International NSAs and international law as the structure in which they are embedded can be studied well from a social constructivist perspective too (Wendt 1999: 9).

We may learn something from Wendt's examination of the (psychological) personhood of the state about personhood of international actors more generally. Wendt identifies three conceptions of personhood: (1) being an intention system, (2) being an organism, and (3) the even thicker conception of having consciousness. The second and third sense are not required in the rational actor model, which conceives of the person as an intentional – purposive or goal-directed – system. The state as intentional system, neither real nor fictitious. But the state is not the only global actor whose members see themselves as part of a group in pursuit of shared ends and which is institutionalized and hierarchical: '[m]ost of the important actors in contemporary world politics – states, MNCs, and most NGOs – have corporate intentionality' (Wendt 2004: 298).

Today, NSAs are interacting increasingly with the ideational system called international law and through that interaction shape the international system as well as their own (social and legal) identity. Arguably, the current reproduction and transformation of the structures of international politics and law involves states as well as international NSAs (Wendt 1999: 310). The latter are slowly but surely being constituted not so much as an ignorable *Other* but as an *Other* with whom ideas – the ideational structure of international law – are shared. Albeit slowly, international NSAs – like MNCs – are internalizing international (human rights and environmental) norms and values. A social constructivism that is less state-centric is possible and necessary. This fundamental change of theory is worth to be examined. Here, I would like to point out that social constructivism allows for international NSAs to be conceived as *real* agents too. They too are self-organizing, constituted by internal social structures (real but non-material), possess intentionality and intrinsic motivational dispositions, and in the self-reproduction of their identity and interests they interact with the international legal system and other (state and non-state) actors (socialization).

Another approach is possible, which draws more on the idea of an ontological foundation of ILP. This would entail a modern conception of what the 'reality' of an entity should be for ILP to emerge; of which capacities the international actor should have for ILP to emerge. Gierke has offered the concept of 'action', a capacity that returns in Teubner's approach though in a less ontological context. Next to the capacity to act, Gierke identified the capacity to will something, hence the capacity to purposive action. Gierke conceptualized the collective entity with a mind and spirit of its own. In his day and age, these notions were loaded with Hegelian connotations and metaphysical realism. Wendt however shows on the basis of the latest insights that to use the word 'mind' no longer means the same as 100 years ago. If today, organized groups work as intentional systems by using their 'mind', there is nothing physical about this qualification of social reality. A contemporary real personality theory may clarify when international NSAs qualify as ILPs; when they are capable of operation at the international stage, within the international legal order; when they are intentional actors capable of purposive action and self-reflexive communication in terms of international law. It could be added – when they are capable of taking responsibility for their international actions. By 'taking' and 'making' international law, NSAs reproduce themselves as international legal persons through interaction with international law.

V. Conclusion

The conclusion to this chapter can be brief. The claim that NSAs have or should have international legal personality (ILP) for the sake of an international rule of law is ever more widely accepted. This claim in turn hinges on the – increasingly accepted – idea that any international actor with factual (social, economic or political) power should also have legal visibility. Such legal visibility can effectively be formalized through the tool of 'international legal personality'. These considerations have rekindled the debate on ILP. This chapter suggests that the prevailing 'fiction theory' on ILP is no longer fitting for the current state of affairs and that legal personality would need grounding in a social, political and/or economic reality. I have argued that it is worth to re-visit the 'real personality' or 'realist' theory on legal personality and to examine whether and how a new generation of this approach can be developed on the basis of contemporary scientific insights on what is 'real' when it comes to collective actors. If we can identify a set of (pre-legal) capacities required by a social reality in order for legal personality to emerge, we may be able to move beyond the current state–non-state dichotomy in ILP theory. In order to set the stage for the much-needed debate on ILP theory and the social grounding of legal personality, this chapter has touched upon the theories of Teubner and Wendt. Read together with the reconceptualization of ILP as a stage of the ethical-moral identity of the individual or collective subject, these approaches suggest that the new realist theory debate need no longer be hindered by the (in)famous organicist legacy of Otto von Gierke, but may profit from the latest insights in philosophy, (social) psychology, sociology. It could be added that a modern version of a 'capacity approach', which includes the capacity for responsibility and accountability, could actually be quite helpful when it comes to the constitution of NSAs as legal persons in international law.

References

Allott, P. 1990. *Eunomia: New Order for a New World*. Oxford: Oxford University Press.

Allott, P. 2002. *The Health of Nations: Society and Law Beyond the State*. Cambridge: Cambridge University Press.

Alston, P. 2005. The 'Not-a-Cat' Syndrome: Can the International Human Rights Regime Accommodate Non-State Actors?, in *Non-State Actors and Human Rights*, edited by P. Alston. New York: Oxford University Press, 3–36.

Anzilotti, D. 1929. *Cours de Droit International*. Volume I. Paris: Recueil Sirey.

Beaulac, S. 2007. An Inquiry into the International Rule of Law. *EUI Working Papers Series*, 14, 1–29.

Bianchi, A. (ed.) 2009. *Non-State Actors and International Law*. Aldershot: Ashgate.

Brierly, J.L. 1949. *The Law of Nations*. 4th Edition. Oxford: Oxford University Press.

Brierly, J.L. 1958. The Basis of Obligation in International Law, in *The Basis of Obligation in International Law and Other Papers by the Late James Leslie Brierly*, edited by H. Lauterpacht and C.H.M. Waldock. Oxford: Clarendon Press.

Brölmann, C.M. 2007a. *The Institutional Veil in Public International Law: International Organizations and the Law of Treaties*. Oxford: Hart.

Brölmann, C. 2007b. Deterritorialization in International Law: Moving Away from the Divide Between National and International Law, in *New Perspectives on the Divide Between National and International Law*, edited by J. Nijman and A. Nollkaemper. Oxford: Oxford University Press, 84–109.

Brownlie, I. 1998. *The Rule of Law in International Affairs: International Law at the Fiftieth Anniversary of the United Nations*. The Hague: Martinus Nijhoff Publishers.

Brownlie, I. 2003. *Principles of Public International Law*. 6th Edition. Oxford: Oxford University Press.

Carty, A. 2005. International Legal Personality and the End of the Subject: Natural Law and Phenomenological Responses to New Approaches to International Law, Review Essay: The Concept of International Legal Personality. *MJIL*, 6(2), 534–552.

Cassesse, A. 2005. *International Law*. 2nd Edition. Oxford: Oxford University Press.

Cavaglieri, A. 1929. Règles Générales du Droit de la Paix, *RCADI*, 26, 311–585.

Chesterman, S. 2008. An International Rule of Law? *Am. J. Comp. L.*, 56(2), 331–361.

Chinkin, C.M. 1989. The Challenge of Soft Law: Development and Change in International Law, *ICLQ*, 38(4), 850–866.

Chinkin, C.M. 2000. Normative Development in the International Legal System, in *Commitment and Compliance, the Role of Non-Binding Norms in the International Legal System*, edited by D. Shelton. Oxford: Oxford University Press, 21–42.

Chinkin, C. 2007. Monism and Dualism: The Impact of Private Authority on the Dichotomy Between National and International Law, in *New Perspectives on the Divide between National and International Law*, edited by J. Nijman and A. Nollkaemper. Oxford: Oxford University Press, 134–163.

Claire Cutler, A. 2001. Critical Reflections on the Westphalian Assumptions of International Law and Organization: A Crisis of Legitimacy, *Review of International Studies*, 27, 133–150.

Clapham, A. 2006. *Human Rights Obligations of Non-State Actors*. Oxford: Oxford University Press.
Clapham, A. 2009. *Non-State Actors*, edited by V. Chetail. Oxford: Oxford University Press, 200–212.
Commission of Global Governance. 1995. *Report of the Commission of Global Governance, Our Global Neighborhood*. New York: Oxford University Press.
d'Aspremont, J. 2008. Softness in International Law: A Self-Serving Quest for New Legal Materials, *EJIL*, 19(5), 1,075–1,093.
Dewey, J. 1926. The Historic Background of Corporate Legal Personality. *Yale Law Journal*, XXXV(6), 655–673.
Dicey, A.V. 1885. *Introduction to the Study of the Law of the Constitution*. London: Macmillan.
Dixon, M. 2005. *Textbook on International Law*. 5th Edition. Oxford: Oxford University Press.
Dworkin, R. 1985. *A Matter of Principle*. Cambridge: Harvard University Press.
Figgis, J.N. 1913. *Churches in the Modern State*. London et al.: Longmans, Green and Co.
Friedmann, W. 1967. *Legal Theory*. 5th Edition. London: Stevens & Sons.
Fuller, L.L. 1969. *The Morality of Law*. Revised Edition. New Haven: Yale University Press.
Georgiev, D. 1993. Politics or Rule of Law: Deconstruction and Legitimacy in International Law. *EJIL*, 4, 1–14.
Gierke, O. 1887. *Die Genossenschaftstheorie und die deutsche Rechtsprechung*. Berlin: Wiedmannsche Verlagsbuchhandlung.
Gierke, O. 1895. *Deutsches Privatrecht,* Erster Band (Allgemeiner Teil und Personenrecht). Leipzig: Duncker & Humblot.
Gierke, O. 1900. *Political Theories of the Middle Age*. Translated with an Introduction by F.M. Maitland. Cambridge: Cambridge University Press.
Gierke, O. 1902. *Das Wesen der menschlichen Verbände*. Berlin: Universität-Buchdruckerei von Gustav Schade.
Habermas, J. 2006. *The Divided West*. Cambridge: Polity Press.
Heilborn, P. 1925. Subjekte des Völkerrechts, in *Wörterbuch des Völkerrechts und der Diplomatie*, Volume 2, edited by K. Strupp. Berlin and Leipzig: De Gruyter.
Heilborn, P. 1926. Les Sources du Droit International. *RCADI*, 11(1), 1–62.
Higgins, R. 1994. *Problems and Process: International Law and How We Use It*. Oxford: Clarendon Press.
Horwitz, M.J. 1992. *The Transformation of American Law, 1870-1960: The Crisis of Legal Orthodoxy*. New York: Oxford University Press.
Jellinek, G. 1905. *Allgemeine Staatslehre*. Berlin: O. Häring.
Jennings R.Y. and Watts, A. (eds) 1992. *Oppenheim's International Law*. 9th Edition. New York: Oxford University Press.
Kaufmann, E. 1935. Règles Générales du Droit de la Paix. *RCADI*, 54(4), 309–620.

Kelsen, H. 1920. *Das Problem der Souveränität und die Theorie des Völkerrechts*. Tübingen: Mohr.

Kelsen, H. 1926. Les Rapports de Système entre le Droit Interne et le Droit International Public. *RCADI*, 14(4), 227–331.

Kelsen, H. 1932. Théorie Générale du Droit International Public, Problèmes Choisis. *RCADI*, 42(4), 116–351.

Kelsen, H. 1952. *Principles of International Law*. New York: Rinehart and Company.

Koh, H.H. 1996. Transnational Legal Process. *Neb. L. Rev.*, 75, 181–207.

Koskenniemi, M. 1989. *From Apology to Utopia: The Structure of International Legal Argument*. Cambridge: Cambridge University Press.

Koskenniemi, M. 1990. Politics of International Law, *EJIL*, 1, 4–32.

Koskenniemi, M. 2002. *The Gentle Civilizer of Nations: The Rise and Fall of International Law 1870–1960*. Cambridge: Cambridge University Press.

Kratochwil, F. 2009. Has the 'Rule of Law' become a 'Rule of Lawyers'? An Inquiry into the Use and Abuse of an Ancient Topos in Contemporary Debates, in *Relocating the Rule of Law*, edited by G. Palombella and N. Walker. Oxford: Hart Publishing, 171–196.

Lauterpacht, H. 1975. The Grotian Tradition of International Law, in *International Law: Being the Collected Papers of Hersch Lauterpacht*, Volume 2, edited by E. Lauterpacht. Cambridge: Cambridge University Press, 307–360.

Le Fur, L. 1927. La Théorie du Droit Naturel Depuis le XVIIe Siècle et la Doctrine Moderne. *RCADI*, 18(3), 259–442.

Lindblom, A.K. 2006. *Non-Governmental Organizations in International Law*. Cambridge: Cambridge University Press.

Maitland, F.W. 1905, 2003. Moral Personality and Legal Personality, in *Maitland: State, Trust and Corporation, Cambridge Texts in the History of Political Thought*, edited by D. Runciman and M. Ryan. Cambridge: Cambridge University Press, 62–74.

Malanczuk, P. 1997. *Akehurst's Modern Introduction to International Law*. 7th Edition. London: Routledge.

McDougal, M. 1953. International Law, Power, and Policy: A Contemporary Conception. *RCADI*, 82(1), 133–259.

Nijman, J.E. 2004. *The Concept of International Legal Personality: An Inquiry into the History and Theory of International Law*. The Hague: Asser Press.

Nijman, J.E. 2007. Paul Ricoeur and International Law: Beyond 'The End of the Subject' – Towards a Reconceptualization of International Legal Personality. *LJIL*, 20, 25–64.

Oppenheim, L. 1920. *International Law: A Treatise*. 3rd Edition. Edited by R.F. Roxburgh. London: Longmans, Green & Co.

Palombella, G. 2009. The Rule of Law Beyond the State: Failures, Promises, and Theory. *International Journal of Constitutional Law*, 7(3), 442–467.

Peters, A. 2007. The Globalization of State Constitutions, in *New Perspectives on the Divide between National and International Law*, edited by J. Nijman and A. Nollkaemper. Oxford: Oxford University Press, 251–308.

Politis, N. 1923. La condition juridique des associations internationales. Rapport préliminaire et avant-projet de convention internationale. Quatorzième Commission de l'Institut de Droit International, Session de Bruxelles. *JDI* (Clunet), 50, 465–487.

Politis, N. 1928. *The New Aspects of International Law*. Washington: Carnegie endowment for international peace.

Ruggie, J.G. 2004. Reconstructing the Global Public Domain – Issues, Actors, and Practices, *EJIR*, 10(4), 499–531.

Runciman, D. 1997. *Pluralism and the Personality of the State*. Cambridge: Cambridge University Press.

Sands, P. 2005. *Lawless World: America and the Making and Breaking of Global Rules*. New York: Viking Press.

Sands, P. 2008. *Torture Team: Deception, Cruelty and the Compromise of Law*. London: Allen Lane.

Scelle, G. 1932a. La doctrine de L. Duguit et les fondements du droit des gens. *Archives de philosophies du droit et de sociologie juridique*, 83–119.

Scelle, G. 1932b. *Précis de Droit des Gens, Principes et Systématique*. Volume I. Paris: Recueil Sirey.

Scelle, G. 1936. Théorie et Pratique de la Fonction Exécutive en Droit International, *RCADI*, 55(1), 87–202.

Séfériadès, S. 1930. Principes Généraux du Droit International de la Paix. *RCADI*, 34(4), 177–492.

Shaw, M.N. 2003. *International Law*. 5th Edition. Cambridge: Cambridge University Press.

Shelton, D.L. 2009. Soft Law, in *Handbook of International Law*, edited by David Armstrong. New York: Routledge, 68–80.

Slaughter, A.-M. 1993. International Law and International Relations Theory: A Dual Agenda. *AJIL*, 87(2), 367–397.

Slaughter, A.-M., Tulumello, A.S. and Wood, S. 1998. International Law and International Relations Theory: A New Generation of Interdisciplinary Scholarship. *AJIL*, 92(3), 367–397.

Spain, A. 2009. Who's Going to Copenhagen?: The Rise of Civil Society in International Treaty-Making. *ASIL Insight*, 13(25).

Tamanaha, B.Z. 2004. *On the Rule of Law: History, Politics, Theory*. Cambridge: Cambridge University Press.

Teubner, G. 1988. Enterprise Corporatism: New Industrial Policy and the 'Essence' of the Legal Person, *American Journal of Comparative Law*, 36, 130–155.

Triepel, H. 1923. Les Rapports entre le Droit Interne et le Droit International, *RCADI*, 1(1), 77–121.

Waldron, J. 2009. Are Sovereigns Entitled to the Benefit of the International Rule of Law?, *IILJ Working Paper*, 3, 1–28.

Weeramantry, C.G. 2004. *Universalising International Law*. Leiden: Martinus Nijhoff Publishers.

Weiss, T.G. 2000. Governance, Good Governance and Global Governance: Conceptual and Actual Challenges. *Third World Quarterly*, 21(5), 795–814.

Wendt, A. 1999. *Social Theory of International Politics*. Cambridge: Cambridge University Press.

Wendt, A. 2004. The State as Person in International Theory. *Review of International Studies*, 30, 289–316.

Chapter 6
Observations on the Desirability of an Enhanced International Legal Status of the Non-State Actor

Noemi Gal-Or

I. Introduction

This chapter arises out of two main observations regarding the rights and obligations of non-state actors (NSAs) under international law. First, there is considerable disagreement as to what the position of the NSA is, (Bianchi 2009, Reinisch 2009) and should be,[1] under international law; and second – flowing from that and from the fragmented state of international law – that there is an urgent doctrinal (Carty 2006)[2] need for an integrated and comprehensive assessment of the status of the NSA in international law.[3] Because it is indisputable that the NSA has already been recognized as enjoying a set of rights and being bound by certain obligations in international law, this paper will investigate the desirability of charting international legal development towards further *enhancement* of the legal status already secured by the NSA. Undeniably, legal status in international law hinges on the elusive concept of international legal personality (ILP), a matter 'negated' (Nijman 2004) for long yet enjoying gradual renewal.

This is a normative, and of course, political, question. The chapter, however, will not explore the value of an NSA's enhanced legal status; rather, it brings forward a proposal outlining *how to examine* the essence of an NSA's legal status and its 'weight' in international law. Such knowledge is invaluable for the maintenance of consistency and coherence in a fast transforming and developing international law (Frank 1995, Hart 1994). Also, it is important to note that our focus is not on whether or not a specific NSA should or should not be recognized as a subject of international law. Rather, the purpose of this chapter is to propose how to explore three fundamental questions from a doctrinal perspective because, as eloquently

1 'The role that non-state actors play and should play in implementing human rights is indeed still largely under-theorized, while nevertheless being at the forefront of current legal, political, and ethical debates' (De Brabandere 2009: 191).

2 Also see Carty (2006) for the meaning of doctrine in international law.

3 Bianchi (2009) is stating this in full and plain language.

observed, '[in] a world where there is no want of information ... somewhat paradoxically, doctrine may still mediate, no longer between primary sources and their potential users but, rather, between secondary sources and interested readers,' (Bianchi 2009: xii) and all the more so, where the subject matter is still suffering from lack of systematic scrutiny (Bianchi 2009, de Brabandere 2009, Noortmann 2001).

The first question is whether the NSA should be recognized as a *general category* of an actor. Specifically, should the NSA be considered as consisting of a 'garden variety' of various types of actors[4] akin to the state[5], and to which a fundamental unitary set of rights and obligations in international law applies.[6] Consequently, the second question is whether the NSA – as a general category or as several single types of NSAs – should be considered a subject of international law *equal* to the state and consequently recognized as bound by the identical and full set of rights and obligations pertaining to the state. Thirdly, should the rights and obligations of the state be adjusted to accommodate the legal status needs (and gains) of the NSA? In other words, would it be desirable to break out from the current doctrinal paradigm of international law?

In reference to the *dictum of* the International Court of Justice (ICJ) that '[t]he subjects of law in *any* legal system are not necessarily identical in their nature or in the extent of their rights, and their nature depends upon the *needs* of the community' (*Reparation* 1949, emphases added), another question arises: Would the NSA's interests and needs – at both domestic and international realms – be

4 Inter-governmental organization (IGO), non-governmental organization (NGO), transnational corporation (TNC), and individuals, and so forth.

5 Of which there are several types, for example national, bi-national, unitary, federal, con-federal, and so forth.

6 The International Law Commission has addressed this question of scope regarding one type of NSA in its First Report on Responsibility of International Organizations:

> 20. While it may be held that a large number of international organizations have a legal personality in international law, the great variety of existing international organizations would make it difficult to state general rules applying to all types of organizations. It would be as if the Commission considered questions of international responsibility concerning States and individuals at the same time. It is clearly preferable only to address questions relating to a relatively homogeneous category of international organizations. If the present study is intended to be a sequel to the draft articles on the responsibility of States for internationally wrongful acts, it is appropriate to limit the scope of this study to questions relating to organizations that exercise certain functions, that are similar, and possibly identical, to those exercised by States. These functions, whether legislative, executive or judicial, may be called governmental. (Gaja, 2003: 11–12)

more appropriately satisfied by applying municipal, rather than international, legal standards? If so, then equality before international law, between international actors, would not require their equality under international law.

Following a discussion on the meaning of 'legal status' and international law, the methodology regarding how to answer the above questions will be addressed from two angles. First, stock will be taken of the current state of the art regarding the status of the NSA in international law and the conditions requisite for possession of ILP including an observation concerning as well as a discussion on the viability of a doctrinal general category of NSA. An analytical model to serve as a methodological tool for further research will be presented. This examination will be followed by the question of whether further changes to the legal status of the NSA are likely to enhance the development of international law. Accordingly, it is suggested to conduct this inquiry by exploring whether international law passes the test of the NSA challenge to the extant doctrine.

II. Legal Status and International Law

The legal discourse on the status of the NSA in international law inevitably touches upon a 'sensitive nerve' of international law. It represents a crucial, perhaps the paramount factor in the fatal crisis of the doctrine (Carty 2006) where it is no longer being assumed 'that standards are universal and everywhere the same not only in space but in time' (Carty 2006: 240).[7] From an epistemological perspective, the difficulties originate in the challenge posed by the NSA – an internationally conscious actor – to the concept of ILP, and its claim to an enhanced international legal status. Can the *ratione materiae* and *ratione personae* parameters of international law be reconciled so as to comfortably incorporate the NSA as a subject of international law? And if so, what rationale would there be for the continuing (co)existence of two systems of law – one national, the other international?

From a *ratione materiae* (nature of the system of law and order) vintage point, would international law not become redundant were the supremacy of the state in international law to be abolished? Arguably, governance considerations point at the European Union's regional international and con-federal law as a model for national and international legal systems' co-habitation, one which has acknowledged NSAs' demands for legal recognition. Whether that experiment proves attractive on a global international scale remains uncertain. Alternatively, the sustainability of two (municipal and international), perhaps three (municipal,

7 Bianchi (2009) appears to be echoing this sentiment when expecting to discover a 'treasure chest' of essays on the NSA and international law, but emerges disappointed at the difficulties he and colleagues were facing, and the wanting results. This serves as yet another confirmation of the state of the doctrine as far as the NSA is concerned.

international and transnational), legal systems has been entertained by advocates of transnational law.[8]

From a *ratione personae* (nature of the actor in the system) perspective, and considering state – NSA relations, a re-evaluation of the legal significance of space is warranted. Is the role played by physical territory in distinguishing between actors and determining the respective laws governing them still viable? Is a reconfiguration of time, of the notion of the state as timeless, and of the NSA's (natural and legal) identity as ephemeral, bound by birth and origin (nationality) and demise and deadlines, still valid? For instance, the discourse contemplating a new identity of the 'global citizen' is certainly an indicator of possible change regarding both traditional *ratione materiae* and *ratione personae* conceptions in international law. Indeed, at this backdrop, ILP emerges as a pivotal legal concept in a transforming international law.

Not surprisingly, the idea of ILP in the sense that '[a] subject of the law is an entity capable of possessing international rights and duties and having the capacity to maintain its rights by bringing international claims' (Brownlie 2003: 57) has survived in spite of recent challenges in the legal discourse (Kerbrat 2005, Nijman 2004). The Westphalian rationale behind ILP appears to remain prevalent, encapsulating the essential and *original* purpose of the inter-state law. This is so even where ILP vaguely transpires in-between the lines as, for instance, in Alan Boyle's and Christine Chinkin's recent work on international law-making. There, the term 'participants' is used to capture the nature of the internationally active NSA:[9]

> What is more problematic is to determine empirically the precise role of such bodies [NSAs] in law-making: do they act as little more than a catalyst to traditional forms of state law-making or can they be accurately described as *free-standing participants* in international law-making? ... Do they represent a paradigm shift away from a state-centric model of international law-making? Further questions follow relating to the desirability, legitimacy and accountability of such bodies: does their participation in law-making processes constitute a *desirable democratisation* of international legal processes, or a new form of *legal imperialism*? (Boyle and Chinkin 2007: 44–45 emphases added)

8 For a discussion on transnationalism, see Math Noortmann, Chapter 7. Political scientists have suggested to consider the age of globalization and the multiplicity of actors operating on a global scene as a modernized version mirroring the medieval pluralist political system; and legal scholars have revived and updated the lex mercatoria by introducing the neologism of transnational law.

9 See also Bianchi (2009) for a discussion on the likelihood that interdisciplinarity has lead to confusion between actor and subject and for a literature review when discussing the international legal theoretical approaches to the NSA.

Compare Hart's (1994) analysis of the sovereign and the subject (in any law) in elucidating the essence of ILP. Taking a culture neutral prism (as much as possible), he sets out to show that the theory of sovereignty represents the 'foundation of *all* legal systems' (Hart 1994: 50, emphasis added). Hart's approach is compelling for it provides a measuring yard to distinguish among different legal systems according to their dogma as well as their independence. The essence of the law is summarized as following:

> The doctrine [of sovereignty] asserts that in every human society, where there is law, there is ultimately to be found latent beneath the variety of political forms, *in a democracy as much as in the absolute monarchy*, this simple relationship between subjects rendering habitual obedience and a sovereign who renders habitual obedience to no one. This *vertical structure* composed of sovereign and subjects is, according to the theory, as essential a part of a society which possess law, as a backbone is of a man. Where it is present, we may speak of the society, together with its sovereign, as a single independent state, and we may speak of *its* law; where it is not present, we can apply none of these expressions, for the relation of sovereign and subject forms, according to this theory, part of their very meaning. (Hart 1994: 50, emphases added)

Accordingly, also in international law, one would expect to identify a sovereign: If the law of the state requires the fusion of society and sovereign, who then, is the sovereign with whom the society of states unites? Is it the *idea* of state sovereignty? Or, is there a global tangible (for example political authority) sovereign? Is there a different law for the blending of states versus the merging of global human society with (whichever) sovereign?

Leaving these grand queries to another forum, this chapter conforms to the positivist approach as a point of departure and proceeds from the traditional premise that the essential character of an international system of law is grounded in its legal personalities. Consequently, the concept of ILP will serve to assess *how* to examine, from a doctrinal perspective, the desirability for international law of developing and recognizing an enhanced international status of the NSA. We therefore now turn to take stock of the current state of the art regarding the legal status of the NSA in international law.

III. The Status of the NSA in International Law: The Current State of the Art

The definition of the NSA is in its name: a grouping of actors comprising of all actors other than the state. As such, the definition includes both groups and individuals. Boyle's and Chinkin's list provides a good sense of NSA heterogeneity:

> Non-state actors today encompass *inter alia* sub-state entities and denied statehood, national and international issued-based NGOs, individuals, 'kitchen-tablers', the corporate and business sector, shareholders, churches and religious groupings, trade unions and employees, academics, think tanks, consumer groups, para-military forces, professional associations, including those of judges, lawyers, parliamentarians and law enforcement agencies, expert communities, sport associations and criminal terrorist associations. (Boyle and Chinkin 2007: 44)

Simply put, the NSA is an actor which does not possess the authority and the power of the state and its organs,[10] but who considers itself, and is increasingly being considered, as potentially possessing some commensurate qualities.[11] All the same, the NSA remains legally dependent on the state.

NSA's State Dependency

As the above tally specifies, the list is open. Today's NSA category may differ from tomorrow's; it may shrink or expand depending on the demise or birth of actors. We may speak of an NSA as possessing a special type of allegiance to the state, akin to (but not formally constituted as) nationality and citizenship. Certainly, the NSA may be considered to possess formal citizenship as individual persons do even though business firms and NGOs cannot come into existence without some form of formal registration, hence without state authorization from within a state's jurisdiction.[12] Moreover any 'collective' group or community, for example an armed

10 Most importantly, '[n]on-state actors cannot sign an international treaty.' *Hamdan v. Ramsfeld* (2005). See also Brownlie 2003: 57).

11 For example, the non-governmental organization according to the Council of Europe European Convention on the Recognition of the Legal Personality of International Non-Governmental Organizations 'laying down the conditions for recognition of the legal personality of these organizations in order to facilitate their activities at European level' (NGO Convention: Preamble), but specifying that the NGO must 'have been established by an instrument governed by the internal law of a Party' (Article 1.b) and subjected to 'restrictions, limitations or special procedures governing the exercise of the rights arising out of the legal capacity and provided for by the legislation of the Party where recognition takes place' (Article 2.2).

12 For example, '... international law has had to recognize the corporate entity as an institution created by States in a domain essentially within their domestic jurisdiction. This in turn requires that, whenever legal issues arise concerning the rights of States with regard to the treatment of companies and shareholders, as to which rights international law has not established its own rules, it has to refer to the relevant rules of municipal law. ... In allocating corporate entities to States for purposes of diplomatic protection, international law is based, but only to a limited extent, on an analogy with the rules governing the nationality of individuals. The traditional rule attributes the right of diplomatic protection of a corporate entity to the State under the laws of which it is incorporated and in whose

opposition group, or an environmental advocacy organization, effectively depends on the sum of its individual members. While similar to the state, its collective identity is a reflection of its membership,[13] its operation and performance depend on legal incorporation.[14] All of these collectivities possess some form of nationality without which they would be deprived of participation in the public domain, whether domestic or transnational/global. An NSA may also possess, or involve the relevance of, one or more (double, triple) state nationalities or citizenships. It may operate within one state's jurisdictional boundaries only, or transcend national borders and conduct affairs concurrently in more than one jurisdiction. Indeed, this *relationship* to the state explains why the NSA is being addressed by both municipal and international law (private and public). As Ian Brownlie puts it:

> The legal consequences of belonging to a political community with a territorial base have not changed a great deal since the feudal era, *in spite of changes in the theory used to describe or explain the relation*. Ties of allegiance, citizenship, and nationality have provided the basis for the legal community of the state, whether the state was regarded primarily as an organic unity expressed in terms of 'personal' sovereignty or as a territorial domain. (Brownlie 2003: 497, emphasis added)

Collective NSAs come with various structures and follow different processes. Their arrangements may extend from loose to tight, informal and formal and so on, and there is as yet neither single nor fixed 'taxonomic address' for this collectivity. In a Hartian sense, to loosen the constraints of nationality or citizenship, and be capable of participating independently in any system of international law, the NSA would have to demonstrate some measure of sovereignty. As it stands, the state is the sole actor capable of satisfying the requirement of sovereignty[15] hence also the ILP benchmark. For want of sovereignty, the NSA is relegated to a lower legal status of as *not possessing in full* the same rights and duties as the state, or completely devoid of any such status in international law. To be sure, indeterminacy regarding the NSA is the order of the day. NSA's partial ILP is reflected in a haphazard and

territory it has its registered office. These two criteria have been confirmed by long practice and by numerous international instruments' (*Barcelona Traction*: 32, 34, 42).

13 The state requires citizens, the collectivity whatever type of members.

14 For instance, even a terrorist organization, which evidently would not be registered as such, may operate, among others, through the agency of a charitable non-profit organization and require access to banking services through accounts registered to individuals who are nationals of a state.

15 So long as sovereignty remains an exclusive quality of the state, the argument will remain tautological.

gradational governance approach (or distinct approaches) devoid of any agreed test to ascertain possession of necessary and sufficient criteria.[16]

Illustrating the above, is the placement of NSAs in descending order of recognition as possessing ILP. Next and located most closely to the 'full' extreme of the ILP spectrum is the protectorate – an entity wanting of separate statehood, followed by s*ui generis* territorial entities, that is to say, mandated, non-state trust territories, condominia and internationally administrated territories, special (historical) cases, IGOs, associations of states, insurgents and belligerents, national liberation movements and states in *status nascendi*, inter-governmental international public companies, transnational corporations, NGOs, and individuals (Shaw 2008, Brownlie 2003). Notably, while the 'scaled' order of NSAs may indicate a ranging from less full to lesser to least ILP, it does not reveal any certain *quality* of legal personality. Furthermore, on this descending scale, the weaker the likelihood of detecting some resemblance of sovereignty in an NSA, the less likely it is for conditions for possession of ILP to be identified.

Statehood – the quality of being of a state – requires not only external[17] but also an internal assessment. Differently put, the state has no existence without some notion of representation and agency.[18] The concept of internal sovereignty links the state not only to other states but to the individual person, whether citizen or not (and to the community governed by the state), and in most recent legal history, increasingly also to the individual as a human being. Consequently, if the state's ILP is to serve as the benchmark for ILP in general, then in order to possess such personality, the NSA must also possess an *endogenous* quality.

At the outset of the chapter, we raised the question of NSA taxonomy: a single analytical category or an assemblage of distinct actors? In order to conceptualize of the NSA as a single general category, a uniform endogenous criterion applicable to all cases of NSA must be ascertained. Community, agency, and participation are some of the concepts which have been circulating in the quest to decipher the internal 'DNA' of the NSA (Graz and Noelke 2007, Claire Cutler 2003). Suppose, for the sake of the argument, that the natural legal person might be perceived as a member of the community of humankind (the 'global citizen'), and that this commonality evidences the NSA's DNA. Even then, it must be admitted, this relationship, falls short of satisfying the sovereignty requirement for it runs counter to the idea of hierarchy and representation inherent to the state. A similar

16 A similar observation is made by Bianchi who finds that 'it is not the same thing' to speak of law arising from a community of states and law arising from a community of participants who are oblivious to state jurisdictional spheres; in fact, it 'hides a fundamental difference in thinking of the international legal system' (Bianchi 2009: xv).

17 Independence of participation and comparative legal status as previously discussed represent aspects of external sovereignty.

18 Presumed in both natural and positivist, as well as more recent, legal theories. Legitimacy, which is a matter relevant to this discussion, is however beyond the scope of this chapter.

observation applies to the relationship, as between NSAs, for instance to the terrorist organization and Amnesty International, and so on.

The combination of endogenous and exogenous qualities of sovereignty endows the state with its capacities and competences in international law – law-making, law enforcement, and adjudication (albeit to a much lesser degree than in municipal law). It is the greater understanding of these qualities and the associated theories, and questioning their *exclusive* attribution to the state, which have been nourishing the growing discourse on, and recognition of, some analogous international legal capacities and competences of the NSA. The statement that '[t]he international legal system has moved far beyond the categorization of the sources of international law in the Statute of the ICJ', (Boyle and Chinkin 2007: 35) is an example and illustration of the acknowledgment of the significant role played by the NSA as an (indirect) source of international law. Further conceptual progress, however, requires engagement in a systematic, empirical, comprehensive, and comparative assessment of the NSA's legal status. Next here comes a short elaboration on rights and duties – warranted as an introduction to the taxonomy of ILP, which follows thereafter.

Rights, Duties, and Reciprocity

Brownlie's definition of subject of the law reads: 'The principal formal contexts in which the question of personality has arisen have been: capacity to make claims in respect of breaches of international law, capacity to make treaties and agreements valid on the international plane, and *the enjoyment of privileges and immunities from national jurisdictions*' (Brownlie 2003: 57, emphasis added). Implicit in this definition is the quality of immediacy or directness of the capacity of possessing international rights and duties.[19] Thus, from a substantive point of view, an entity is recognized as a legal subject when featuring, within a single system of law, as an addressee of one or more rights (for example a state's right to self-defence against an aggressor state) *and* carrying with correlate legal duties (for example a state's duty to refrain from aggression against another state).[20] Procedurally, the addressee of the right and bearer of the duty possesses the capacity of directly defending one's

19 Although state responsibility is also triggered indirectly. See, Draft Articles of Responsibility.

20 The discussion in this section is informed by the theories of law influenced by Hohfeld's analysis (Eleftheriadis 2008). 'Hohfeld's tables of legal relations explain the various ways in which we are able in law to act (liberty) or to claim that others act in a certain way towards us (claim) or shape legal relations in certain ways (power) or to stand protected in our present legal relations (immunity). Hohfeld's instances of law explain the work of legal doctrine in various domains ...' (Eleftheriadis 2008: 6–7). Bentham saw legal right as conditioning that its holder was the beneficiary of an obligation (Eleftheriadis 2008: 6–7). In Hart's view, there is a 'bilateral liberty of the right holder. In the central case of a claim-right the idea is that of the 'one individual being given by the law exclusive control, more or less extensive, over another person's duty so that in the area of conduct covered

own right and being held responsible via institutional administrative instances that control the implementation of international norms.[21]

The legal acknowledgement of rights is effected through law-making (in international law regarding both conventional and customary law) via legislation and adjudication. Accountability and compliance[22] are for a duty what interest and claims are for a right and are effected through law enforcement and adjudication. Since the legal system is essentially a social system which governs *relations* between and among social actors, rights and duties are meaningful only as *reciprocal between* these actors.[23] Rights are divided into negative and positive rights (Gal-Or 2009).[24] International law recognizes more negative than positive rights.[25] Negative rights (largely civil rights which form part of human rights) comprise of those interests or claims requiring protection against intrusion with the right holder by another right holder. Interests and claims requiring protection in support of maintaining a right through positive action are known as positive rights (largely other than civil rights and also encompassed within the umbrella of human rights). As both a social and legal construct, a right is meaningless without the *reciprocal* and correlate duty, namely the obligation of the 'intruder' to refrain from intervening with the negative right of a right holder, and the duty of the 'protector' to actively foster the positive right of the right holder.

Both state and NSA are each holders of rights, which govern the three prong relationship of NSA-to-NSA, state-to-state, and state-to-NSA. Each state and NSA is legally and materially capable of enjoying rights in this threefold relationship. Moreover, none of these three relationships is exclusively governed by one set of rules. In other words, state-to-state relations are governed by their municipal law and international law, NSA-to-NSA relations by both municipal, private, and to some extent also public, international law, and state-NSA relations largely by municipal law, but in criminal, some economic, and other matters, also by international law. In comparison with this wide scope and large number of addressees of rights (NSAs and predominantly the individual), the range of bearers of duties is significantly

---

by that duty the individual who has the right is a small-scale sovereign to whom the duty is owed' (Eleftheriadis 2008: 10).

21 'The neutral theories effectively say that the action-guiding features of legal rights are only the results of a procedure' by officials and institutions (Eleftheriadis 2008: 80).

22 The discussion of the relationship between responsibility and duty is being left out for lack of space and because it is less relevant to the construction of the empirical model.

23 Rawls explains the legitimacy of political power as conditioned by the 'duty of civility' which, as Eleftheriadis explains, 'derives from public justification that respects reciprocity between equals and requires that we give great prominence to the need for consensus' (Eleftheriadis 2008: 65). Arguably, the 'idea of equal respect and reciprocity among citizens' (Eleftheriadis 2008: 165) is transferrable to the international level where it applies as between international actors – in the prevalent doctrine – as between states.

24 See Eleftheriadis (2008) for a discussion of moral versus legal rights.

25 In municipal law, the type of political regime, and often of political ideology, determine the extent of preponderance of negative versus positive rights.

narrower.[26] Notably, the capability to carry with the duties corresponding to *positive* rights has largely been the preserve of the state. IGOs and TNCs have been developing some similar international legal responsibilities accompanied by the ability to create material circumstances necessary to back up the duty. When considering duties attached to *negative* rights, the debate surrounding, for instance, the obligations of distinct NSAs such as private military enterprises and terrorist groups and networks in the context of armed conflict, appear to be significantly lesser developed.[27] The upshot of these incongruent developments has been an emphasis on recognition of rights applicable to the NSA (for example in law-making).[28] By comparison, the responsibility of the NSA in international law for carrying with duties, and the capability necessary to protect rights, or refrain from infringing on them, are of rather limited scope.[29]

In the next section, we describe the preliminary draft of a model designed to ascertain the capacities of the NSA as an international legal person. It serves as an empirical tool to take stock of the NSA. It addresses the chapter's first question concerning the conceptualization of a general category of NSA and the uniformity of ILP in its application to both NSA and state.

26 The discussion of the range of the bearers of duties is trailing far behind the impressive advancements in the development of rights, and especially human rights. Reinisch observes that while a sense is prevailing among lawyers that guarantees to ensure protection of human rights no longer form the ultimate and only preserve of state goodwill or responsibility, '... these developments have not affected the basic conceptual premise that human rights are limitations of state power, that they apply in the public sphere, and that they protect the (weak) individual against the (strong) state [although] [t]hey seem to have contributed to a new awareness of the need to protect human rights beyond the classic paradigm of the powerful state against the weak individual, to include protection against increasingly powerful non-state actors' (Reinisch 2009: 38).

27 Consider, for instance, the discussions surrounding Common Article 3 of the Geneva Conventions and the principle of the distinction between combatant and civilian (Blum 2009, Corn and Jensen 2009, Vöneky 2007, Niels 2009).

28 Indeed, law-making is the area most conspicuously representing the NSA's contention for more substantive endogenous and exogenous sovereignty. This process figures as cardinal in advancing and encouraging the NSA's endeavour to secure fuller ILP.

29 A discussion of this legal phenomenon, the revival of natural law, and the development of transnational law is beyond the scope of this chapter. Suffice it here to draw attention to the theoretical confusion regarding the desirability of an enhanced international legal status for the NSA, which is flowing not only from the gap between legal capacity and material capability to uphold the law, but also from the difficulty of reconciling this gap with the justice requirement of reciprocity. It arises in both contexts of reciprocity discussed above, namely as between actors (*ratione personae*) and as between right and duty (*ratione materiae*). It is precisely because of their 'participation' that NSAs have been shedding light on the fading of this distinction between person and matter, and the broadening frame for matters, which are *erga omnes*.

IV. Categorizing the NSA, Modelling a Taxonomy

Based on the previous discussion concerning legal status and ILP, the first model represents a framework for analysis constructed along three main properties of the ILP – possessing,[30] maintenance, and creation (without order of preference).[31] To be sure, these properties represent categories, each of which contains a detailed tally of personality qualities normally associated with the conditions of sovereignty and exercise of jurisdiction by the state.[32] For instance, law creation (or law-making) consists of activities ranging from the incipient idea concerning a particular legal need, through lobbying, informing and creating public awareness, engaging in conduct congruent with the idea, or challenging an already established law, drafting 'soft' and 'hard' law, running consultations, concluding and signing treaties (conventional law), committing to the reciprocal acknowledgment of practice (custom), and more. Law maintenance consists of two main sub-categories – law adjudication and law enforcement. The selection of adjudicatory methods spans from formal to less and lesser formal modes of dispute settlement. Similarly, law enforcement ranges from the use of force, for example as per Articles 42 and 43 of the UN Charter, through the application of various sanctions and up to public shaming.

Considering the state's ILP as generic, the model provides a uniform and conclusive benchmark against which to canvass the selection of NSAs (and future NSAs). A detailed outline of the characteristics of each capacity will be developed, representing the spectrum of the relevant factors. The model requires a systematic assessment of NSAs' sets of rights and obligations corresponding to the three main ILP capacities of possession, maintenance, and creation of law. In this way, it accomplishes three tasks. For one, the systematic assessment will draw the commonalities and differences in rights and obligations of various NSAs. The knowledge gained will advance us a step further towards conceptualizing the categories of the NSA and determining whether the NSAs represent a consist class of cases justifying membership in one legal theoretical general category. Second, it will measure and position the NSAs along an ILP[33] spectrum (of fullness to no

30 The capacity to possess is a theoretical concept too complex to be elaborated on here. At this stage of legal development, the capabilities to create and maintain law suffice for the purpose of ascertaining the degree of development of the ILP of any given NSA.

31 As already mentioned, these qualities are borrowed from Brownlie's (2003) definition.

32 Each of the three capabilities encompasses a correlate set of rights and duties. Taken together, they form a stand-alone legal system of the state as a 'system of normative regulation' (Cotterrell 1989: 37) representing a coercive order with authoritative and monopolistic power to settle disputes for a political community.

33 Bianchi's anthology is a step in this direction. It includes an empirical part organizing various NSAs according to the role they play in law-making, law-adjudication, and law-enforcement as well as a part addressing NSA accountability. I contend that a more rigorous, coordinated, and consistent effort in this direction needs to be undertaken.

ILP) thus ranking NSAs according to the quality of their ILP. The ensuing account of the spectrum of international legal persons will offer a convenient reference point for the purpose of maintaining consistency and coherence in international law. Third, this juxtaposition – of NSA against the state in matters personality – will assist in ascertaining whether a fundamental normative transformation is indeed underway and necessitating respective paradigmatic legal shifts for. After all,

> [t]o designate as 'law' in modern Western societies normative systems other than those of state law is to raise the hypothesis that the problem with which lawyers concern themselves – about the justifications of legal decision-making, the interpretation, development, generalisation and systematisation of rules, the relationship between rule and secretion and between justice and certainty in law – may be problems that arise in some form in many normative systems, not only in lawyer's law. (Cotterrell 1992: 31)

An application of the model to different NSAs will show that NSAs occupy various placements along the continuums of possession, maintenance, and creation of law reflecting differences in corresponding rights and duties. Most obviously, individual persons and organizations/groups differ in their ILP capacities in many ways, depending also on context and circumstances. For instance, it is evident that the individual natural person does not possess the capacity to create law unless it is part of a group. Law-making is a collective act generated by a collective effort whether deliberate or not.[34] The group might be the state, and the individual engaging law creation employed by, or representing, the state, for example the diplomat, negotiator, or an official in any other capacity delegated by the state; the group might be consulting government (for example think tank), lobbying government (for example business and legal profession), protesting against government (union, any civil society grouping); or, it might be operating separately and apart from government (for example civil society 'norm entrepreneurs', intellectuals), and so on. After all, law pertains to society (an individual alone on an isolated island is not in need of law) hence originates in the collectivity (habitually a community) also where the particular legislative act is carried out by an individual who is an absolute dictator. Arriving at answers as to how this difference affects the conceptualization of law creation as a necessary condition of ILP, and what implications flow from the individual – group dichotomy with respect to their ILPs, will be facilitated by the systematic and detailed approach of the proposed model.

---

34 This does not contradict the conceptualization of the individual as the fundamental addressee of the law or that the '... individual answers to the question how international law is made may depend[ing] upon what one understands as comprising international. [And] [i]n turn this determines the sources utilized and processes identified as "law-making"' (Boyle and Chinkin 2007: 10).

Arguably, the group possesses the substantive capacity to create law because its very plurality represents the idea of collectivity. Representation (whether democratic or not) is a necessary condition for law creation and legislative power. In the proposed model, the question will arise as to what *extent* the group NSA may be representing its members in a sense akin to the state's representation of its citizenry. Obviously, this question triggers consideration also of the nature of the NSA's legitimacy.[35] Even if different from the state, the NSA type of representation and legitimacy must not be contradictory to, hence reconcilable with, that of the state. Such a result will have implications with regard to their respective ILPs. An example of the NSA as a legitimate 'representative actor' is that of the IGO, for example the United Nations (UN) when serving as an instrument by which states create international law.[36] Similarly, the NGO, for example the International Law Association (ILA), is capable of developing and promoting soft law which eventually finds its way into hard law, (Boyle and Chinkin 2007) that is to say, becomes representative and likely legitimate. In these examples, the group differs from the individual in its immediate and direct capacity of possessing rights and duties.[37] Two observations follow: first, differences in the quality of the NSA – group versus individual – result either in a gradation concerning the capacity to create law, or in a qualitative and essential variance. Second, this gradation does not apply to the law among states, all of which share identical law creation capacity. It is expected that the systematic comparative inquiry built into the model will elicit thoughts concerning this distinction and implications for ILP.

Similar to the inquiry into law creation, the model also breaks law maintenance into its component parts. Accordingly, law maintenance refers to the ability to effectively exercise both rights and duties in the context of a wide spectrum of possibilities. For instance, law maintenance comprises of the capacity to bring a claim before an international adjudicative forum and secure enforcement of the judgment, on the one hand, and the capacity of defending against a claim filed in an international court or tribunal, and be held accountable and capable of complying with the judgment, on the other hand. Here as well, the NSA is not monolithic in its maintenance capacity. Both individual and group enjoy a degree of standing in international law. For instance, in investment law, the business

35 Legitimacy is a necessary condition for just law creation and is discussed by Cedric Ryngaert 2009 in Chapter 4.

36 For lack of space, the discussion on the legitimacy of the UN Security General as a legislative and representative body is deferred for a later time. Suffice it to note that the question of the legislative powers of the UN have been source to an ongoing controversy, see (Higgins 1963, Schwebel 1966).

37 While it may be argued that the individual is participating indirectly in the creation of international law, for example mediated through election processes, referendums, and other means administered by the state or through the group designed to elicit the individual's approval; or as a member of the state legislature or an NSA's board of directors; the group NSA enjoys more direct law creation capacity than the individual NSA. The model will assist in assessing whether this difference is of any significance, and if so, what.

corporate legal person and the individual natural person both share maintenance capacity, which applies to rights and duties[38] (Gal-Or 2005). By comparison, the non-profit NGO's capacity to maintain has been saliently uneven as rights, rather than the corresponding duties, have often been more effectively maintained. This may be attributed to the fact that the law has been articulated more clearly and extensively concerning the collective public good and rights rather than regarding associated duties. It is also a function of the shortcoming of NGOs, which operate as activist advocates of rights, in developing corollary duty-bound regulations for themselves (Abiew and Kieting 2004).

It is expected that the models' proposed systematic inquiry will elicit whether a pattern of maintenance continuum exists along which to rank the individual, group, and state consequently shedding light on the nature of the NSAs ILP in matters law maintenance.

The capacity to possess rights and duties is the most difficult to reconcile conceptually. Ontologically, a theoretical and philosophic inquiry would be engaged, of a sort which is beyond the scope of this chapter. However, for the purpose of establishing whether the NSA can be classified as a general category, we note again that it suffices to address only two out of the three components of the model (law creation and maintenance) in order to conclude in the negative.

Our model is benefitting from a previously developed, practical and systematic, model designed to ascertain in great detail the above three characteristics of the ILP. It was developed as part of a German project regarding NGOs only (Kissling 2006), and is based on a selection of criteria for ILP as elucidated by international lawyers ('legal doctrine has never agreed upon the exact combination of the criteria which would map out the scope of the concept')[39] (Kissling 2006: 4–5). Claudia Kissling's model considers ILP as a gradually developing quality leading to the recognition of a partial personality, yet not excluding the potential of reaching full ILP.[40] Outlining a table addressing amongst others accountability, responsibility, and normative power, it offers a valuable reference point and guidance towards constructing a comprehensive NSA properties stock-taking tool conducive to

38 For the development of corporate social responsibility standards see Reinisch 2009. Individual rights and duties in matters law maintenance have been developing in the area of human rights, specifically international criminal law (Shabas 2009, Gal-Or 2009b).

39 For a discussion of ILP in the sense of subject of international law and the argument that the concept does not represent a homogenous and unitary system of rights and duties, see Menon (1992).

40 For a related discussion of various qualifications of the legal personality, for example partial, original, derived, functional, direct, and relative personality, see Kissling (2006). Note that the paper evaluates the legal rights and duties of NGOs based on their cooperation with more than 30 international organizations.

ascertaining the adequacy of attributing some international personality traits to the NSA.

By way of recapturing, determining the desirability of a further enhanced legal status of the NSA requires first to establish whether the NSA should be recognized as a *general category* of an actor or a 'garden variety' of various types of actors to which a fundamental unitary set of rights and obligations in international law applies. We submit that the model described will prove instrumental in this quest. We offered to compare the various 'legal statuses' of NSAs to determine whether or not several general categories of the NSA are conceptually discernable, and whether any might satisfy the necessary conditions of ILP intrinsically similar to that of the state. We hope that an organized and empirical model-based debate will ensue and pool together the many loose and scattered threads that characterize the burgeoning debates on the role of NSAs.

V. NSA's ILP: A Contribution to the Development of International Law?

We now turn to examine whether fostering the NSA's status would contribute to a more cohesive and coherent international law.

The view that the days when 'traditional doctrine provided a neat framework of analysis' (Bianchi 2009: xiv) are over suggests that change is imperative. Surely, an international political actor, the NSA has emerged as a chief critic of international law's performance whether as NGO expressing disappointment and distrust (for example regarding environmental, economic, and human rights, matters), as a challenger of the system altogether (for example international terrorists), of state supremacy (for example, sub-federal governance entities and regional cross-border associations), or otherwise. Correlate pressures were exerted on the legal system through processes of juridification, legalization and constitutionalization (Cotterrell 1992) as unfolding, for instance, in the so-called privatization of the public and the development of transnational law; and a perception of a further diminishing remedial capacity of the legal system (Cotterrell 1992). Attributed to deficiencies of the state in living up to its ILP obligations (and consequently, impacting its rights) this process would come to expose the limits of the effectiveness and efficiency of both the municipal and international legal systems. Would then enhancing the NSA's ILP provide the only solution to bridging over the gap separating legal 'reality' from NSA commensurate expectations from the law?

In the following section, we suggest to entertain the question of the *desirability* of enhancing the NSA's legal personality as an examination of whether such development is *necessary* for international law's 'best' performance.[41] This corresponds to the third question posed at the outset of the chapter: Should the

41 The question has been raised in the context of human rights law (Clapham 2006, Ruggie 2008, Kennedy 2001). We are proposing to expand the perspective to include the entire spectrum of international law.

rights and obligations of the state be adjusted to accommodate the legal status needs (and achievements) of the NSA? In other words, would it be desirable to break out from the current doctrinal mould of international law? The following section offers preliminary thoughts regarding the overarching question on the law's *capabilities* as a pre-requisite for assessing its effectiveness and efficiency. First, it will be suggested to re-assess the presumption of the NSA's interest in possessing ILP. Second, desirability will be examined as a function of capability: Is international law capable of satisfying the challenge of the NSA without change to the underlying premise of the subject of international law? And specifically, is such a possibility congruent with the law's requirement for unity?

VI. Does International Law's Performance Pass the Test of the NSA Challenge?

Is the NSA Interested in International Legal Status?

A most illustrative example to elucidate international law's responsiveness to the NSA is found in the field of (state) security[42] and the use of armed force. Often, it is here where a fundamental rupture between the NSA and the state surfaces.

Security related NSAs, for example terrorist organizations, (Hollis 2007) and to some extent pirates, (Kontorovich 2009) have been instrumental in encouraging the development of international law not through advocacy, civil disobedience, and legal action but rather by legal transgression.[43] Indeed, the challenge posed to international law by these NSAs stems from their thriving on disrespect of either system of law – municipal and international.[44] This is explained on the one hand, by permissive conditions in fragile and failed states, which are lacking capacity to develop and enforce municipal law; (Gal-Or 2009b) and on the other hand, as a result of capable states' unwillingness to harness the municipal legal system in confronting the challenge (Newton 2009). The NSA engaged in armed violence denotes a widespread category including both national and international terrorist organizations and networks; warlords in pursuit of political office; anarchists desirous of the abolition of the state, para-military wings of national liberation movements, and so on. Across this spectrum, it is the international terrorist who currently represents the greatest challenge to international law for its comportment often defies exclusive 'compartmentalization' within any certain area of the

42 Other examples pertaining to the international law of trade and investment were mentioned previously in this contribution and are also addressed elsewhere in this anthology.

43 For an interesting account of the difference between types of international law-breakers see Gooding (2009).

44 I am refraining here from discussing dilemmas concerning the interface between criminal law, human rights law, and the law of armed conflict for lack of space.

law (Corn and Jensen 2009, Watkin 2005). Unlike the NGO and TNC, terrorist groupings of the religious and global 'al-Qaida type', appear to be oblivious to ILP. Manifestly disdainful of extant international law, they aspire for an alternative international legal regime. Enhancement of this NSA's ILP is therefore irrelevant.[45]

Given the diversity of NSA interests concerning their international legal status, it would be interesting to capture this aspect by placing NSAs along a continuum ranging from strongly seeking ILP, through moderately interested in, indifferent to such status, to entirely rejecting the international legal regime. It is reasonable to expect transnational criminal organizations to differ from terrorist networks in this regard. Surely, civil society non-profit organizations have exhibited a stronger interest and claim in joining in the extant legal regime, notably, in order to reform it from within.[46]

NSAs interest in enhancing their ILP transpires through various pressures (diverse and sometimes contradictory) they exert on governments and IGOs. On the one hand, NGOs have been urging governments to comply with extant legal doctrine, for instance, the International Committee of the Red Cross regarding the need to reconcile international humanitarian law and international human rights and criminal, law (Melzer 2009). On the other hand, NGOs have been strongly advocating for the development of new and progressive international legal rules as illustrated, for instance, in the case of corporate social responsibility (CSR) (Gal-Or 2009). Similarly, sub-federal governmental entities and regional cross-border organizations have been seeking increased autonomy within the extant international legal regime. A Canadian example of a sub-federal government entity seeking legal status in conformity within international law is the province of Quebec, which enjoys a special (state constitutional) status concerning certain international relations. Across the European Union, regions have often, and continuously, been pushing both the regional and international proverbial

45 An interesting approach deserving more attentive consideration in the debate about the adequate legal regime to counter the threat emanating from this type of NSA is offered by the studies of culture and cross-cultural interactions. They might prove valuable in the search for a valid doctrinal re-conceptualization of the international legal status of the NSA. See, for instance Arbuckle (2006) and Bagayoko (2010).

46 Invariably, this type of NSA has been playing the role of self-appointed guardian of pertinent rights and promoter of (international and municipal) legal development. Certainly, it is unconceivable to think of the establishment of the International Criminal Court without acknowledging the significant influence exerted by human rights NGOs. 'What has been novel about the new transnational advocacy networks has been their ability to mobilize information strategically to create new issues and categories and to persuade, pressure, and gain leverage over much more powerful organizations and governments. They usually operate in issues areas characterized by high value content and informational uncertainty. ... Transnational advocacy networks were crucial in the 'road to Rome' which resulted in the Rome Statute of the International Criminal Court on July 17, 1998' (Del Buono 2001: 202, 205).

envelopes (Gal-Or 1990). Some have been successful in establishing associations and organizations, which have been institutionalized within the European area in various forms,[47] representing a regional (integration) *sui generis*, hence new, paradigm of international law. These examples serve to show that NSAs' interests in possessing ILP represents a subject that would benefit from further elucidation when assessing the desirability of an enhanced ILP of the NSA.

The 'Management of Law' Approach.

Sir Robert Jennings' observation that 'a discussion about legal personality conducted in terms of *broad generalizations and theoretical dogma* has outlived any relevance to real issues that it might once have had', (1998: 2, emphasis added) eloquently summarizes the imbalance within the international legal system and as such offers a tempting place to begin our discussion. Sir Jennings attributed the imbalance to the abundance of court decisions interpreting and applying the law, on the one hand, and the lack of complementary court procedures related to government[48] policy review, on the other hand.[49] Directing us to pay closer attention to, and improve, the 'machinery of policy decisions', (Jennings 2004: 129–130) his proposed reform focuses on developing a 'clever international regime of management',[50] (Jennings 2004: 128) which finds application in a number of legal regimes. While on its face, this scheme elegantly circumvents the ILP challenge, we must query whether this machinery preferably includes the NSA with enhanced ILP capacity. Or alternatively, *can international law do better without attributing an ILP to the NSA?* And if so, how?

As example of the 'management approach', Sir Jennings discusses the Antarctic Treaty of 1959, hailed as 'one of the great triumphs of international law' (Jennings 2004: 128). It represents a typical inter-state context focusing on territorial claims, which was subsequently supplemented by the 1991 Protocol on Environmental Protection. The latter offers a more adequate management test case for it reflects a conscious decision to take the NSA and its interests seriously. Established in Article 11 of the Environment Protocol, its Committee for Environmental Protection (CEP) consists of representatives from all Parties to the Protocol and observers from

47 The Association of European Border Regions (AEBR) operates as a European union for only five amalgamations of border regions from Northern and Central Europe, out of 14 such large-size cross-border groupings across Europe.

48 Presumably meaning 'governance'.

49 'The function of the courts in the policy areas of government is to review the competences of the bodies which have the task of making these decisions and ensure that they act *intra vires*. This is the kind of law that, in developed societies, we call constitutional and/or administrative law. Such constitutional international law as we have is inadequate' (Jennings 2004: 127).

50 The question whether the management approach is exclusively procedural or whether procedure and substance are inseparable must be deferred for another time.

Parties to the Treaty (but not to the Protocol) as well as observers from designated institutions and other invited organizations (CEP Rules of Procedure). The 1991 Protocol has thus transformed a system established in 1959 into a transparent and more inclusive international legal forum for the NSA. In our previously discussed model, this development might be considered as a step towards enhancing the NSA's legal personality.

Forty years after the Antarctic Treaty embracement of an inclusionary management strategy, and seven years after the Protocol, the Aarhus Convention (1998) offers another similar example (Fitzmaurice 2009). The Convention reinforces the endorsement of NSA participation with an arguably even stronger articulation of rights. It provides for any person, presumably natural or legal, access to a review procedure before 'a *court* of law or another independent and impartial body established by law' (Article 9.1 Aarhus Convention 1998, emphasis added). The NSA's enhanced maintenance capacity stops right there, as the Convention is silent as to any specifications.

By comparison, the legal status of investors, achieved in over 2,000 inter-state bilateral investment treaties (BITs) and international trade agreements (ITAs) (Gal-Or 2005),[51] represents yet another medium whereby the NSAs maintenance capacity is being extended with regard to both rights and duties.[52]

Notably, inclusion reflects the weight of the NSA as a political actor but pointedly – also the NSA's dependence on recognition by the 'absolute' international person – the state. And while management is critical to bringing the law up to speed with reality, it must also be noted that the *de jure* enhancement of the NSA's status in international law remains integrated within conventional law, the bastion of the state's ILP. To be sure, the management approach does not mandate full 'legal personification' of the NSA, even though it might be a by-product. Its rationale – the development of an international inclusive policy review mechanism to bolster international law's efficiency and effectiveness – remains to be studied.

The upshot of the management approach, if successful, is in facilitating a more practical and down-to-earth interlocution between state and NSA and among NSAs themselves in international legal matters. A so inclined 'cleverer' regime of international management will require not only the state, but also the NSA, to develop institutions and institutional procedures that satisfy all three ILP requirements: capacity to possess, to maintain, and to create law. In addition to extant provisions concerning access to justice (for example amicus briefs, specialized international and transnational courts and tribunals), the emphasis would have to expand to securing the administrative and constitutional processes governing also the NSA and ensuring its responsibility. Self regulating international administrative 'oversight' or 'auditing' bodies and procedures do already exist and

51 A development prompted by the North American Free Trade Agreement (NAFTA) Investment Chapter 11 (NAFTA 1994).

52 See also Muchlinkski, Chapter 2.

have originated in the collaborative work of NSAs as demonstrated in the practice of international certification in various trades, industries, and professions.[53] Additional benefits to efficiency and effectiveness of international law might potentially ensue as management unfolds as instrumental in controlling the proliferation of NSAs, reducing the number of NSAs possessing enhanced legal status,[54] encouraging inter-NSA dialogue,[55] and streamlining the development of international law. Should the management approach result in satisfactory answers to the NSA challenges, the conclusion might well be that a partial ILP within the extant doctrine of international law proves to be the adequate answer to the question regarding the desirability of an enhanced NSA ILP. However, where the NSA remains discontent, the managerial approach might stimulate the opposite reaction and serve as a lever propelling the NSA to further develop ILP capacities and re-opening of the doctrinal debate.

Based on the discussion above, the question whether international law's performance has passed the test of the NSA's interests and claims, remains open.

VII. Conclusion

This chapter has set out to offer preliminary observations regarding the doctrinal challenge posed by the NSA to international law, and propose directions for further reflection and debate on the NSA status and role in international law. The leading question has been whether it would be *desirable* to further enhance the legal status in international law already secured by some NSAs, considering international law's requirements for cohesion and consistency. The purpose of the chapter was to address this question by proposing a *methodology*, and offering an organizational framework, for a focused debate in a discourse, which has so far been characterized by a prolific but disjunctive discourse. The chapter opened by exploring the first question of the study, namely whether, from a doctrinal orientated perspective, the various NSAs lend themselves to a classification that would group them within a single *general category* of NSA and facilitate a uniform application of ILP criteria. The discussion addressed the concept of legal status in *any* legal system, including international law, noting that the essential character of an international (global)

53 See Rheinisch 2009 for detailed examples.

54 For instance, where there is a *ratione materiae* overlap between the NSA and the natural person, and where their claims for legal status overlap, it would be reasonable to expect the management approach to address the important subject of NSA representation.

55 For instance, in matters of CSR under various institutional auspices. Again, it is not unreasonable to expect similar management applications regarding other types of NSA actors, for example private military companies, which operate in an area for which a state-NSA and NSA-NSA international legal management system could be developed (Corn 2008, Roche 2010).

system of law was grounded in its legal personalities. This justified the use of the ILP concept as the standard to ascertain the desirability for international law in further enhancing the NSA's personality.

After an examination of the contemporary status of the NSA in international law, a discussion of its ranking in a descending order of recognition as possessing ILP, followed suit. A model was proposed to address the second question of the chapter, namely, whether (at least some of) the NSAs might be candidates for doctrinal treatment similar to that of the state. It was designed as a guideline for a more concrete and empirical study of the chapter's overarching question regarding desirability. The model borrowed Brownlie's (2003) characteristics of the state's legal personality consisting of the three capacities of law creation, maintenance, and possession. Kissling (2006) model focusing on NGO's legal personality contributed the idea of gradation in ILP. It proved useful for further development into a measuring yard to establish the extent of capacities of *all* NSAs. An empirical comparison of various NSAs on a continuum ranging from less-than-full (that is to say, less than state) ILP to no ILP at all might serve as an indicator for the practicability of further NSA legal status development. Consequently, the model proposed may assist in synthesizing the knowledge concerning the NSA in international law. This has been growing by leaps and bounds, and would certainly benefit from some theoretical systematization in the legal discourse on the NSA in general, and regarding to the desirability of an enhanced legal status of the NSA, in particular.

Another angle to approach the question regarding the desirability of further enhancing the NSA's ILP was contemplated in the paper's third question regarding international law's capability to satisfactorily address the NSA challenge. This was discussed in two main sections: one focusing on the NSAs' interest in possessing ILP and the other – on international law's management potential. It was suggested that the presumption that all NSAs aspire to possess ILP must be carefully scrutinized for diverge intentions may potentially affect international law's development. While management was found to result in the partial enhancement of the ILP capacities of some NSAs via inclusion in both law creation and law maintenance, it remained doubtful whether, from an NSA perspective, such a solution would prove satisfactory.

References

Abiew, F.K. and Keating, T. 2004. Defining a Role for Civil Society, in *Building Sustainable Peace*, edited by T. Keating and W.A. Knight. Edmonton: The University of Alberta Press, 93–117.

Arbuckle, J. 2006. *Military Forces in 21st Century Peace Operations. No Job for A Soldier?* London: Routledge.

Bagayoko, N. 2010 (forthcoming). La notion de 'culture tactique', un instrument pour l'analyse des normes du maintien de la paix?, in *Après la Guerre*, edited by N. Gal-Or and K.-G. Giesen. Paris: La documentation française, forthcoming.

Bianchi, A. 2009. Introduction: Relativizing the Subjects or Subjectivizing the Actors: Is That the Question?, in *Non-State Actors and International Law*, edited by A. Bianchi. Farnham, England: Ashgate, xi–xxx.

Blum, G. 2009. The Dispensable Lives of Soldiers. *Harvard Public Law Working Paper No. 09-52*.

Boyle, A. and Chinkin, C. 2007. *The Making of International Law*. Oxford: Oxford University Press.

Brownlie, I. 2003. *Principles of Public International Law*. 6th Edition. Oxford: Oxford University Press.

Carty, A. 2006. Renewed Place for Doctrine as the Source of International Law in a Time of Fragmentation, in *L'influence des Sources sur l'Unité et la Fragmentation du Droit International*, edited by H. Vinaixia and K. Wellens. Bruxelles: Bruyalnt, 239–261.

Cassesse, A. 1986. *International Law in a Divided World*. Oxford: Clarendon Press.

Claire Cutler, A. 2003. *Private Power and Global Authority: Transnational Merchant Law in the Global Political Economy*. Cambridge: Cambridge University Press.

Clapham. A. 2006. *Human Rights Obligations of Non-State Actors*. Oxford: Oxford University Press.

Corn, G. 2008. Bringing Discipline to the Civilianization of the Battlefield: A Proposal for a More Legitimate Approach to Resurrecting Military Criminal Jurisdiction Over Civilian Augmentees. *University of Miami Law Review*, 62, 401 ff.

Corn, G. and Jensen, E. 2009. Untying the Gordian Knott: A Proposal for Determining Applicability of the Law of War to the War on Terror. *Temple L. Rev.* 81 (3) 787 ff.

Cotterrell, R. 1992. *The Sociology of Law: An Introduction*. 2nd Edition. London: Butterworths.

De Brabandere, E. 2009. Non-State Actors, State-Centrism and Human Rights Obligations. Review Essay, *Leiden Journal of International Law* 22, 191–209.

Del Buono, V.M. 2001. International Advocacy Networks and the International Criminal Court, in *The Changing Face of International Criminal Law. Selected Papers*. Vancouver, BC: The International Centre for Criminal Law Reform and Criminal Justice Policy, 201–216.

Eleftheriadis, P. 2008. *Legal Rights*. Oxford: Oxford University Press.

Fitzmaurice, M. 2010 (forthcoming). Participation of Civil Society in Environmental Matters. Case Study: The 1998 Aarhus Convention on Access to Information, Public Participation in Decision-making and Access to Justice in Environmental

Matters, in *Non-State Actors, Special Issue of Human Rights and International Legal Discourse*, edited by C. Ryngaert and M. Noortmann.

Franck, T. 1995. *Fairness in International Law and Institutions*. Oxford: Clarendon Press.

Gal-Or, N. 1990. *Europe after 1992. The Completion of the Single Market: Towards the Weakening of the Nation-State and the Rise of Ethnic-Regionally Based Boundaries? 1989–1990 Award for Research into European Integration*. Brussels: Commission of the European Communities.

Gal-Or, N. 2005. NAFTA Chapter Eleven and the Implications for the FTAA: The Institutionalisation of Investor Status in Public International Law. *Transnational Corporations*, 14(2), 121–158.

Gal-Or, N. 2009. The Investor and Civil Society as Twin Global Citizens: Proposing a New Interpretation in the Legitimacy Debate. *Suffolk Transnational Law Review*, 32(2), 271–301, forthcoming.

Gilbert, M. 2006. *A Theory of Political Obligation*. Oxford: Oxford University Press.

Goodin, R.E. 2005. Toward an International Rule of Law: Distinguishing International Law-Breakers from Would-Be Law-Makers. *The Journal of Ethics*, 9(1/2), 225–246.

Graz, J.-C. and Noelke, A. (eds). 2007. *Transnational Private Governance and Its Limits*. London: Routledge.

Hart, H.L.A. 1994. *The Concept of Law*. 2nd Edition. Oxford: Oxford University Press.

Higgins, R. 1963. *The Development of International Law Through the Political Organs of the United Nations*. Oxford: Oxford University Press.

Jennings, Sir R. 1989. *Collected Writings of Sir Robert Jennings*. Volume 1. The Hague: Kluwer.

Jennings, Sir R. 2004. The Imbalance of the International Law System. *International Law FORUM du droit international*, 6, 126–130.

Kennedy, D. 2001. The International Human Rights Movement: Part of the Problem? *Eur. H.R.L,* 6, 245 ff.

Kerbrat, Y. (ed.) 2005. Le colloque du Mans de la Société française pour le Droit International (4 et 5 juin 2004): le Sujet de 'Sujet'. *International Law FORUM du droit international*, 7, 63–65.

Kissling, C. 2006. The Legal Status of NGOs in International Governance and its Relevance for the Legitimacy of International Organizations, Bremen, Germany: TranState Working Papers No. 38.

Melzer, N. 2009. *Interpretive Guidance on the Notion of Direct Participation in Hostilities under International Humanitarian Law.* Geneva: ICRC.

Menon, P.K. 1992. The International Personality of Individuals in International Law: A Broadening of the Traditional Doctrine. *Journal of Transnational Law and Policy*, 1, 151–182.

Newton, M. 2009. Exceptional Engagement: Protocol I and a World United Against Terrorism. *Texas International Law Journal,* 45(2), 323 ff.

Nijman, J.E. 2004. *The Concept of ILP. An Inquiry into the History and Theory of International Law*. The Hague: T.M.C. Asser Press.

Nijman, J.E. 2007. Paul Ricoeur and International Law: Beyond 'The End of the Subject'. Towards a Reconceptualization of International Legal Personality, in *Non-State Actors and International Law*, edited by A. Bianchi. Farnham, UK: Ashgate, 79–118.

Reinisch, A. 2009. The Changing International Legal Framework for Dealing with Non-State Actors, in *Non-State Actors and Human Rights,* edited by A. Bianchi. Oxford: Oxford University Press, 37–89, reproduced in *Non-State Actors and International Law*, edited by A. Bianchi. A. Farnham, UK: Ashgate, 411–464.

Roche, J.-J. 2010 (forthcoming). 'Contractors, Mode D'emploi', in *Après la Guerre*, edited by N. Gal-Or and K.-G. Giesen. Paris: La documentation française.

Schabas, W. 2002–2003. Punishment of Non-State Actors in Non-International Armed Conflict. *Fordham International Law Journal*, 26, 907–933, in *Non-State Actors and International Law*, edited by A. Bianchi. Farnham, UK: Ashgate.

Schwebel, R. 1966. Book Review. *Yale Law Journal*, 75, 677 ff.

Shaw, M.N. 2008. *International Law*. 6th Edition. Cambridge: Cambridge University Press.

Vöneky, S. 2007. *Response* – The Fight against Terrorism and the Rules of International Law – Comment on Papers and Speeches of John B. Bellinger, Chief Legal Advisor to the United States State Department. *German Law Journal* 8(7), 743 ff.

Watkin, K. 2005. Warriors Without Rights? Combatants, Unprivileged Belligerents, and the Struggle Over Legitimacy. *Harvard University Occasional Paper Series* Winter No. 2, 1–75.

PART THREE

Chapter 7

Understanding Non-State Actors in the Contemporary World Society: Transcending the International, Mainstreaming the Transnational, or Bringing the Participants Back In?

Math Noortmann

I. Introduction

According to Rosalyn Higgins (Higgins 1999: 50):

> [i]t is not particularly helpful, either intellectually or operationally, to rely on the subject-object dichotomy that runs through so much of the writings. It is more helpful and closer to perceived reality to return to the view of international law as a particular decision making process. Within that process (which is a dynamic and not a static one) there is a variety of *participants*, making claims across state lines, with the object of maximizing various values.

The distinguished terminology of the policy-orientated jurisprudence of Myres S. McDougal and Harold D. Lasswell (Lasswell and McDougal 1992, McDougal and Reisman 1981) is difficult to miss in the opinion of the former President of the International Court of Justice. In the 1950s, the jurisprudence of the New Haven School was one of the 'new beacon(s) to those impatient with the process of international law and dissatisfied with much of its content' (D'Amato 1961: 458). One particular cause of that dissatisfaction was the conceptual neglect and the politics of exclusion of 'entities not being states' by the disciplinary elites.

At the same time, that McDougal and Lasswell presented their policy-orientated jurisprudence, Phillip C. Jessup (1956), introduced a less radical and therefore perhaps the more acceptable notion of *transnational law*. Both approaches indirectly acknowledged the International Court of Justice's observation in the *Reparation for Injuries Case* of 'instances of action upon the international plane by entities which are not states'[1] and moved away from the traditional state centred internationalism of international law. To the post-war radical and less traditional scholarship, international law was no longer exclusive to nations.

McDougal and Lasswell in contrast to Jessup, however, took that understanding to its conceptual logic and introduced the term 'participants' thereby avoiding the discriminatory distinction between states and non-states in the law-making process. Jessup merely noted the existence of non-state entities as an empirical fact.

While both approaches had lost much of their attraction in the early 1970s in legal circles, the idea of transnationalism was kept alive in international relations circles by a growing neo-liberal critique on Realism. That dominant IR theory had – much like its positivistic counterpart in international law – effectively shaped and marginalized the discourse on entities not being states within the political science discourse (Charney 1983, Huntington 1973, Judge and Skjelbaek 1975, Keohane and Nye 1977). The first wave of IR 'trans-nationalism' in the 1970s and 1980s however also failed to trigger a paradigmatic turn on the notion of non-state actors. The so-called neo-neo debate between neo-realist and neo-liberals became a paradigmatic clash, which effectively pushed the question of non-state entities to a lower level of scientific awareness.

The collapse of the Soviet empire and the subsequent developments in the intergovernmental and non-governmental realms, however, caused non-state entities to prominently reappear in the spotlights of the ivory towers of international relations and international law. It first provoked social and political scientists and later international law scholars to engage in what was considered to be a new transnational reality (Bennet 1995, Risse-Kappen 1995). Since then, a neo-transnationalist terminology has permeated the languages of international law and international relations, but not without critique (Pries 2008) and what is more important, like the old-transnationalism, it has apparently not resulted in a paradigmatic reconsideration of non-state entities in mainstream thinking.

In much of international law's contemporary writings, non-state actors are at most empirically acknowledged as 'special cases' (Shaw 2003), 'selected anomalies' (Wallace 2006), 'special types' and 'controversial candidatures' (Brownlie 2003) or '*Sonderfälle*' and '*andere Rechstellungen*' (Hobe and Kimminich 2004). Conceptually, however, non-state actors are still structurally excluded from the textbooks and discourses in international law. In those rare instances where non-

1 See Introduction. The advisory opinion of the International Court of Justice in the Reparation for Injuries case (1948) might indeed be considered to be one of the first recognitions of a world beyond the state and as a confirmation of the NSA exception to the state centred paradigm of international studies. However, the Court's observation did not trigger a paradigm shift beyond the emerging recognition of international governmental organizations as new actors and new 'persons' in international law.

state actors have been made the explicit subject of international legal or political investigation, they are posited in a dialectical relationship with international law.[2]

The continuing trend to exclude non-state actors from the general international legal discourse however has not gone by unnoticed. Critical and other obstreperous legal scholarship has vigorously commented on the trend to marginalize entities, which are not governmental.[3] That marginalization, however, cannot be attributed to 'the other' only. Philip Alston (2005) is right! By consistently referring to 'non-state actors', we indeed seem to suffer from the 'not-a-cat syndrome'. In adopting the term non-state, we implicitly admit that our main and sole point of reference is the state. We thereby marginalize our subject of research and 'reinforce the assumption that the state is the only central actor' (Alston 2005).

In this chapter, I will, first of all, argue that the transnational/international dichotomy is not helpful and in fact counterproductive in understanding the amalgam of non-state entities in the mainstream theories of international relations and international law. Secondly, and instead, I will argue that the albeit imperfect notion of *participants* – as originally conceptualized by McDougal and Lasswell – provides us with a far better starting point to assess and understand the role of – what is nowadays fashionably referred to as – 'non-state actors' in the international law-making process.[4]

II. Transnationalism I: Masking the Shortcomings of Internationalism

The post-world war discourse in international law was characterized by a growing displeasure in the state-centred focus of international law (McDougal and Feliciano 1961, Jessup 1956, Schwarzenberger 1952). The policy-orientated approach and the transnational law approach can be seen as two different expressions of that discomfort. Both explicitly address the problematic of non-state entities in a state dominated international legal order. While McDougal and associates adopted a rather radical interdisciplinary legal-political approach, Jessup choose to stay closer to the positivistic tradition, and methodological and theoretical confinements of the international legal discipline.

---

2 For scholars perceiving the relationship in terms of 'and' rather then 'in' (see Alston 2005, Bianchi and Naqvi 2004, Higgott et al. 2000). For scholars perceiving the relationship as an embedded one see: (Arts and Noortmann et al. 2001, Josselin and Wallace 2001, Noortmann 2001).

3 The terminological change at this point from 'states' to 'governmental' reflects the established position and acceptance of intergovernmental organizations in the debates and writings of international law and international relations. These 'non-state actors' act in a league that is closer to the 'state' then to other non-state actors.

4 The term 'participant' has recently reappeared in a number of significant publications, however, without explicit clarification or clear reference to the policy-orientated approach (see for example: Boyle and Chinkin 2007, Ku and and Diehl 2003).

In the first publications bearing the title *Transnational Law* (which was not accidentally published by the Yale University Press), Phillip C. Jessup (1956: 1) considered international law 'inadequate' to describe and analyse the legal problems related to the 'complex interrelated world community.' In Jessup's conception, transnational law included both 'all law which regulates actions or events that transcend national boundaries' and 'situations [that] involve 'individuals, corporations, states, organizations of states or other groups' (Jessup 1956: 1). But unlike his colleagues in New Haven, Jessup (1956: 9) was not thinking of non-state entities as participants in the law-making process but as 'affected by rules' that is to say, they are 'law-takers'. In Jessup's opinion (1956: 9), non-state actors are at most confronted with an 'infinite variety of transnational situations [which are governed by] a number of applicable legal rules and they may conflict with each other' either between 'rules of different national laws' or between 'a rule of national law and a rule of 'Public International Law'. To Jessup, transnational law was first of all a meditative institution between conflicting laws in a transnational situation. Non-state entities were objects rather than subjects of the law, whether international or transnational. Indeed, while the use of the term 'transnationalism' signaled the need for a paradigmatic change, it did not however require a substantial theoretical reconsideration of the world of states, which would require the majority of international legal scholars to perform the proverbial leap over ones own shadow.[5]

By 1972, a possible transnational momentum was gone in international law circles. The collection of essays in the honor of Phillip C. Jessup, entitled *Transnational Law in a Changing Society*, awkwardly demonstrates that both the whole concept as well as the idea of transnational law had become extremely thin. Wilfried Jenks contribution on multinational companies – the only contribution that dealt with non-state entities – displays the disconnect between ones socio-political worldview and ones perception of the international legal order.

> The world society is, and must by its nature be, a pluralistic society. It is because it is a pluralistic society that the doctrine of sovereignty is so unhelpful to the progress of world organization. It is because it is a pluralistic society that the status within it of a wide range of varied types of multinational entity constitutes one of the central problems of international law [but] no *inter*national status for multinational corporations can be created in the foreseeable future by a mandatory decision and the status would become a significant reality only insofar as corporations sought it and governments recognized it. (Jenks 1972: 73)

5 The discrepancy between the contents and the titles of the Columbia and Vanderbilt transnational law journals reflect the conceptual unease with the new terminology. Except for a one-and-a-half page article by Phillip Jessup entitled *The Concept of Transnational Law: An Introduction*, the term transnational is nowhere to be found in the first three volumes of the Columbia journal.

The impossibility to transcend the international and intergovernmental level and the indiscriminate use of the transnational language is symptomatic, which I consider to be the core methodological and theoretical problem in the analysis of contemporary world order and justice.

The end of transnationalism in the legal discourse however was not the end of the idea of transnationalism or the transnational discourse. In IR circles a critique was growing against the realist conception of world order as a state of affairs between nation-states. A critique that would ultimately culminate in the famous debate between neo-realist and neo-liberals.

The acclaimed founder of the neo-realist school, Kenneth Waltz (Waltz 1979) excluded non-state actors in his *Theory of International Politics*, from the structure of *international* politics, in the same manner as his positivistic colleagues had excluded non-state entities from the structure of international law: empirically they existed, but conceptually they did not To the extend that neo-realists applied their rational choice based methodologies and power political theories to non-state entities, these entities entered the arena of world politics, but not that of international relations, that is to say, the relations between states (Walt 2002). Neo-realists, however, became the first to effectively seek to conceptualize the difference between a *trans*national realm and the *inter*national realm as different governance spaces, that is to say, political spaces that either included or excluded non-state actors as participants in the international decision-making process. While neo-realists conveniently accepted the existence of a transnational realm, they maintain that 'neorealism has little to say about *transnational relations*' (Krasner 1995) and that just might explain their inclination to simply identify '*trans*national movements among the processes that go on *within* … the system's [state-centric] structure' (Waltz 1979). From a neorealist's perspective then, *trans*national relations and *inter*national relations are therefore not necessarily 'logically two sides of the same coin' as van Apeldoorn (van Apeldoorn 2004:143) suggests.

Neo-realists' paradigmatic problem to accommodate the transnational within the international becomes apparent in Krasner's *Power Politics, Institutions and Transnational Relations* (Krasner 1995), in which transnational actors are identified in terms of '[national] institutional structures' and 'relational power'. The neo-realist distinction between 'international' and 'transnational' is more than mere terminology.[6]

The neo-realist critique that students of transnational movements (1) called the 'state centric view of the world into question' and (2) have 'developed no theory of their subject matter or international politics in general' (Waltz 1979: 95) has created a Catch-22 in which states became the ontological and epistemological points of cross reference. States, according to Waltz 'are the units whose interactions form the structure of the international political system' (Waltz 1979:

6 Many approaches and publications including Thomas Risse-Kappen's *Bringing Transnational Relations Back In*, unfortunately contribute to blurring the difference by adhering to indiscriminate and interchangeable terminology.

95). Non-state entities can – in the opinion of neo-realists – only be positioned in that structure through internal institutional structures of the state. In the anarchical conception of the interstate realm, 'the transnational actor must be a *natural* component of a sovereign state system' according to Krasner (1995: 257). The neo-realist conception of power and its attributes constitutes the second hurdle in understanding and explaining non-state actors in world politics from a neo-realist perspective. Once again, Krasner's position is telling. While he acknowledges that 'power politics … analyses outcomes as a manifestation of the powers and conflicting interests of *actors*', he fails to provide an understanding of the relative and relational aspects of power in such a way as to accommodate non-state actors (Krasner 1995: 277).

The impossibility to conceptualize the distinction between international and transnational in an inclusive global political framework was not unique to neo-realism. Neo-liberalism and the English School had equal difficulties with developing a theoretical framework that would include both states as well as non-state actors in the quest for global order and justice.

As Robert Keohane and Joseph S. Nye's *Power and Independence* (1977) was published two years before Waltz's *Theory of International Relations*, they might very well be credited for opening the discourse on transnationalism (Waltz 1979).[7] At the same time that Waltz and Keohane 'discovered' the transnational dimension to international order, Hedley Bull recognized in *The Anarchical Society* (2002) such phenomena as 'transnational solidarity' and 'transnational groups,' which he considered relevant for the 'world international society' but obviously not for the 'international society' of states. Bull's underdeveloped – or rather undeveloped distinction between an 'international society' and a 'world society', is by Andrew Hurrell considered to be a 'somewhat neglected legacy of Bull's approach.'[8] Hurrel's *On Global Order* (2007) takes Bulls notion of an 'international society' to the next level of contemplation, but except for observing a higher level of 'transnational solidarity', there does not seem to have been a development of transnationalism over the last three decades, that warrants a publication on 'world society'.

7 For decades, the apostles of Keohane and Waltz have indulged themselves in a debate that has entered the history of international relations theory as the 'neo-neo debate' or the inter-paradigm debate, which suggests the succesfull exclusion of Marxist and Critical IR theory (Weber 2005, Linklater 2007). Recently, constructivist scholarship has positioned themselves between neo-realism and neo-liberalism in an attempt to engage that specific debate and become accepted as a mainstream IR theory (see for example Wendt 1999, Risse 2002). There is no counterpart of the neo-neo debate in international legal discourse, due to the oppresing dominance of legal positivism. Non-positivistic theories as pushed to the perifery of international legal discourse, notwithstanding the fact that the non-positivistic theories and their proponents are widely recognized (Marks 2008, Meteyard et al. 2004, McDougal and Reisman 1985, Beck and Arend et al. 1996, Koskenniemi 2006, 2001, Noortmann 2005, Ratner and Slaughter 2004).

8 See Andrew Hurrell's foreword to the 3rd edition. p xviii.

III. Transnationalism II: Masking the Shortcomings of Transnationalism I

According to Thomas Risse (Risse-Kappen 1995), 'the original concept of transnational relations was ill-defined. It encompassed everything in world politics except state to state relations.' His *Bringing Transnational Relations Back In: Non-State Actors, Domestic Structures, and International Institutions* was one of the first publications that addressed the increased non-state activism in the post-Cold War era. The increased global activities of international governmental organizations and their non-governmental counterparts, provoked scholars from a broad variety of disciplines to once again question the conceptions and workings of the classical international system.[9]

In an attempt to 'bringing transnational relations back in' Thomas Risse defines transnational relations as 'regular interactions across national boundaries when at least one actor is a non-state agent or does not operate on behalf of an national government or an international organization' (Risse-Kappen 1995a: 3).

In order to assess 'what we have learned', Risse again juxtaposed the international and the transnational arenas, arguing that 'we need to bring transnational relations back in, if we want to understand international relations.' (Risse-Kappen 1995b: 313). Risse could not have put it more clearly; understanding *international* relations is the theoretical objective and *transnational* relations, the methodological tool.

A comparable trend can be identified in international legal discourses. When Harold Koh claims that 'the New Haven School was among the first to recognize the emerging importance of transnational law', the question as to what is meant by 'transnationalism' must be asked again! 'Transnational' to Koh is a two-fold concept, relating to 'substance' and 'process'. Transnational legal substance is the transnationalism of Jessup; a transnationalism that bridges the 'previously accepted dichotomies ... domestic and international, public and private' (Koh 2007: 566).

Perhaps the best operational definition of transnational law, is according to Koh threefold (1) 'law that has been downloaded from international to domestic law' (2) law that has been 'uploaded' and then 'downloaded' and (3) law that has been 'horizontally transplanted', which in Koh's comparison with computers would be called 'synchronization' whereby the syncing units general have the option to either 'sync' from A to B or vice versa, or to sync A and B at the same time. Where the transnational legal process concerns the process of domestication,

9 Much of the groundwork was already done by regime theorists (Rittberger 1993) and neoliberal institutionalists (Keohane 1984) who also drew a closer link between international relations and international law. Robert Keohane and Oran Young call for an interdisciplinary IR/IL project, was pursued for a while by legal and interdisciplinary scholars such as Beck (1996) and Slaughter et al. (1998). The IR/IL approach seems to have lost of much of its popularity among legal scholarship and the (inter)disciplinary development is more towards re-entrenchment.

however the difference between the process of downloading and the process of domestication becomes unclear.

Hillary Charlesworth and Christine Chinkin have referred to 'more radical suggestions [that] have been made for new methods of international law-making that focus less on the role of states and consider the actions of other actors within the international arena …' (Charlesworth and Chinkin 2000: 172). One of such propositions would allow 'the activities of NGOs as constitutive of practice for determining rules of customary international law' (Charlesworth and Chinkin 2000: 172). Such a proposition is perhaps not as radical as Charlesworth and Chinkin suggest, as article 38 of the Statute of the International Court of Justice (ICJ) does not specify international custom, as evidence of a general *state* practice accepted as law. Nevertheless, a different intersubjective constructed interpretation of article 38 of the ICJ Statute as Charlesworth and Chinking do, includes 'evidence of a general non-state practice' and that is a novel perspective on the sources of international law. In that way, non-state entities would not merely be vehicles in a transnational legal process but figures in that process. Non-state entities like the International Committee of the Red Cross would not only perform acts of codification, but instead their acts would become intrinsically relevant to a world order process of law-making; as much as the opinion and practices of armed opposition groups would become relevant to the interpretation of the land-mine ban treaty and the formation of customary international law in that field; the 'peace' treaties concluded between these groups and governments, would become relevant to the interpretation of the law of peace and armed conflict or international humanitarian law.

According to ICRC President Jakob Kellenberger: 'it is rather obvious that the disrespect of international humanitarian law by non-state actors is an enormous problem.'[10] That problem, however, is not simply a problem that states can unilaterally solve. It is a problem that transcends the conventional international armed conflict and includes an amalgam of non-state actors. The problem can also no longer be confined to questions concerning the rights and duties of these actors as defined and enforced by their state counterparts.

The problem goes to the theoretical and conceptual foundations of international law and concerns the question whether the opinions and practices of these actors are taken into account when determining the normative state of the art of humanitarian law.[11] Can an effective and functional system of humanitarian law any longer be based on the difference between law-makers and law-takers? Who determines who is in and who is out? The problematic is best illustrated by the classical opinion of Sir Hersch Lauterpacht:

---

10 Simon Bradley, Genfer Konventionen an neuen Entwicklungen anpassen, swissinfo.ch, accessed 12 August 2009. '*Es ist ziemlich klar, dass die Nicht-Respektierung des humanitären Völkerrechts durch nicht-staatliche Akteure ein großes Problem ist.*'

11 For a discussion of the practical and theoretical considerations of this problem see Noortmann (2010) Chesterman and Lehnardt (2007), Pfanner (2006) and Scahill (2007).

> The rules of the Geneva Convention apply intoto if the legitimate Government is a party to them and if the *recognized* insurgents formally accept and apply the provisions of these conventions. Failing this, the accepted customary rules of war apply as between the parties in this as in other spheres. (Lauterpacht 1955: 212, emphasis added)

In the same manner, one could take the formulated opinions and actions of normative entrepreneurs, interest organizations or companies into account in the formulation, interpretation and implementation of world society norms. The problem is one of legitimacy as Cedric Ryngaert correctly asserts in Chapter 4. We must critically question whether rules can apply to institutions and individuals, which have not had the change to participate in the formulation of those rules. The 'take-it-or-leave-it' approach might apply to the politics of international humanitarian law, but should not refrain scholars from voicing a different opinion on the growing gap between those who make the rules of international law and those who are supposed to take them.

The question than, as to who is to be considered relevant for that (trans)formative socio-legal process, is a conceptual and perhaps normative one rather than a practical one. It is not 'the range and diversity of non-state actors [that] make it impossible to do more than generalize about their law-making activities' as Boyle and Chinkin (2007: 44) contend, but the adherence to the politics of formulating their 'contribution' in a language that is alien to the determination of the role of states in international law-making. It is not in the research questions we ask, but in the methodological and conceptual tools we employ that we might construct a more participatory orientated approach to the process of law-making. There can be no doubt about the legal questions we have to ask: what role do 'non-state actors play in the constitutive process of legal rules' (Clark Arend 1996: 294–95) or 'can they be accurately described as free-standing participants in international law-making? (Boyle and Chinkin 2007: 44). However, if these questions are investigated from a traditional point of view they are rhetorical at the least and counterproductive at the most. It is remarkable that the bulk of answers to this question are formulated in the exclusive socio-political language of impact and influence. The answer to these questions requires a critical and methodological reconsideration of the hegemonic assumptions of both internationalism and transnationalism. It is in the formulation of a counter hegemonic language, which avoids references to international and transnational arenas that we start constructing a participatory model of world order.

IV. Bringing the 'Participants' Back In

In appraising the methods of international law, Steve Ratner and Anne-Marie Slaughter (2004: 6) conclude that 'perhaps the New Haven's school greatest contribution has been its emphasis on both what actors say and what they do.' The term 'actors' of course begs the question: where Ratner and Slaughter thinking in either the conceptual language of the New Haven School or within the conceptual confinements of any other theoretical discourse.[12] One does not need to reject the term actor or any other term denoting participatory involvement for reasons of terminological purity or New Haven nostalgia, but on the basis of conceptual content.[13] Using the term 'actors' is unfortunately more frequently dictated by terminological fashion than conceptual consideration. The term 'participants' is also not completely immune of that trend. Unfortunately, the concept of 'participants' is perhaps also the least developed and most inconsistent element in the New Haven jurisprudence notwithstanding the crucial function of that concept in the policy-orientated jurisprudence.[14]

'Participants in the world social process are' according to McDougal and Lasswell (1959: 8) 'acting individually in their own behalf and in concert with others with whom they share symbols of common identity and ways of life of varying degrees of elaboration.' From the beginning, the New Haven School made clear that 'participants' was an all-inclusive, non-discriminatory concept containing such diverse participants as individuals, states and social groupings. In response to the suggestion that a 'New' New Haven School was emerging, Michael Reisman, Siegfried Wiessner and Andrew Willard (2007: 578) explained some 50 years later, the New Haven School's preoccupation with 'participants' as a 'conceptual technique for mapping relevant social processes':

> The Participants in any decision process include those formally endowed with decision competence, such as executives, legislators and judges, and all those other actors who, though not endowed with formal competence, may nonetheless play important roles in influencing decision outcomes. In international decision, this means examining, in addition to formal international organizations, state officials, non-governmental organizations, interest groups, gangs and individuals who act on behalf of other participants and their own.[15]

From the perspective of the policy-orientated approach, there is little doubt that at the lowest (or should one say highest) level of mapping the legal system as a

12 One could be thinking for example of the Actor-Network Theory or Social Movement Theory. See for example Keck and Sikkink (1998), Tarrow (2005), Clark (2001), Boli and Thomas (1999), van Schendelen (2002), Arts (1998), Noortmann (2006). These theories will not be discussed explicitly in this chapter.

13 Another frequently employed phrase by policy-orientated scholarship is 'members of a community'. See for example Wiessner and Willard (2004).

14 The failure to include a substantial part of the case book of the New Haven School to participants reflects that inconsistency and constitutes a serious flaw in the teaching of policy-orientated jurisprudence. See McDougal and Reisman (1981).

15 On the concept of 'participants' see also Chen (1989), Higgins (1994) McDougal and Reisman (1985) and Reisman (1999).

participatory social process it is the individual human being that constitutes the first 'participant', 'actor', 'member' or 'agency'. In addition to the individual is a standardized element in any contemporary enumeration of non-state actors; however, there is no conceptual barrier to direct any research focuses to institutionalized actors, activities and arenas.[16] The main difference between the 'participants' and 'actors' approach is not one of empirical focus but one of concept and theoretical outlook, it is not the unit of reference, but the unit of analysis.

Therefore, one must critically ask what 'New' New Haven School means when referring to 'a *flexible* approach to *actors of* international law [that has] its roots in the work of core New Haven scholars.' The question that comes to mind when contemplating Laura Dickinson's (2007) terminology is whether the 'New' New Haven term 'actor' equals the 'Old' New Haven term 'participant', or whether the younger generation is simply conforming to modern and trendy terminology or whether it signifies a less radical and less critical understanding of the role of the partakers and stakeholders in the world order's authoritative decision making process.

Participants, both individuals as well as organizations and institutions, were and still are 'the 'shapers' and 'sharers' of power' according to Lasswell and McDougal (1992). They could not have put it more parsimoniously. In scrutinizing institutionalized 'shapers' and 'sharers' of power McDougal and Lasswell roughly distinguish between: (1) communities, including nation-states[17], sub-national communities (provinces, metropolitan areas, localities) and intergovernmental organizations, (2) classes and (3) interest groups, which are 'classified according to the scope value at stake' (Lasswell and McDougal 1992: 421). The later group, which has been labelled as non-governmental by other policy-orientated scholarship contains all organizations and associations beyond the individual and the governmental (Chen 1989). Perhaps the most interesting element of the conceptualization of 'participants' is that one is able to categorize participants and participation along the lines of the eight different value categories or preferred events identified by the New Haven School: *Power*, *Affection, Wealth*, *Well-Being*, *Enlightenment*, *Rectitude*, *Respect* and *Skill*; (Chen 1989: 16, Lasswell and McDougal 1992: 31). If we exclude – for the sake of argument – possible overlap between values and participants, which intend to pursue more than one of preferred events, that is to say, assuming that participants are exclusively

---

16 For a recent reconsideration of the political and legal role of the masses in contemporary world public order see the discourses on 'empire' and 'multitude' (Hardt and Negri 2001, 2000, Borón 2005, Douzinas 2007, Marks 2003, Passavant 2004, Petras and Veltmeyer 2005).

17 Policy-orientated scholars may have moderated the role of the nation state in the world order processes; they have never excluded the state from 'world order processes'. Overall Policy-orientated scholarship has time and again acknowledged states as the 'major and most significant participants' (McDougal and Feliciano 1961, see also McDougal Lasswell 1959, Reisman and Willard 1988, Wiessner and Willard 2004.

concerned with one value, the following categories of institutionalized participants can be associated with one the respective values indicated above: political parties and liberation movements, educational organizations and epistemic communities (*enlightenment*); business, trade and financial organizations (*wealth*); pelief and development organizations (*well-being*); professional, sports and leisure organizations (*skills*); family and gender organizations (*affection*); religious organizations (*rectitude*) and human dignity organizations (*respect*).

Linking actors and values in order to determine their practice as relevant to the constitution of customary international law for example would offer a solution to Christine Chinkin's (2003) problem to 'determin[e] which of the [activities of the] literally thousands of NGOs in existence … would be relevant as evidence of practice'. That methodological problem extents to the appraisal of *opinio iuris*.[18]

The preferred values of the respective participants are neither to be confused with their functions in the *process* of authoritative decision-making (intelligence, promoting, prescribing, invoking, applying, terminating and appraising) nor with the manipulative *tools* they employ for realizing preferred events: influence, pressure and coercion, which could form additional or separate analytical tools for appraising participatory impact. Each and every participant is theoretically capable to exercise one of the functions through one of the manipulative tools, depending solely on the contextual status of the participant and their material and immaterial resources.

An actor with actual or potential influence is a candidate for participation in the decision-making process and by grasping the totality of the international process of decision-making, policy-orientated jurisprudence enables scholars, advisers and decision-makers to be maximally effective while empowering non-state entities to play a greater role in decision-making. The individuals and organization can then be taken as involved in different modalities of participation, which vary from context to context (Wiessner and Willard 2004).

V. Conclusions or a Trans-Disciplinary and Critical After Thought

In conclusion, I will balance the policy-orientated opinion by one member of the International Court of Justice in the beginning of this article with a 'modern positivist' opinion from another member of the Court: 'The New Haven approach, by conflating law, political science and politics plain and simple, fails to provide the very guidance that real-life decision makers expect from their lawyers' (Simma and Paulus 2004). Positivism and policy-orientated jurisprudence is generally

18 One is reminded here that the relevance of state practice is considered to differ according to the relative position of states, that ias to say, whether states have or have not the political or material capacity to practice a specific behaviour. The position of land-locked states in the formation of the territorial sea is intrinsically different than coastal states, as are the practices of states with nuclear testing capacity.

considered to constitute mutually exclusive approaches. The notions of providing 'guidance to real life decision makers' and 'providing guidance to scholar, adviser or decision-maker for directing attention to the relevant features of particular contexts for purposes of inquiry and effective intervention' (Wiessner and Willard 2004:48) not only reveals a different conception of the function of legal education but also a completely different *Weltanschauung*.

The development of a methodology for the determination of international legal rule, which 'draw[s] on the insights of both positivism and the New Haven School while attempting to avoid the pitfalls of these approaches' (Clark Arend 1999: 87) can therefore not be completed without serious conceptual amputations. In Anthony Clark Arend's *Towards an Understanding of International Legal Rules*, that amputation is found in the removal of the concept of participants, since the concept of 'members of the international community' ... is too vague to put into practice. Moreover, at present international law is created by states. As a consequence, he considers the decision-making elites in the states as the pre-dominant actors in the law-creating process (Clark Arend 1999: 89). It seems to me that this amputation of participants and the implicit return to the subject-object dichotomy was precisely what Rosalyn Higgins was warning us of, but it demonstrates beyond the shadow of a doubt what we loose, which is not always clear in the rhetoric of transnational influence and impact on that decision-making process called law.

A first step and perhaps crucial step on the way to a more participatory orientated approach to the process of law-making is found in asking the right questions; questions that transcend the exclusive socio-political analytical terminology which most international law scholars amazingly have adopted, to the involvement of non-state entities: 'can they be accurately described as free-standing participants in international law-making? (Boyle and Chinkin 2007: 44). Those international legal scholars, who are willing to investigate these questions, cannot but adopt a non-traditional outlook and a methodology towards law-making that also solicits the cooperation of non-state actors.

In opting for a participatory approach to the creation of law, we cannot but avoid to adopt two essential 'guiding themes' of the New Haven Approach and which should with all due respect be leading principles in the research approach of every scholar, who is genuinely interested in understanding that normative complexity of multi-actor law-making processes: 'trans-disciplinarity' and 'critical' (Dickinson 2007, Koh 2007).

In 2002, I already made a plea for an interdisciplinary research program on non-state actors (Noortmann 2002). Today, I must reconsider that suggestion and propose a trans-disciplinary program. Such a program would foster 'the elaboration of a new language, logic, and concepts to permit genuine dialogue' (Thompson Klein 2004: 516) very much in the same way as McDougal and Lasswell developed their approach that transcended the disciplinary confinements of international law and international relations. Such an approach facilitates the identification of stakeholder and community values, interest and inputs in the social process of norm formation.

A critical approach is necessary, because it reminds us to be conscious of the power political dimensions and choices involved in our subject of research. The term non-state actor for example is everything but politically neutral as indicated above. The political dimension in our discursive languages must be clear. In this respect, one must applaud all approaches that do not conceal anti-participatory politics of internationalism behind the veil of transnationalism and non-state actors.

References

Alfredsson, G. and Ring, R. (eds). 2001. *The Inspection Panel of the World Bank; A Different Complaints Procedure*. Den Haag: Martinus Nijhoff Publishers.

Alston, P. (ed.) 2005. *Non-State Actors and Human Rights*. Oxford and New York: Oxford University Press.

Alston, P. 2005. The 'Not-a-Cat' Syndrom: Can the International Human Rights Regime Accommodate Non-State Actors?, in *Non-State Actors and Human Rights*, edited by P. Alston. Oxford and New York: Oxford University Press, 3–36.

Arts, B. 1998. *The Political Influence of Global NGOs – Case Studies on the Climate and Biodiversity Conventions*. Utrecht: International Books.

Arts, B., Noortmann, M. and Reinalda, B. (eds). 2001. *Non-State Actors in International Relations*. Aldershot: Ashgate Publishing Company.

Beck, R.J. 1996. International Law and International Relations: The Prospects for Interdisciplinary Research, in *International Rules; Approaches from International Law and International Relations*, edited by R.J. Beck, A.C. Arend and R.D.V. Lugt. Charlottesville, Virginia: Oxford University Press.

Beck, R.J., Arend, A.C. and Lugt, R.D.V. (eds). 1996. *International Rules; Approaches from International Law and International Relations*. Charlottesville, Virginia: Oxford University Press.

Bennet, A.L. 1995. *International Organizations – Principles and Issues*. London: Prentice-Hall International.

Bianchi, A. and Naqvi, Y. 2004. *Enforcing International Law Norms Against Terrorism*. Oxford: Hart Publishing.

Boli, J. and Thomas, G.M. (eds). 1999. *Constructing World Culture*. Stanford: Stanford University Press.

Borón, A. 2005. *Empire and Imperialism: A Critical Reading of Michael Hardt and Antonio Negri*. London and New York: Zed Books.

Boyle, A.E. and Chinkin, C.M. 2007. *The Making of International Law*. Oxford and New York: Oxford University Press.

Brownlie, I. 2003. *Principles of Public International Law*. Oxford: Clarendon Press.

Bull, H. 2002. *The Anarchical Society*. Houndmills: Palgrave.
Charlesworth, H. and Chinkin, C.M. 2000. *The Boundaries of International Law: A Feminist Analysis*. Manchester: Manchester University Press.
Charney, J.I. 1983. Transnational Corporations and Developing Public International Law. *Duke Law Journal*, 748–788.
Chen, L.-C. 1989. *An Introduction to Contemporary International Law – A Policy-Oriented Perspective*. New Haven: Yale University Press.
Chesterman, S. and Lehnardt, C. (eds). 2007. *From Mercenaries to Market: The Rise and Regulation of Private Military Companies*. Oxford and New York: Oxford University Press.
Chinkin, C. 2003. The Role of Non-Governmental Organizations in Standard Setting, Monitoring and Implementation of Human Rights, in *The Changing World of International Law in the Twenty-First Century, A Tribute to the Late Kenneth R. Simmons*, edited by J.J. Norton et al. The Hague: Kluwer Law International, 45–66.
Clark Arend, A. 1996. Towards an Understanding of International Legal Rules, in *International Rules: Approaches from International Law and International Relations,* edited by R.J. Beck, A.C. Arend and R.D.V. Lugt. Charlottesville, Virginia: Oxford University Press, 289–310.
Clark Arend, A. 1999. *Legal Rules and International Society*. Oxford: Oxford University Press.
Clark, W. 2001. *Activism in the Public Sphere: Exploring the Discourse of Political Participation*. Aldershot: Ashgate.
D'Amato, A. 1961. Studies in World Public Order, book review. *Harvard Law Review*, 75, 458–459.
Dickinson, L. 2007. Toward a New New Haven School of International Law? *Yale Journal of International Law,* 32, 547–552.
Douzinas, C. 2007. *Human Rights and Empire: The Political Philosophy of Cosmopolitanism*. New York: Routledge-Cavendish.
Hardt, M. and Negri, A. 2000. *Empire*. Cambridge, Mass.: Harvard University Press.
Hardt, M. and Negri, A. 2004. *Multitude: War and Democracy in the Age of Empire*. New York: The Penguin Press.
Higgins, R. 1994. *Problems and Process: International Law and How We Use It.* Oxford: Clarendon Press.
Higgott, R.A., Underhill, G.R.D. et al. (eds). 2000. *Non-State Actors and Authority in the Global System*. London: Routledge.
Hobe, S. and Kimminich, O. 2004. *Einführung in das Völkerrecht*. Tübingen: A. Francke Verlag.
Huntington, S.P. 1973. Transnational Organizations in World Politics. *World Politics*, 253, 333–368.
Hurrell, A. 2007. *On Global Order: Power, Values, and the Constitution of International Society.* Oxford and New York: Oxford University Press.

Jenks, W.C. 1972. Multinational Entities in the Law of Nations, in *Transnational Law in a Changing Society; Essays in Honor of Philip C. Jessup*, edited by W. Friedmann, L. Henkin and O.J. Lissitzyn. New York: Columbia University Press: 70–83.

Jessup, P.C. 1956. *Transnational Law*. New Haven: Yale University Press.

Josselin, D. and Wallace, W. (eds). 2001. *Non-State Actors in World Politics*. Hampshire: Palgrave.

Judge, A.J.N. and Skjelbaek, K. 1975. Transnational Associations and their Functions, in *Functionalism: Theory and Practice in International Relations,* edited by A.J.R. Groom and P. Taylor. London: London University Press, 190–224.

Keck, M.E. and Sikkink, K. 1998. *Activists Beyond Borders – Advocacy Networks in International Politics.* London: Cornell University Press.

Keohane, R.O. and Nye, J.S. 1977. *Power and Interdependence: World Politics in Transition*. Boston: Little Brown.

Keohane, R.O. 1984. *After Hegemony; Cooperation and Discord in the World Political Economy*. Princeton: Princeton University Press.

Koh, H.H. 2007. Is there a New New Haven School of International Law? *Yale Journal of International Law*, 32, 559–557.

Koskenniemi, M. 2001. *The Gentle Civilizer of Nations: The Rise and Fall of International Law 1870–1960*. Cambridge: Cambridge University Press.

Koskenniemi, M. 2006. What is International Law For?, in *International Law*, edited by M.D. Evans. Oxford: Oxford University Press, 57–82.

Krasner, S.D. 1995. Power Politics, Institutions and Transnational Relations. Bringing Transnational Relations Back In, in *Non-State Actors, Domestic Structures and International Institutions*, edited by T. Risse-Kappen. Cambridge: Cambridge University Press, 257–297.

Ku, C. and Diehl, P.F. 2003. *International Law: Classic and Contemporary Readings*. Boulder, Colo.: Lynne Rienner Publishers.

Lasswell, H.D. and McDougal, M.S. 1992. *Jurisprudence for a Free Society*. New Haven and Dordrecht: Martinus Nijhoff Publishers.

Lauterpacht, H. 1955. *Oppenheim's International Law*. London: Longmans, Green and Co. Ltd.

Linklater, A. 2007. *Critical International Relations Theory: Citizenship, State and Humanity*. New York, NY: Routledge.

Marks, S. 2003. Empire's Law. *Indiana Journal of Global Legal Studies*, 10 (1), 449–466.

Marks, S. 2008. *International Law on the Left: Re-Examining Marxist Legacies*. Cambridge and New York: Cambridge University Press.

McDougal, M.S. and Feliciano F.P. 1961. *Law and Minimum Public Order*. New Haven: Yale University Press.

McDougal, M.S. and Lasswell, H.D. 1959. The Identification and Appraisal of Diverse Systems of Public Order. *American Journal of International Law*, 531, 1–29.

McDougal, M.S. and Reisman, W.M. 1981. *International Law in Contemporary Perspective – The Public Order of the World Community*. New York: The Foundation Press, Inc.

McDougal, M.S. and Reisman, W.M. 1985. *Power and Policy in Quest of Law.* Dordrecht: Martinus Nijhoff Publishers.

Noortmann, M. 2001. Non-State Actors in International Law, in *Non-State Actors in International Relations*, edited by B. Arts, M. Noortmann and B. Reinalda. Aldershot: Ashgate.

Noortmann, M. 2002. Globalisation, Global Governance and Non-State Actors: Researching Beyond the State. *International Law FORUM du Droit International* 4, 36–40.

Noortmann, M. 2005. *Enforcing International Law; From Self-help to Self-contained Regimes*. Aldershot: Ashgate.

Noortmann, M. 2006. The Role of Civil Society in International Institutional Reform: Decreasing the Private by Increasing the Private, in *International Institutional Reform*, edited by A.A. Fijalkowski. Cambridge: Cambridge University Press, 320–328.

Noortmann, M. 2010 (forthcoming). Aufständische Gruppen und Militärische Privatunternehmen: Theoretische und Praktische Überlegungen zur Position der Nicht-staatlichen Bewaffneten Gruppen im Humanitären Völkerrecht, in *60 Jahre Genfer Konventionen*, edited by H.J. Heintze and K. Ipsen. Berlin: Springer Verlag.

Passavant, P.A. 2004. From Empire's Law to the Multitudes Rights: Law, Representation, Revolution, in *Empire's New Clothes: Reading Hardt and Negri*, edited by P.A. Passavant and J. Dean. New York: Routledge: 95–120.

Petras, J. and Veltmeyer, H. 2005. *Empire with Imperialism; The Globalization Dynamics of Neo-Liberal Capitalism*. London: Zed Books Ltd.

Pfanner, T. (ed.) 2006. Private Military Companies. *International Review of the Red Cross*. Geneva: International Committee of the Red Cross.

Pries, L. 2008. *Rethinking Transnationalism: The Meso-Link of Organizations*. Milton Park, Abingdon, Oxon and New York: Routledge.

Ratner, S.R. and Slaughter, A.-M. (eds). 2004. *The Methods of International Law*. Washington: The American Society of International Law.

Reisman, M.W. and Willard, A.R. (eds). 1988. *International Incidents: The Law That Counts in World Politics*. Princeton: Princeton University Press.

Reisman, W.M. 1999. *Law in Brief Encounters*. New Haven: Yale University Press.

Reisman, W.M., Wiessner, M.S. and Willard, A. 2007. The New Haven School: A Brief Introduction. *Yale Journal of International Law*, 322, 575–582.

Risse, T. 2002. Constructivism and International Institutions: Towards Conversations Across Paradigms in *Political Science; State of the Discipline,* edited by I. Katznelson and H.V. Milner. New York: W.W. Norton & Company, 597–623.

Risse-Kappen, T. (ed.) 1995. *Bringing Transnational Relations Back In: Non-State Actors, Domestic Structures, and International Institutions*. Cambridge and New York: Cambridge University Press.

Risse-Kappen, T. 1995. Bringing Transnational Relations Back In: Introduction, in *Bringing Transnational Relations Back In: Non-State Actors, Domestic Structures, and International Institutions*, edited by T. Risse-Kappen. Cambridge and New York, Cambridge University Press, 3–33.

Rittberger, V. (ed.) 1993. *Regime Theory and International Relations*. Oxford: Oxford University Press.

Scahill, J. 2007. *Blackwater: The Rise of the World's Most Powerful Mercenary Army*. New York: Nation Books.

Schwarzenberger, G. 1952. *A Manual of International Law*. London: Stevens & Sons Ltd.

Shaw, M. 2003. *International Law*. Cambridge: Cambridge University Press.

Simma, B. and Paulus, A.L. 2004. The Responsibility of Individuals for Human Rights Abuses in Internal Conflicts: A Positivist View, in *The Methods of International Law*, edited by S.R. Ratner and A.-M. Slaughter. Washington: The American Society of International Law, 23–46.

Tarrow, S.G. 2005. *The New Transnational Activism*. New York: Cambridge University Press.

Thompson Klein, J. 2004. Prospects for Transdisciplinarity. *Futures,* 36, 515–526.

Van Apeldoorn, B. 2004. Theorizing the Transnational: A Historical Materialist Approach. *Journal of International Relations and Development*, 7, 142–176.

Van Schendelen, R. 2002. *Machiavelli in Brussels; The Art of Lobbying the EU*. Amsterdam: Amsterdam University Press.

Wallace, R.M. 2006. *International Law*. London: Sweet & Maxwell Ltd.

Walt, S.M. 2002. The Enduring Relevance of the Realist Tradition, in *Political Science; State of the Discipline*, edited by I. Katznelson and H.V. Milner. New York: W.W. Norton & Company, 197–234.

Waltz, K.N. 1979. *Theory of International Politics*. Reading, Mass.: Addison-Wesley Pub. Co.

Weber, C. 2005. *International Relations Theory: A Critical Introduction*. London and New York: Routledge.

Wendt, A. 1999. *Social Theory of International Politics*. Cambridge and New York: Cambridge University Press.

Wiessner, S. and Willard, A.R. 2004. Policy-Oriented Jurisprudence and Human Rights Abuses in Internal Conflict: Toward a World Public Order of Human Dignity, in *The Methods of International Law*, edited by A.-M. Slaughter and S.R. Ratner. Washington: American Society of International Law, 47–78.

Chapter 8

International Law-Making by Non-State Actors: Changing the Model or Putting the Phenomenon into Perspective?

Jean d'Aspremont

Introduction

The international legal system has weathered sweeping changes over the last decades, for new participants have emerged. Indeed, international law-making and law-enforcement processes have become multi-layered and the number of actors involved herein has proven unprecedented. This growing importance of non-state actors at the law-making and law-enforcement levels has generated a lot of new scholarly studies on the topic.[1] While it has remained uncontested that non-state actors like individuals, insurgents, multinational corporations and even terrorist groups are nowadays – albeit differently – playing an important role on the international plane, international legal scholars have failed to identify what really has changed in the international legal system.

Swayed by the impression that the emergence of non-state actors constitutes an utterly new and radical change in the international arena, international legal scholars have been prone to put the existing model of international law into question and claim that international law-making processes had become more heterogeneous from the standpoint of the actors involved. By focusing on the question of the law-making status of these new actors, it is the ambition of this chapter to show that the failure of the current international legal system to accommodate the phenomenon of non-state actors is as much the consequence of its inherent limits as a direct effect of the inclination of scholars to magnify the new phenomena which they witness. After an empirical appraisal of the extent to which non-state actors wield some law-making powers at the international level (II), this chapter will attempt

1 Just to mention a few: Andreopoulos and Kabasakal Arat 2006, Arts and Noortmann 2001, Boyer and Drache 1996, Boyle and Chinkin 2007, Clapham 2006, Danilenko 1993, Heinz 1997, Franck 1999, Genugten 2006, Gowlland-Debbas and Tehindrazanarivelo 2004, Heere 2003, Held 1995, Higgott and Underhill, 2000, Kunugi and Schweitz 1999, Meron 2006, Slaughter 2004, Wolfrum and Röben 2005.

to evaluate the degree to which the alleged inadequacy of the current legal system is directly affected by our respective perceptions of the role played by non-state actors in international law. In doing so, this section will try to demonstrate that much of the controversy yielded by the law-making status of non-state actors stems from an attempt to bolster the scope, the expertise and the legitimacy of international legal scholarship (III). This chapter ends with a few remarks on the consequences of the absence of any law-making status of non-state actors on their overall place in the international legal system. On this occasion, it will be argued that non-state actors, instead of being seen as law-makers, should be rather seen as law-consumers, *that is to say*, entities which, instead of making the law, constitute great consumers of it (IV).

The inquiry that is undertaken here cannot be seriously carried out without formulating an important preliminary caveat as to the relativity of any conclusion regarding the status of non-state actors in international law. Indeed, it is acknowledged that the manner in which one construes the role of non-state actors is intrinsically relative, for it hinges on the each scholar's respective understanding of law. This chapter accordingly starts with some introductory remarks about the necessity to clearly explain how we understand the international legal system before venturing into any examination of the status of the actors involved therein (I).

It is important to note that, for the sake of our inquiry, the question of the international legal personality is seen as incidental and is thus left aside. Indeed, from the functionalist perspective endorsed by the International Court of Justice in its advisory opinion on the *Reparation for Injuries Suffered in the Service of the United Nations*[2], international legal personality usually follows the attribution of rights and duties to non-state entities. It does not necessarily precede them. In that sense, the question of the international legal personality, being only the necessary consequence of the attribution of rights and duties to an actor, does not seem to constitute the appropriate lens through which the law-making status of these actors must be examined.

I. Preliminary Caveats: Which International Legal System?

It cannot be disputed that the manner in which scholars construe the role and status of non-state actors is, to a very large extent, *dependant upon their own understanding of international law as a whole*. Some critical distance is accordingly indispensible, for we must acknowledge that each scholar's elementary understanding of international law is instrumental in his perception of the role and status of non-state actors.

The relativity of the manner in which one understands the law-making status of non-state actors can be illustrated by the diverging visions provided by the

2 ICJ Rep 1949, 11 April 1949, 174, at 178–179.

mainstream schools of thought in international law.[3] Each of them carries a different conception of the role and status of non-state actors. For instance, (Cattaneo and Parker 2008) liberal approaches – which place the individual at the centre – are prone to recognize a role and a status to non-state actors.[4] The same, although for different reasons, is true for constitutionalist approaches[5] or those based on global administrative law.[6] The latter purports to identify overarching principles that regulate the behavior of regulating agencies in global governance. In contrast, positivists defend the continued relevance of inter-state international law and argue that current categories are sufficient to grapple with the problems raised by the growing role of non-state actors (d'Aspremont 2009). Yet, positivist accounts of the position of individuals in international law are not always uniform, This is well illustrated by the Kelsenian approaches which provide a unique understanding at odds with mainstream positivism, for the monism defended by Kelsen allows one to grant non-state actors a clear legal status under international law (Kammerhofer 2009). Likewise, it is no surprise that those that have construed international law as a process – that is to say, those belonging to the so-called policy-orientated school – have been prone to categorize these actors as 'participants' (Lasswell and McDougal 1992).[7] Eventually, the critical legal studies (CLS) – who classically advocate the indeterminacy of legal categories – construe the understanding of the role and status of non-state actors as merely reflecting how one wants power to be distributed within the international legal order (Koskenniemi 2007).

The diverging conceptions of the role of non-state actors can also hinge on some geographical perspectives in that the understanding of the role and status of non-state actors is fragmented along regional lines. For instance, the pragmatism that permeates American legal scholarship underpins the great amenability of American scholars towards the recognition of a role and status to non-state actors. By contrast, French scholars, who are commonly more formalist, have generally proved more reluctant to embrace new categories that accommodate the growing role of non-state actors (Jouannet 2006). The same may be true, although for different reasons, with respect to Asian scholars who are very attached to the idea of sovereignty (d'Aspremont 2008). The constitutionalist inclination of German

3 For a brief account of the various mainstream traditions of international law, see (Simma and Paulus 1998).

4 For some liberal approaches, see (Franck 1995, Allott 1998, Slaughter 1995, 2000).

5 See for example (Tomuschat 1999, Delbrück and Heinz 1997, De Wet 2006a, 2006b, Mosler 1982, Peters 2006, Simma 1994, Dupuy 2005, Weiler 2004).

6 See the project carried out at New York University (http://www.iilj.org/global_adlaw/). See the special issue of the 37 *New York Journal of International Law and Politics* 2005, n. 4. See also (Krisch 2006, Kingsbury and Krisch 2006).

7 On a criticism of this movement, see for example Richard Falk (1995) and Math Noortmann in the previous chapter.

scholars that one can single out in the German school of international law is not without effect on their vision of the law-making status of non-state actors.[8]

It will not come as a surprise that one's understanding of the role and status of non-state actors can eventually be influenced by the substantive features of the area of law in which one is specialized. In other words, the conception of the role and status of non-state actors may also hinge on the content of the substantive rules at stake. This may first be influenced by the overall function of the rules concerned. But this may more simply be the result of the actual role and status of non-state actors within that area of law.[9]

These few examples suffice to show the relativity of any inquiry about the law-making role of non-state actors. To a large extent, one's conception of the law-making status of non-state actors hinges on his understanding of law as a whole. The relativism to which we are led could leave the impression that any inquiry about the law-making role of non-state actors is futile and useless. Indeed, this relativity may convey the idea that, after all, this question is all contingent and no firm conclusion can ever be formulated, for they are premised on each observer's basic understanding of law. This radical scepticism to which relativism leads largely echoes some of the basic tenets of the critical legal studies in international law (Koskenniemi 2007). This chapter nonetheless backs away from such a radical scepticism, as it adopts an approach that seeks to confront the existing practice with the positivist and systemic conception of international law. More particularly, it is the ambition of this chapter to appraise whether the classical positivist conception of international law can accommodate the recent practice pertaining to the rise of new actors.

In this respect, it is important to explain that from the perspective of the positivistic standpoint adopted here, international law is not construed as *given* but as a formal language *created* by those that have been granted a law-making power by the international legal system. From that perspective – which echoes a Hartian understanding of international law (Hart 1997, d'Aspremont 2009) – international law *presupposes the existence of an international legal system*. In other words, the system is a constitutive element of law, for there can hardly be any law – except in some prehistoric and rudimentary form – without a system.[10] In that sense, the creation of law – and hence the determination of those entrusted with a law-making power – is regulated by the system. Such a conception of international law does not amount to saying that the legal system is completely hermetical to external

8 On the German approaches to international law, see the special issue of the *German Yearbook of International Law* (2007), vol. 50.

9 Compare for instance the diverging functions ascribed to the concept of attribution of a conduct to an individual in the international case-law. Comp. ICTY (Appeals Chamber), *Prosecutor v Dusko Tadic* (IT-94-1), 15 July 1999, paras. 99 ff. and ICJ, Application of the Convention on the Prevention and Punishment of the Crime of Genocide (*Bosnia and Herzegovina v. Serbia and Montenegro*), Merits, 26 February 2007, paras 396 ff.

10 For some refinement of Hart's theory, see (Raz 1979; 1994, Coleman 2001).

factors like the practice. The positivist approach embraced here assumes that there cannot be any legal system that is not effective, that is when the addressees of the norms and those empowered to apply them do not abide by the rules of the system (Hart 1997: 107–110), thereby making the practice a central element of the understanding of that system.

It is in the light of the abovementioned conception of the legal system that the law-making status of non-state actors is evaluated here. In doing so, the present chapter will try to evaluate whether classical positivist model – and the elementary blueprints on which the latter rests – have been put into jeopardy by the emergence of new actors on the world plane.

II. Empirical Observations: State-Centrism of International Law-Making Processes

It is beyond doubt, that over the last two decades non-state actors have been expending their say in international law-making processes and nowadays constitute an important 'material source' of law.[11] They also potentially wield some influence in the review[12] and amendments[13] procedures of conventional instruments. While the extent of their influence is probably new, the role of non-state actors cannot in any way be considered as unprecedented. Steve Charnovitz (1997) has shrewdly demonstrated that NGOs have been involved in international law-making for more than 200 years. In fact, NGOs have aroused the initiative or have been granted a formal participatory role in various international law-making conferences as early as the nineteenth century. To name but a few, this is well illustrated by the role of the American Peace Society in the first plan for the Permanent Court of Arbitration (Charnovitz 1997); the role of the Geneva Public Welfare Society in the adoption of the 1864 Geneva Convention for the Amelioration of the Condition of the Wounded in Armies in the Field (Bennet 2005); the role of all the peace societies which sent representatives to the First and Second Hague Peace Conferences (Rosenne 2001) the role of the Inter-Parliamentary Union and the World Court League in the establishment of the Permanent Court of International Justice (Hudson 1943); and the occasional role of NGOs in the committees and conferences of the League of Nations (Zimmern 1939). In the same period, a similar role was played by the private sector on several occasions, as is illustrated

11 On the concept of 'Material source', see (Fitzmaurice 1958, Oppenheim 1955: 24).

12 See Article 12 of the Convention on the Prohibition of the Use, Stockpiling, Production and Transfer or Anti-Personnel Mines and on Their Destruction (adopted 18 September 1997, entered into force 1 March 1999) *36 ILM* 1507 and the Dublin Convention on Cluster Munitions (adopoted 30 May 2008, not yet in force) CCM/77.

13 See Article 13 of the Convention on the Prohibition of the Use, Stockpiling, Production and Transfer or Anti-Personnel Mines and on Their Destruction.

by the meetings of the International Telegraph Union (Meyers 1914, Codding 1952), the annual conferences of the International Labour Organization (Jenks 1937)[14] or the Pan American Conferences (Crawford 1997, Bourne 1999).

Although the role of non-state actors in international law-making processes is not entirely new, it must be acknowledged that the extent of their contribution has undergone a noteworthy increase (Weiss and Gordenker 1996). For instance, their formal presence and participation in international law-making processes has swollen, as is demonstrated by their (potential) involvement within the framework of the UN Economic and Social Council (ECOSOC) (Noortmann 2003), the UN Global Compact (Judge 2000), the UN Human Rights Council,[15] the UN Security Council[16] (to a very limited extent), the World Trade Organization[17] and within the cooperation policies of the European Community with the Group of African, Caribbean and Pacific Countries (ACP countries).[18] Some notorious

14 Article 7.1 of the Constitution of the International Labour Organization (ILO), Paris Peace Conference (28 June 1919).

15 UN General Assembly Indonesia. Badan Pengendalian Dampak Lingkungan. Wilayah Denpasar. (1998). Indonesia: BAPEDAL Wilayah Denpasar institutional strengthening project: project design document. [Denpasar, BAPEDAL Wilayah Denpasar. Res 60/251 (3 April 2006) UN Doc A/*RES/60/251*.

16 This is the so-called Arria formula devised in 1993 whereby Security Council members are allowed to invite other members to an informal meeting which they chair with a view to receiving information from the NGO concerned on a specific issue. For an example, see UN Security Council (UNSC) Resolution 1325 on Women and Peace and Security (31 October 2000) UN Doc S/RES/*1325*.

17 See Article V (2) of the Agreement Establishing the World Trade Organization (adopted 15 April 1994) 33 ILM 1125; see also the Guidelines for Arrangements on Relations with Non-Governmental Organizations (23 July 1996) WTO Doc WT/L/162. See the critical comments of (Boyle and Chinkin 2007, Van den Bossche 2008).

18 See Article 4 of the Partnership Agreement between the members of the African, Caribbean and Pacific Group of states of the one part, and the European Community and its member states, of the other part (signed in Cotonou 23 June 2000) [2000] OJ L 317. The ACP states shall determine the development principles, strategies and models of their economies and societies in all sovereignty. They shall establish, with the Community, the cooperation programmes provided for under this Agreement. However, the parties recognize the complementary role of and potential for contributions by non-state actors to the development process. To this end, under the conditions laid down in this Agreement, non-state actors shall, where appropriate:

- be informed and involved in consultation on cooperation policies and strategies, on priorities for cooperation especially in areas that concern or directly affect them, and on the political dialogue;
- be provided with financial resources, under the conditions laid down in this Agreement in order to support local development processes;
- be involved in the implementation of cooperation project and programmes in areas that concern them or where these actors have a comparative advantage;
- be provided with capacity-building support in critical areas in order to reinforce the

recent convention-making conferences have also weathered a renewed NGO involvement as is illustrated by the conferences leading to the adoption of the 1997 Convention on the Prohibition of the Use, Stockpiling, Production and Transfer or Anti-Personnel Mines and on Their Destruction,[19] the 2008 Convention on Cluster Munitions (Anderson 2000, Cameron and Lawson 1998)[20] or the well-known examples of the processes leading to the adoption of 1984 Torture Convention (Boyle and Chinkin 2007), the 1990 Convention on the Rights of the Child (Price Cohen 1990), and the 1999 Rome Statute of the International Criminal Court.[21] In these situations, it can hardly be denied that non-state actors, through their formal role, have left their imprint in the substance of the rules finally adopted. The same is true with respect to the ILC which has engaged in regular consultations with NGOs, as is illustrated by the work of the Special Rapporteur Eduardo Valencia-Ospina on the Protection of Persons in the Event of Disaster.[22]

The major role of non-state actors in international law-making is not limited to treaty-making procedures. They can also be instrumental in the tentative codification of new rules of customary international law as is exemplified by the International Committee of the Red Cross' (ICRC) study on Customary International Humanitarian Law (Henckaerts 2005) and the report of the International Commission on Intervention and State Sovereignty (Evans and Sahnoun 2001). While the potential impact of the latter still remains unclear and subject to deep

capabilities of these actors, particularly as regards organization and representation, and the establishment of consultation mechanisms including channels of communication and dialogue, and to promote strategic alliances.

19 See Convention on the Prohibition of the Use, Stockpiling, Production and Transfer or Anti-Personnel Mines and on Their Destruction. Preamble: 'Stressing the role of public conscience in furthering the principles of humanity as evidenced by the call for a total ban of anti-personnel mines and recognizing the efforts to that end undertaken by the International Red Cross and Red Crescent Movement, the International Campaign to Ban Landmines and numerous other nongovernmental organizations around the world'. On this convention and the role of non-state actors.

20 See Convention on Cluster Munitions. Preamble: 'Stressing the role of public conscience in furthering the principles of humanity as evidenced by the global call for an end to civilian suffering caused by cluster munitions and recognizing the efforts to that end undertaken by the United Nations, the International Committee of the Red Cross, the Cluster Munitions Coalition and numerous other non-governmental organizations around the world.'

21 See for instance the role of the Coalition for the International Criminal Court, www.iccnow.org/?mod=icchistory (last accessed 22 June 2009).

22 See the Preliminary Report on the protection of persons in the event of disasters, 5 May 2008, A/CN.4/598, para. 6; see the second report on the protection of persons in the event of disasters, 7 May 2009, A/CN.4/615, paras. 10–12.

questioning,[23] the role of the former has been particularly remarkable, however controversial its methodology may have been.

The abovementioned developments, while they are undeniable, do not however suffice to suggest a major upheaval of the entire international law-making system. There is no doubt that, whatever the influence of these non-state actors may be, states remain the exclusive international law-makers. The upstream influence wielded by some non-state actors can help ignite new law-making initiative or orientate ongoing law-making undertakings but this is insufficient to elevate these actors to the status of law-makers. Indeed, no formal international law-making powers have been bestowed upon these actors[24] and states always retain the final word (d'Aspremont 2008).

It is true that, besides internationally personified international organizations, it cannot be excluded that some of these non-state actors may have been endowed with international legal personality. However, as has been explained above, the likelihood that some of them have acquired international legal personality[25] – although to an extent that may be more limited than some have claimed[26] – is less the result of a direct conferral of international legal personality upon non-state actors. Rather it is an indirect consequence stemming from them having rights and duties.[27] That means that these actors may well now have a formal international legal personality derived from their rights and duties but that has not endowed them with any formal and actual law-making powers (Abi-Saab 1987, Weil 1992).

---

23 See the Proceedings of the Société Française pour le Droit International, *La responsabilité de protéger – Colloque de Nanterre* (Paris, Pédone 2008). See also (Stahn 2007).

24 Even within the UN Economic and Social Council (ECOSOC), the status and the role of NGOs remain entirely determined by states. See Merle 2005.

25 *Reparations for Injuries Suffered in the Service of the United Nations* (Advisory Opinion) [1949] ICJ Rep 174. See also La Grand (*Germany v United States*) [2001] ICJ Rep. paras 77 and 89, (Trebilcock and Howse 1999), Giorgio Gaja, 'First Report on Responsibility of International Organizations' UN Doc A/CN.4/532, para 17). For a forceful opinion argument about extending legal personality, see (Green 2008).

26 A lot of controversy has been swirling around the question of the legal personality of the (ICRC), especially following the decision of the International Criminal Tribunal for the Former Yugoslavia (ICTY), Prosecutor *v* Simic et al., Decision on the Prosecution Motion Under Rule 73 for a Ruling Concerning the Testimony of a Witness, 27 July 1999, para 72l. It is worth noting that the unique character of the ICRC has been incidentally recognized in the ILC First report on responsibility of international organizations, A/CN.4/532, 26 March 2003, para 21. A majority of authors seems to concur with the idea that the ICRC is endowed with international legal personality. See for instance (Kamminga 2005, Dominicé 1984).

27 See generally, (Dominicé 1996). In the context of the debate about the responsibility of transnational corporations, see (De Schutter 2006). This has led scholars to deem that the question of international legal personality was described as 'circular', 'sterile' and boiling down to an 'intellectual prison'. See (Reinisch 2005, Clapham 2006: 60).

Moreover, it must be understood that the rights and duties that non-state actors may now hold remain the result of a state-centric law-making process. The question of the international legal personality of these actors should accordingly be seen as separate to the question of their law-making status.

Likewise, individuals and non-governmental organizations are sometimes entitled to institute proceedings against a state before regional Courts.[28] Insurgents and multinational companies can also be party to international arbitral procedures as is illustrated by international commercial arbitration[29] or by the recent award of the Permanent Court of Arbitration in the 2009 arbitration between the Government of Sudan and the Sudan People's Liberation Movement/Army.[30] The standing that individuals, insurgents, multinational companies, and non-governmental organizations may have before these judicial bodies does not confer upon them any law-making power. At most, their initiative can encourage some judges to engage in some form of law-making (Raimondo 2007). But their influence in the institution of the proceedings stands apart from the question of whether they can actually make law.

The inaccuracy of the claim that international law-making processes have proven more diverse and heterogeneous *ratione personae* because of a growing role of non-state actors is also underpinned by the exact opposite phenomenon. Indeed, while the role of non-state actors has swollen, we simultaneously witness that states have reinforced their grip over global law-making processes. A similar feeling is shared by Andrew Clapham. According to him, whether 'globalization is really leading to the demise of nation state is still open to question. It may be argued that, in at least some contexts, the globalization of certain decision-making processes is actually leading to a greater role for the state, and for international law, and international decision-making processes' (Clapham 2006: 5–6). This reinforced state dominance may take various forms. First, it is the result of a more intensive law-making activity through the classical state-centric convention-making system[31]. This is also manifest in the light of the unprecedented resort to

28 See for instance Article 34 of the European Convention for the Protection of Human Rights and Fundamental Freedoms (adopted 4 November 1950, entered into force 3 September 1953) 213 UNTS 222 or the article 5(3) and article 34(6) of the Protocol to the African Charter on Human and Peoples' Rights on the Establishment of an African Court of Human and Peoples' Rights (adopted 10 June 1998, entered into force 25 January 2004) Organization of African Unity (OAU) Doc OAU/LEG/EXP/AFCHPR/PROT (III).

29 See for example the 1965 Convention on the Settlement of Investment Disputes between States and Nationals of Other States (ICSID).

30 See the arbitration between the Government of Sudan and the Sudan People's Liberation Movement/Army, Final Award, 22 July 2009, available at http://www.pca-cpa.org/. The tribunal recognized that arbitration agreement is not an international treaty but boils down to an agreement between the government of Sudan and a political movement. See para. 427.

31 See for instance the area of international economic law (for example the overhaul of the international economic order through the final Act of the 1986–1994 Uruguay Round

existing institutional law-making mechanisms within international organizations where states still wield a sweeping clout and, in particular, a more frequent use by states of the UN Security Council to create wide-ranging and binding rules.[32]

The renewed dominance of states over international law-making processes is not only the upshot of a greater use of the classical channels of law-making. The emergence of new forms of law-making, outside the normal abovementioned blueprints, also contribute to reinforcing the dominance of states. For instance, the development of the so-called 'governmental networks' (Slaughter 2002) illustrates how the power of states has been thriving outside traditional law-making frameworks. It is true that the state itself may be undergoing an internal diversification of its organization and of the allocation of powers within its machinery (Patterson and Afilalo 2008). In that sense, the state is in the midst of a process of disintegration (Slaughter 2002). However, this segregation of the state can essentially be seen as a reinforcement of its powers, for it allows the state to be even more present and influential, even in areas traditionally adverse to it. These developments do not accordingly lead to a multiplication of law-makers. They only show that, if a diversification is truly taking place, it is mostly *within* the state machinery.

In sum, the assertion that international law-making is turning more heterogeneous *ratione personae* because of the multiplication of non-state actors is not entirely convincing from an empirical perspective – and, hence, the concerns for the excessive role of non-states actors could be exaggerated (Bolton 2001).[33]

III. Non-State Actors in the International Legal Scholarship: An Invention?

The practice reported above shows that, from an empirical perspective, the law-making status of non-state actors remains significantly limited. Despite these glaring facts, it is central to the argument developed here to note that, on the whole, legal scholars have remained very amenable to the idea that non-state actors have become some sort of law-makers on the world stage. If one sticks to an empirical perspective, such a position proves exaggerated if not entirely illusory. It is accordingly the aim of this section to appraise the reasons of this common inclination of scholars. Before attempting to explain this leaning of legal scholars, it must nonetheless be repeated that the manner in which the practice is analysed

of trade negotiations or the United Nations Framework Convention on Climate Change (adopted 9 May 1992, entered into force 21 March 1994) 1771 UNTS 107).

32 See e.g., UNSC Res 1373 (28 September 2001) UN Doc S/RES/1373. On this issue, see generally S Talmon, 'The Security Council as World Legislature' (2005) 99 *American Journal of International Law* 175.

33 See also the opinion of Gilbert Guillaume, *Legality of the Threat or Use of Nuclear Weapons* (Advisory Opinion) [1996] ICJ Rep 266.

hinges to a large extent from one's understanding of the international legal system as a whole.

Legal scholars have been very prompt to see in some of the aforementioned developments the emergence of a new international law-making framework, within which non-state actors enjoy a fledging status of law-maker (Teubner 1997, Reisman 2000, Kamminga 2005). Others like Alan Boyle and Christine Chinkin remain slightly ambiguous on the characterization of the role of non-state actors: while recognizing that states do in any case retain the final word, they assert that 'it would be myopic to insist on the classical view of states as the sole makers of international law; rather we must recognize the multi-layered, multi-partite nature of the international law-making enterprise' (2007: 97). However, a substantial group of scholars, while acknowledging that contemporary law-making processes are still fundamentally state-centric, have come to the conclusion that granting a law-making status to non-state actors should be at least advocated and promoted (Arend 1999, Falk and Strauss 2000). To a lesser extent, it has also been defended that the behaviour of non-state actors should be taken into account for the sake of customary international law (Gunning 1991: 211), as is underpinned by the methodology used in the abovementioned study of the ICRC on the customary rules of international humanitarian law (Henckaerts 2005).[34] And even when legal scholars back away from this idea and stand by the daily reality of state-centrism, they remain somehow attracted by this image. Many international legal scholars thus prove, in one way or another, amenable to the idea of a law-making role of non-state actors (Thomas 1998).[35] It is therefore of great interest to embark on an examination of the reasons explaining why the heterogeneity *ratione personae* of international law-making constitutes such a powerful temptation.

There are probably many reasons underlying the abovementioned inclination of scholars. It would be too ambitious to strive to describe them all. Although such a choice condemns the argument developed here to offering only a partial explanation, this chapter will expound on what I see as the three main reasons explaining why legal scholars are so enticed to embrace the image of a heterogeneous and diverse international law-making.

I have argued elsewhere that the development of heterogeneous international legal *instruments* (especially through the idea of *soft* legal instruments) reflects an attempt by international legal scholars to redefine the 'rules of recognition' of the international legal system with a view to poaching new materials of study in areas

34 See the critique of (Boyle and Chinkin 2007, Bellinger and Haynes 2007). For a counter-reaction see (Henckaerts 2007).

35 It is also particularly well illustrated by the fact that we have witnessed the creation of a special law journal devoted to the question (*Non-State Actors and International Law* – published by Brill until 2005) or that of a book series initiated by Math Noortmann (*Non-State Actors in International Law, Politics and Governance*), which is published by Ashgate. Anne-Marie Slaughter is not far from recognizing such a law-making role for individuals (Slaughter 1997). See also (Beigzadeh 2008).

which are intrinsically outside the realm of international law and which would have originally fallen within the expertise of scholars of other disciplines (d'Aspremont 2008).[36] It is the aim of the following paragraphs to develop this argument further and to apply it to the idea of the heterogeneity of international law-making *as a whole*. More precisely, this section will try to demonstrate that the contemporary assertion that international law-making has become more heterogeneous is less the result of an actual practice than the outcome of an inclination of scholars to expand their material of study.[37]

While the aspiration for the import of new legal materials into the ambit of international legal scholarship can provide a rational explanation of the proneness of international scholars to depict international law-making processes as diverse and heterogeneous, it is not sufficient to explain all the underlying motives of such a leaning. It is submitted here that, in a few circumstances, the tendency to play down the state-centrism of international law-making processes and the magnification of their heterogeneity can also be traced back to a more general and fundamental endeavour of international legal scholars to convey a cosmopolitan vision of international law with a view to fostering the legitimacy of their object of study. The following observations also explain the attraction of scholars to these heterogeneous representations of international law-making as an attempt by international legal scholars to preserve the importance of their expertise and that of their discipline in areas where they have been subject to the competition of other social sciences.

Firstly, mention will be made of the need of scholars to find new legal materials and new objects of study for the sake of their own scholarship: (1). Secondly, it will be argued that these portrayals of international law-making as heterogeneous boil down to a means to preserve the relevance of the expertise of international legal scholars in fields where other disciplines have been overshadowing international legal scholarship (2). Ultimately, it will be explained that the representation of international law-making as heterogeneous conveys a cosmopolitan image of law-making processes, thereby reinforcing the legitimacy and the acceptance of the rules that are adopted therein (3).

There is little doubt that all the abovementioned reasons are intertwined as they all point to fostering the place and the role of international legal scholarship. Whether by providing new objects of studies, bolstering the relevance of international law or enhancing its legitimacy, all the tendencies examined below are directed at preserving the credibility of international legal scholarship. A few words will accordingly have to be said about why international legal scholars have felt the need to defend the place of international law and fight for its credibility (4).

36 For a different approach, see (Boyle and Chinkin 2007).

37 On the general tendency of academic lawyers to expand and extend changes, see (Dugard 2007).

IV. The Quest for an Expansion of the Objects of International Law

The introduction of non-state actors in the scheme of international law-making through their elevation to the status of lawmaker provides a great advantage in that it allows scholars to extend the limits of international law. Firstly, the law-making status granted to non-state actors enable scholars to create a new object of study as such. In that sense, the role of non-state actors itself becomes the object of scholarly examination. By including non-state actors in their representations of international law-making procedures, international scholars also increase the number of processes that can be deemed to yield international legal rules. In other words, by including non-state actors in the making of international law, they simply multiply the number of international law-making processes. This possibility ultimately allows them to stretch the limit of international law and to include non-legal materials into the scope of their study.

Leaving temporarily aside the question of whether this constitutes a *relevant* topic for a legal analysis, there is little doubt that the question of the role of non-state actors is a wide-ranging one, simply because there is a broad, rich, diverse and complicated practice. The inclusion of this complex practice in the fields that allegedly fall within the expertise of international legal scholars provides them with a spacious 'new' area of study. For those scholars that are interested in how law is made, the role of non-state actors thus becomes a new issue in the same vein as questions pertaining to treaty making or the formation of customary international law. But the benefit of granting non-state actors a law-making role for scholars interested in the procedural aspects of law-making is even greater than that. It not only makes the role of non-state actors a new object of study in itself, it also brings into the scope of legal scholarship new *processes* that would have classically been deemed alien to the making of international law. Indeed, once endowed with an international law-making role, non-state actors interacting with one another can be considered as involved in an international law-making process. This means that granting a formal law-making role to non-state actors can help transform non-legal processes into international law-making processes, which, in turn, can become new objects of study.

Awarding a law-making role to non-state actors is not solely tempting for legal scholars interested in the study of law-making. It can also benefit legal scholars interested in the substance of the law. Indeed, granting a law-making role to non-state actors not only leads to a transformation of non-legal processes into international law-making processes but also makes the *product* of these new law-making processes legally relevant. In that sense, it provides legal scholars with new 'legal' material that allegedly falls within the ambit of their expertise and the scope of their study. The argument of the heterogeneity of law-making processes is thus also a means to capture non-legal material and shroud them with the trappings of a legal object.

However it manifests itself, the general attempt to extant the scope of international law partly originates in an all-out enthusiasm for the 'international'

(Kennedy 1994: 136, Marks 2003: 146)· that is to say, an assumption that law is necessarily good. There is indeed a widespread proneness among lawyers to consider the development of law necessarily constitutes an improvement. Seen in this light, law is thus conceived as an essential condition of any systematized form of community (Fitzmaurice 1957, Abi-Saab 1987) and is construed as the only alternative in the *hobbesian* brutal state of nature.[38] Regulating new areas constitutes a step towards a greater integration of the community away from the anarchical state of nature. I have explained elsewhere that such a basic assumption is oversimplifying (d'Aspremont 2008). Many recent developments – like networks among governmental officials or transnational law (Jessup 1956, Slaughter 2002) – have shown that non-legal instruments may prove more adapted to the speed and the complexity of modern international relations and are more and more resorted to in practice (Klabbers 1996: 121). Non-legal instruments can be as integrative for a community as legal ones (Boyle and Chinkin 2007: 229).[39] This means that the use of non-legal *instrumentum* is not a sign of the disintegration of a community. It simply shows that the members of a community have found more practical and convenient means to regulate the relationships with one another. Be that as it may, the calling for international law is one of the reasons, which explains why legal scholars have sought to expand the limits of international law. The image of multi-layered law-making processes involving state and non-state actors has been one of the linchpins of this quest.

V. The Quest for the Continuous Relevance of International Legal Scholarship

While widening the field of international legal research and giving some cosmopolitan clothing to international law, a representation of contemporary international law-making as being diverse and heterogeneous can eventually help international legal scholars preserve their authority in an area where it has been jeopardized. Indeed, globalization has created normative spaces that are detached from all forms of state's grip (Alston 1997, Jouannet 2007: 395) for which legal categories have proven insufficient. This is especially true with respect to the substantive and factual influence of non-state actors, which legal scholars can hardly grasp and

38 Hobbes has traditionally been interpreted as having offered the best depictions of the international state of nature. See Hans Morgenthau (1948) for a classical realist interpretation of Hobbes and see Hedley Bull (1977) for a more subtle interpretation offered by the English School. On Grotius' appeal to Hedley Bull and the discrepancies between Grotius and Bull see (Kingsbury 1997). For a neo-Hobbesian account of international law, see more recently (d'Aspremont 2008).

39 Boyle and Chinkin (2007) rightly highlight that non-binding instruments do not have necessarily less weight than ungratified or poorly ratified treaties. As is argued here, this does not underpin in any manner the need for the concept of 'soft law'.

identify with formal legal concepts. This means that the expertise of international legal scholars does not extend beyond the formal and procedural role of non-state actors (Hollis 2005). In that sense, it is not certain that international legal scholars are well equipped to engage in the analysis of the factual and substantive role of non-state actors in international law-making. From the perspective of international law, non-state actors can only be mere 'participants' (Higgins 1999, Knop 2002), endowed with a few participatory rights (Chinkin 2001). The need to bring the 'participants' back in, as Math Noortmann argues in the previous chapter, is at least controversial. This means that, even though international legal scholars can probably contribute to clarify the 'formal' and 'procedural' roles of these non-state actors, their technical expertise is of little relevance as to the determination of the 'substantive' influence of non-state actors.

Against that backdrop, the idea of the heterogeneity of law-making processes can be seen as a means to alleviate the unease of international legal scholars towards their inability to gauge the substantive influence of non-state actors beyond their formal and procedural role. The idea of heterogeneous international law-making proves very useful in sustaining the belief that international legal scholars could engage in an analysis of this phenomenon despite the uncertainties pertaining to the relevance of their expertise in that area (Jouannet 2007: 854). In that sense, the idea of the heterogeneity of international law-making and the correlative law-making 'status' granted to non-state actors may seem to guarantee the relevance of the legal expertise and, hence, the authority of legal scholars for subject-matter where the usefulness of their role is anything but certain.

VI. The Quest for More Legitimacy: A Cosmopolitan Representation of International Law

It is contended here that the portrayal of international law-making as more heterogeneous than it actually is, also originates in the attempt of many legal scholars to *convey a more cosmopolitan image of international law*. This is especially true with respect to those authors that have tried to magnify the participation of individuals and NGOs in international law-making processes. This move rests on the assumption that those international law-making processes where states and international organizations have yielded to a greater role of individuals and NGOs would be more cosmopolitan and more democratic – to the extent that this latter concept is applicable to the global forms of governance (Weiler 2004). This attitude also draws upon the belief that regulations produced by such participatory processes would be seen as more legitimate as Cedric Ryngaert seems to argue in Chapter 4 (see also Anderson and Rieff 2005: 26). Even though it is far from certain that this assumption is empirically true,[40] it certainly constitutes one

40 For some general and critical remarks about the legitimacy of international law-making, see (Boyle and Chinkin 2007: 24–35).

of the reasons why international legal scholars are so enticed by the idea of the heterogeneity *ratione personae* of international law-making processes.

VII. A Need to Rehabilitate International Legal Scholarship in a Post-Westphalian World?

As has been explained, the three abovementioned reasons are interconnected, for they pertain to a more general strive to reaffirm and reinforce the place and the role of international legal scholarship, whether by providing new objects of studies, bolstering the relevance of international law or enhancing its legitimacy. This inevitably begs the question why international legal scholars have felt the urge to foster the role of their discipline.

To answer that question, it must be recalled that the twentieth century helped international law gain recognition as an autonomous and fully-fledged area of law. Before that, the idea that international law was only a set of moral principles was rife, even among positivist thinkers (Austin and Rumble 1995). Despite a brief revival in the aftermath of WWII, the realist critique also took a back seat and accordingly failed in its attempt to disqualify international law (Morgenthau 1948, Shimko 1992). As a result, international legal scholars felt emboldened and more confident in their discipline; a confidence, which was further, reinforced by the dramatic growth of international law in the second half of the twentieth century. The self-confidence of international legal scholars grew enough to keep the question of the theoretical foundations of international law at bay.

The all-out confidence of international legal scholars in the sustainability of the standards, on which their understanding of international law rests, nonetheless proved short-lived. The influence of structuralism and the Frankfurter School, which constituted to the breeding ground for critical approaches to law (Koskenniemi 2007), started to trickle in the legal scholarship, thereby shaking the foundations of the entire discipline and igniting a great unease among scholars. The simultaneous emergence of new phenomena – like the one examined here as well as the growing attention paid by other social science to international law – led international legal scholars to doubt about the sustainability of the classical model of international law. In particular, globalization began to compound international relations to an extent that has left spaces that are detached from all forms of state's intervention (Alston 1997, Jouannet 2007) and for which legal categories have proven insufficient. All in all, international legal scholars started to encountered a severe crisis of self-confidence, which has manifested itself in the unease described above and the – witting or unwitting – resort to the illusion that international law-making had been overhauled as to include non-state actors.

The present chapter has attempted to demonstrate that the crisis of self-confidence riddling international legal scholarship today is, to a significant extent, ill founded and unjustified. As is illustrated by the role played by non-state actors, there is no reason for legal scholars to doubt about the potential of their model.

The elementary standards of international law, subject to a few exceptions, still offer adequate instrument to apprehend contemporary developments. This does not mean that the current model is entirely satisfactory. There is a much-needed modernization. This is nonetheless not the first time that international law categories undergo some fine-tuning. On the contrary, it seems anything but abnormal that a regulatory language be occasionally updated. It is nonetheless important to realize that this necessary update of the current model is not one that requires an upheaval of the existing categories of law-makers. Legal scholars have accordingly many reasons to keep the faith in a model, which – because it is simple and mostly uncomplicated – has the capacity to accommodate the most complex phenomena of this new era. The contemporary increased involvement of non-state actors in international rule making is no exception to that.

VIII. Concluding Remarks: From Law-Makers to Law-Consumers

This chapter has tried to show that non-state actors, although endowed with a decisive influence in law-making processes, have remained at the periphery of international law-making processes. Only states and international organizations are actually entrusted with a law-making power in international law. Contemporary practice shows that the image of international law-making as including a multiplicity of actors is mostly an illusion. Despite strong empirical evidence, many scholars have been lured by this idea or have tried to promote it. This chapter has addressed three reasons explaining why international legal scholars are so inclined (or tempted) to defend the law-making status of non-state actors.

Although influential, non-state actors are thus not formal law-makers. It is argued here that they however are vivid *law-consumers*. Indeed, one cannot deny that non-state actors extensively resort to the discourse of international law on the international plane. They also invoke the law in their own interest or the interest of others. This requires that they be familiar with the subtleties of international regulatory instruments. For this reason, non-state actors too are advised by lawyers and legal experts. And it is probably because they are so well versed in the existing international legal rules that certain non-state actors prove so influential. In that sense, their status of great consumer of the law is closely intertwined with the influence that they wield in the international arena. Influence in international law-making processes and law-consumption go undoubtedly hand-in-hand.

Consuming the law rather than making the law? After all, it all boils down to a question of image. Indeed, whether as maker or consumer, non-state actors' existence in the international legal system is no longer disputed and it does not matter what their formal place in the system is as long as the latter can accommodate them. The rest simply is a matter of perspective.

References

Abi-Saab, G. 1987. *Cours général de droit international public*. Leiden: Brill.

Allott, P. 1998. Reconstituting Humanity – New International Law. *European Journal of International Law,* 3, 219–252.

Alston, P. 1997. The Myopia of Handmaidens, International Lawyers and Globalization. *European Journal of International Law*, 8, 435–448.

Anderson, K. 2000. The Ottawa Convention Banning Landmines, The Role of International Non-Governmental Organizations and the Idea of International Civil Society. *European Journal of International Law*, 111, 91–120.

Anderson, K. and Rieff, D. 2005. Global Civil Society, A Skeptical View, in *Global Civil Society*, edited by H. Anheier, M. Glasius and M. Kaldor. London: Sage, 26–39.

Andreopoulos, G.J. and Kabasakal Arat, Z.F. 2006. *Non-State Actors in the Human Rights Universe*. Bloomfield, CT: Kumarian Press, Inc.

Arend, C. 1999. *Legal Rules and International Society*. Oxford: Oxford University Press.

Arts, B., Noortmann, M. and Reinalda, B. (eds). 2001. *Non-State Actors in International Law, Politics and Governance. Non-State Actors in International Relations*. Aldershot: Ashgate.

Austin, J. and Rumble, W.E. 1995. *The Province of Jurisprudence Determined.* Cambridge and New York: Cambridge University Press.

Barile, G. 1979. Caractère du Comité International de la Croix Rouge. *Rivista Diritto Internazionale* 62, 111–119.

Beigzadeh, E. 2008. L'évolution du Droit International Public, in *Regards d'une Génération sur le Droit International Public*, edited by E. Jouannet and H. Ruiz-Fabri. Paris: Pédone.

Bellinger, J.B. and Haynes, W.J. 2007. A US Government Response to the International Committee of the Red Cross's Customary International Humanitarian Law Study. *International Legal Materials*. 46, 514.

Bennet, A. 2005. *The Geneva Convention, The Hidden Origins of the Red Cross*. Sutton: Stroud.

Bolton, J. 2001. Should We Take Global Governance Seriously? *Chicago Journal of International Law* 1, 205–223.

Bourne, C.B. 1999. The International Law Association's Contribution to International Water Resources Law, in *International Law Association Rules on International Water Resources,* edited by S. Bogdanovic. London, Kluwer.

Boyer, R. and Drache, D. 1996. *States Against Markets, The Limits of Globalization*. London and New York: Routledge.

Boyle, A.E. and Chinkin, C.M. 2007. *The Making of International Law*. Oxford and New York: Oxford University Press.

Bull, H. 1977. *The Anarchical Society; A Study of World Order in World Politics*. Houndsmills: Palgrave.

Cameron, M., Lawson, R. et al. (eds). 1998. *To Walk Without Fear, The Global Movement to Ban Landmines*. Toronto: Oxford University Press.

Cattaneo, S. and Parker, S. 2008. *Implementing the United Nations Programme of Action on Small Arms and Light Weapons, Analysis of National Reports Submitted by States from 2002–2008*. Geneva: Nations Institute for Disarmament Research.

Charnovitz, S. 1997. Two Centuries of Participation, NGOs and International Governance. *Michingan Journal of International Law,* 18, 183–286.

Chinkin, C.M. 2001. Human Rights and the Politics of Representation: Is there a Role for International Law?, in *The Role of Law in International Politics; Essays in International Relations and International Law*, edited by M. Byers. Oxford: Oxford University Press.

Clapham, A. 2006. *Human Rights Obligations of Non-State Actors*. Oxford and New York: Oxford University Press.

Codding, G.A. 1952. *The International Telecommunication Union; An Experiment in International Cooperation*. Leiden: E.J. Brill.

Coleman, J. 2001. Incorporationism, Conventionality and the Practical Difference Thesis, in *Hart's Postscript, Essays to the Postscript to the Concept of Law,* edited by J. Coleman. Oxford: Oxford University Press, 99–148.

Craig, P. 1998. *Lawmaking in the European Union.* The Hague: Kluwer Law International.

Crawford, J. 1997. The International Law Association from 1873 to the Present. *Uniform Law Review*, 2, 68–86.

d'Aspremont, J. 2008. The Inhumanity of International Law. *Journal of Intervention and State-Building,* 2, 107–110.

d'Aspremont, J. 2008. International Law in Asia, The Limits to the Western Constitutionalist and Liberal Doctrines, in *Asian Yearbook of International Law*, edited by B.S. Chimni, K.S. Sik, M. Masahiro, M.C.W. Pinto and S.P. Subedi. Leiden: Brill, 89–111.

d'Aspremont, J. 2008. Softness in International Law, A Self-Serving Quest for New Legal Materials. *European Journal of International Law,* 19, 1,075–1,093.

d'Aspremont, J. 2009. The Doctrinal Illusion of the Heterogeneity of International Lawmaking Processes, in Proceedings of the ESIUL Biannual Conference, edited by R. Wolfrum, Oxford: Hart Publishing.

d'Aspremont, J. 2009. Hart and Postmodern Positivism in International Law. *Revue Générale De Droit International Public*, 113, 635–654.

Danilenko, G.M. 1993. *Law-Making in the International Community*. Dordrecht and Boston: M. Nijhoff.

De Schutter, O. 2006. The Challenge of Imposing Human Rights Norms on Corporate Actors, in *Transnational Corporations and Human Rights*, edited by O. De Schutter. Oxford: Hart Publishers, 1–39.

De Wet, E. 2006. The Emergence of International and Regional Value Systems as a Manifestation of the Emerging International Constitutional Order. *Leiden Journal of International Law*, 193, 611–632.

De Wet, E. 2006. The International Constitutional Order. *International and Comparative Law Quarterly*, 55, 51–76.

Delbrück, J., Heinz, U.E. et al. 1997. New Trends in International Lawmaking, International Legislation in the Public Interest, in *Proceedings of an International Symposium of the Kiel Walther-Schücking-Institute of International Law, March 6 to 8, 1996*. Berlin: Duncker & Humblot.

Dominicé, D. 1984. La Personnalité Juridique Internationale du CICR, in *Studies and Essays on International Humanitarian Law and Red Cross Principles in Honour of Jean Pictet*, edited by D. Swinarski. The Hague-Geneva: Nijhoff-ICRC, 663–673.

Dominicé, D. 1996. La Personnalité Juridique dans le Système du Droit des Gens, in *Theory of International Law at the Threshold of the 21st Century, Essays in Honor of K. Skubiszewski*, edited by J. Makarczyk. The Hague: Kluwer.

Dugard, J. 2007. The Future of International Law, a Human Rights Perspective – With Some Comments on the Leiden School of International Law. *Leiden Journal of International Law*, 20, 729–739.

Dupuy, P.M. 2005. Some Reflections on Contemporary International Law and the Appeal to Universal Values, A Response to Martti Koskenniemi. *European Journal of International Law*, 161, 131–137.

Evans, G. and Sahnoun, M. 2001. *The Responsibility to Protect*. New York, Report of the International Commission on Intervention and State Sovereignty, Vol. I. New York.

Falk, R. 1995. Casting the Spell, The New Haven School of International Law. *Yale Law Journal,* 104, 1991–2008.

Falk, R. and Strauss, A. 2000. On the Creation of a Global Peoples Assembly, Legitimacy and the Power of Popular Sovereignty. *Stanford Journal of International Law*, 36, 191–220.

Fitzmaurice, G.G. 1957. *The General Principles of International Law Considered from the Standpoint of the Rule of Law*. Leiden: Brill.

Fitzmaurice, G.G. 1958. Some Problems Regarding the Formal Sources of International Law, in *Symbolae Verzijl*. Martinus Nijhoff: The Hague, 153–170.

Franck, T.M. 1995. *Fairness in International Law and Institutions*. Oxford and New York: Oxford University Press and Clarendon Press.

Franck, T.M. 1999. *The Empowered Self, Law and Society in the Age of Individualism*. Oxford and New York: Oxford University Press.

Gowlland-Debbas, V. and Tehindrazanarivelo, D.L. 2004. *National Implementation of United Nations Sanctions, A Comparative Study*. Leiden and Boston: M. Nijhoff Publishers – Brill.

Green, F. 2008. Fragmentation in Two Dimensions, the ICJ's Flawed Approach to Non-State Actors and International Legal Personality. *Melbourne Journal of International Law*, 9, 47–77.

Gunning, I. 1991. Modernizing Customary International Law, The Challenge of Human Rights. *Virginia Journal of International Law,* 31, 211–247.

Hart, H.L.A. 1997. *The Concept of Law.* Oxford: Oxford University Press.

Heere, W.P. (ed.) 2003. *From Government to Governance – The Growing Impact of Non-State Actors on the International and European Legal System.* Den Haag: T.M.C. Asser Press.

Held, D. 1995. *Democracy and the Global Order, from the Modern State to Cosmopolitan Governance.* Stanford: Stanford University Press.

Henckaerts, J.-M. 2005. Study on Customary International Humanitarian Law, A Contribution to the Understanding and Respect for the Rule of Law in Armed Conflict. *International Review of the Red Cross*, 87, 175–212.

Higgins, R. 1999. International Law in a Changing International System. *Cambridge Law Journal*, 581, 78–95.

Higgott, R.A., Underhill, G.R.D. et al. (eds). 2000. *Non-State Actors and Authority in the Global System.* London: Routledge.

Hollis, D.B. 2005. Why State Consent Still Matters – Non-State Actors, Treaties, and the Changing Sources of International Law. *Berkeley Journal of International Law,* 23, 137–174.

Hudson, M.O. 1943. *The Permanent Court of International Justice, 1920–1942, A Treatise.* New York: MacMillan.

Indonesia. Badan Pengendalian Dampak Lingkungan. Wilayah Denpasar. 1998. *Indonesia, BAPEDAL Wilayah Denpasar Institutional Strengthening Project, Project Design Document.* Denpasar: BAPEDAL Wilayah Denpasar.

Jenks, C.W. 1937. The Significance for International Law of the Tripartite Character of the International Labour Organization. *Transactions of the Grotius Society,* 22, 45–47.

Jessup, P.C. 1956. *Transnational Law.* New Haven: Yale University Press.

Jouannet, E. 2006. French and American Perspectives on International Law, Legal Cultures and International Law. *Maine Law Review*, 582, 291–336.

Jouannet, E. 2007. Universalism and Imperialism, The True-False Paradox of International Law. *European Journal of International Law*, 18, 379–407.

Jouannet, E. 2007. What is the Use of International Law? International Law as a 21st Century Guardian of Welfare. *Michigan Journal of International Law,* 28, 815–862.

Kammerhofer, J. 2009. Kelsen – Which Kelsen? A Reapplication of the Pure Theory to International Law. *Leiden Journal of International Law*, 22, 225–249.

Kamminga, M.T. 2005. The Evolving Status of NGOs under International Law, A Threat to the Inter-State System?, in *Non-State Actors and Human Rights*, edited by P. Alston. Oxford and New York: Oxford University Press.

Kennedy, D. 1994. A New World Order, Yesterday, Today, And Tomorrow. *Transnational Law and Contemporary Problems*, 4, 329–375.

Kingsbury, B. 1997–1998. A Grotian Tradition of Theory and Practice? Grotius, Law and Moral Skepticism in the Thought of Hedley Bull. *Quinnipac Law Review,* 17, 3–33.

Kingsbury, B. and Krisch, N. 2006. Global Governance as Administration – National and Transnational Approaches to Global Administrative Law. *European Journal of International Law,* 17, 1–13.
Klabbers, J. 1996. *The Concept of Treaty in International Law*. The Hague: Kluwer.
Knop, K. 2002. *Diversity and Self-Determination in International Law*. Cambridge and New York: Cambridge University Press.
Koskenniemi, M. 2007. The Fate of Public International Law, Between Technique and Politics. *Modern Law Review*, 701, 1–30.
Krisch, N. 2006. The Pluralism of Global Administrative Law. *European Journal of International Law,* 17, 247–278.
Kunugi, T. and Schweitz, M. 1999. *Codes of Conduct for Partnership in Governance, Texts and Commentaries.* Montreal and Tokyo: United Nations University.
Lasswell, H.D. and McDougal, M.S. 1992. *Jurisprudence for a Free Society*. New Haven and Dordrecht: New Haven Press and Martinus Nijhoff Publishers.
Marks, S. 2003. *The Riddle of All Constitutions*. Oxford: Oxford University Press.
Merle, M. 2005. Article 71. La Charte des Nations Unies, in *Commentaire Article par Article*, edited by J.P. Cot, A. Pellet and M. Forteau. Paris: Economica.
Meron, T. 2006. *The Humanization of International Law*. Leiden and Boston: Martinus Nijhoff.
Meyers, P. 1914. Representation in Public International Organs. *American Journal of International Law*, 8, 81–108.
Morgenthau, H.J. 1948. *Politics Among Nations*. New York: Alfred A. Knopf, Inc.
Mosler, H. 1982. *The International Society as a Community*. Alphen aan den Rijn: Sijthoff & Noordhoff.
Noortmann, M. 2003. Who Really Needs Article 71? A Critical Approach to the Relationship between NGOs and the UN, in *From Government to Governance; the Growing Impact of Non-State Actors on the International and European Legal System,* edited by W. Heere. The Hague: Martinus Nijhoff Publishers, 320–328.
Oppenheim, L. 1995 *International Law*. Vol. 1, 8th Edition. London: Longmans.
Patterson, D.M. and Afilalo, A. 2008. *The New Global Trading Order, The Evolving State and the Future of Trade.* Cambridge and New York: Cambridge University Press.
Peters, A. 2006. Compensatory Constitutionalism; The Function and Potential of Fundamental International Norms and Structures. *Leiden Journal of International Law*, 19, 579–610.
Price Cohen, C. 1990. The Role of Non-Governmental Organizations in the Drafting of the Convention on the Rights of the Child. *Human Rights Quarterly*, 12, 137–147.

Raimondo, F.O. 2008. *General Principles of Law in the Decisions of International Criminal Courts and Tribunals*. Brill: The Hague.

Raz, J. 1979. *The Authority of Law*. Oxford: Oxford University Press.

Raz, J. (ed.) 1994. *Ethics in the Public Domain, Essays in the Morality of Law and Politics*. Oxford: Oxford University Press.

Reinisch, A. 2005. The Changing International Legal Framework for Dealing with Non-State Actors, in *Non-State Actors and Human Rights*, edited by P. Alston. Oxford and New York: Oxford University Press.

Reisman, M. 2000. Unilateral Action and the Transformation of the World Constitutive Process; The Special Problem of Humanitarian Intervention. *European Journal of International Law,* 11, 3–18.

Rosenne, S. (ed.) 2001. *The Hague Peace Conferences of 1899 and 1907 and International Arbitration, Reports and Documents.* The Hague: T.M.C. Asser Press.

Shimko, K.L. 1992. Realism, Neorealism and American Liberalism. *The Review of Politics*, 54, 281–301.

Simma, B. 1994. *From Bilateralism to Community Interest in International Law*. Leiden: Brill-Martinus Nijhof.

Simma, B. and Paulus, A. 1998. The International Community, Facing the Challenge of Globalization. *European Journal of International Law*, 3, 266–277.

Slaughter, A.-M. 1994. The Liberal Agenda for Peace, International Law in a World of Liberal States. *Transnational Law and Contemporary Problems,* 4, 377–419.

Slaughter, A.-M. 1995. International Law in a World of Liberal States. *European Journal of International Law*, 6, 503–538.

Slaughter, A.-M. 1997. A Real New World Order. *Foreign Affairs*, 76, 183–197.

Slaughter, A.-M. 2000. A Liberal Theory of International Law. *American Society of International Law Proceedings*, 94, 240–253.

Slaughter, A.-M. 2002–2003. Global Government Networks, Global Information Agencies, And Disaggregated Democracy. *Michigan Journal of International Law*, 24, 1,041–1,075.

Slaughter, A.-M. 2004. *A New World Order*. Princeton: Princeton University Press.

Stahn, C. 2007. Responsibility to Protect, Political Rhetoric or Emerging Legal Norm. *American Journal of International Law*, 101, 99–120.

Teubner, G. 1997. Global Bukowina, Legal Pluralism in the World Society, in *Global Law Without a State*, edited by G. Teubner. Aldershot: Dartmouth, 3–28.

Thomas, C. 1998. International Financial Institutions and Social and Economic Rights, An Exploration, in *Human Rights Fifty Years On, A Reappraisal*, edited by T. Evans. Manchester: Manchester University Press, 161–185.

Tomuschat, C. 1999. *International Law, Ensuring the Survival of Mankind on the Eve of a New Century, General Course on Public International Law*. Leiden: Brill-Martinus Nijhoff.

Trebilcock, M.J. and Howse, R. 1999. *The Regulation of International Trade*. London: Routledge.

Van den Bossche, 2008. NGO Involvement in the WTO, A Comparative Perspective. *Journal of International Economic Law*, 11, 717–749.

van Genugten, W.J.M. 2006. *The United Nations of the Future, Globalization with a Human Face*. Amsterdam, KIT-Publishers.

Weil, P. 1992. *Le Droit International en Quête de son Identité, cours général de Droit International Public*. Leiden: Brill.

Weiler, J.H.H. 2004. The Geology of International Law – Governance, Democracy and Legitimacy. *Zeitschrift für ausländisches öffentliches Recht und Völkerrecht*, 64, 547–562.

Weiss, T.G. and Gordenker, L. (eds). 1996. *NGOs, The UN, And Global Governance*. Providence: Brown University Press.

Wolfrum, R. and Röben, V. 2005. *Developments of International Law in Treaty Making*. Berlin; New York: Springer.

Zimmern, A. 1939. *The League of Nations and the Rule of Law 1918–1935*. London: MacMillan.

Chapter 9

Non-State Actors: Law-Takers or Law-Makers? Is That the Question?

Math Noortmann and Cedric Ryngaert

Indeed, one could argue that the question could have been raised centuries ago when the Dutch and British West and East Indies Companies (Van Ittersum 2006, de Roever 2002) assumed a political and legal status that could be compared to the sovereigns which flags they were flying. The question could equally have been raised just a few decades ago, when multinational companies were considered to determine the laws and politics of developing countries (Kokkini-Iatridou and de Waart 1983, Charney 1983, Hymer 1976). Moreover, it can be said that non-state actors are not necessarily either law-takers or law-makers; like states, non-state actors, in particular multinational companies could be both.

With the exception of intergovernmental organizations and – nowadays to a lesser extent – with liberation movements, multinational companies are considered one of the proto-types of non-state actors; the type that in organization, power and status comes most close to the features of modern states. The numerous socio-political debates and academic discourses on multinational companies, not only demonstrate the contentious position of MNCs in the global arena, but also the complexity of their legal status and political position. Leyla Davarnejad's and Peter Muchlinski's contributions to this publication can only lead the reader to one conclusion: multinational companies at the same time regulate and are being regulated. If the international law-making process is indeed increasingly less exclusive, we are not only confronted, with the practical questions of accommodating new participants in the law-making process, by redesigning procedures and institutions. Above all, we must accommodate new forms of law-making at a global level, which is increasingly multileveled and multilayered.

Does that imply that we have to make choices between governmental and non-governmental forms of regulation; policy measures and legal measures; hard and soft regulation, alter regulation or self-regulation? Considering the ongoing violation of human rights, the enduring degradation of the global environment and the continuing exploitation of less developed communities, empirical evidence indicates that neither governmental, nor intergovernmental or non-governmental initiatives are in themselves sufficient to overcome those issue. According to Leyla Davarnejad, both 'state and non-state actors are invaluable for the realization of

CSR standards'[1], but she also argues that these 'contributions' are actor-specific and their 'roles are not interchangeable.' She implicitly agrees with Jean d'Aspremont, who voices a sceptical opinion on the non-state actor boom among international legal scholarship. To d'Aspremont empirical relevance does not equal conceptual or theoretical relevance. The transformation of non-state actors from the empirical to the theoretical and conceptual requires what d'Aspremont calls an international legal scholarly 'invention';[2] an invention to help international legal scholarship to expand the inherent limits of their discipline. Indeed, the demonstrated (political) influence of non-state actors on international law-making, does in itself not justify a paradigmatic upgrading of non-state actors to a law-making category. If, according to d'Aspremont, non-state actors are first of all law 'consumers', they are no more the producers of law as the consumers of material goods are not necessarily the producers of those material goods.

Whether we consider non-state actors law-takers or law-makers, or law-consumers or law producers, in doing so we maintain a dichotomy between two different kind of involvements in the legal process, a differentiation which according to Peter Muchlinski is not that obvious, as the law is not one homogeneous set of rules. The law creates different sets of obligations and rights for different actors/stakeholders. Different actors (even within the corporate community) will seek to soften their (quasi) legal obligations and harden their (quasi) legal rights or in case these rights and obligations are directed towards other: harden obligations and soften rights as the case might be. The dynamic complexity of the different involvement of non-state actors in norm creation becomes clear if we investigate the relationship between connected rights and obligations in terms of hard and soft as Davarneyad and Muchlinski did.[3] How can this dynamic normative complexity be translated into the fiction called legal personality?

Where d'Aspremont observes a scholarly trend to 'invent' an international law that included non-state actors, Muchlinski stresses the 'Positivist Restriction'.[4] Were international legal personality is only 'incidental to the inquiry of d'Aspremont, the lack of legal personality, that is to say, the legal 'invisibility of MNE is considered fundamental to the position of those NSA in international law according to Muchlinski. However, in terms of the practical consequences, Muchlinski argues that the interest of MNE can be served without explicit recognition of legal personality, because the latter concept is a 'functional' and 'fluid' one.[5] Those qualifications of 'legal personality' however cannot mask the fundamental character of the 'subjects of international law' discourse and the paradigmatic position of 'legal personality', in international law as both Janne Nijman and Noemi Gal-Or point out.

---

1 p. 60.

2 p. 180.

3 See Part One, Chapters 3 and 2 respectively.

4 p. 10.

5 p. 196.

Both authors agree that the traditional concept of legal personality in international law is in some need of revision. While Nijman argues to 'revisit the realist theory' and to reconsider a 'social grounding' of the general concept of legal personality,[6] Gal-Or argues more in particular to 'further enhancing the NSA's personality'.[7] Both authors, however, come to the same conclusion: the legal personality of non-state actors can not be accommodated by creating a new exclusive single category of legal personality. Non-state actors are too diverse, even within such broad classifications as MNE and NGOs, to construct one exclusive legal concept of personality. One seize does not fit all in the case of non-state actors.

The question as to which form of legal personality should be granted to which NSAs, can be answered on the basis of different theoretical and practical perspectives, but cannot be exclusively confined to the discourse on non state actors. Whether one departs from the traditional state centred doctrine of international legal personality, which is based on the dual capacities of law creation and enforcement and the possession of rights and duties, or one develops a catalogue of 'real' capacities, which is then translated into a variety of different forms of international legal personality, including both full, partial and rejected subjects of international law, one cannot ignore the state in either revising international legal personality or enhancing the status of NSA.

The notion of 'capacity' prominently recurs as an idea to measure power, influence and indeed legal status of actors. According to Davarnejad, MNEs '*capacity* to bring about change in the policies and practices of governments and IGOs is limited'.[8] Muchlinski, however, warns not to 'confuse[s] the reality of MNE power and influence with legal *capacity*'.[9] Indeed, the translation of socio-political capacity into a legal capacity is a tricky one unless again one adheres to the view that the legal personality of the state is unquestionable and that loss of political capacity does not effect the qualification of its legal personality as full; *that is to say,* the concept of international legal personality is only, fluid, functional, partible and limited with respect to non-state actors. Can it be said that 'the extent of ILP reached will not parallel that of the state' as Noemi Gall-Or opines,[10] or must we agree with the 'realist' approach of Janne Nijman that '*any* [italics MN and CR) international actor with *factual* (social, economic and political) power … should have *legal* visibility … effectively formalized through the tool of "international legal personality".'[11] An *a contrario* reasoning, must lead us to conclude that any international actor without that factual power should not have legal visibility. Does this equally apply to failed

6 See Chapter 5.
7 p. 145.
8 p. 60.
9 p. 13.
10 p. 86.
11 p. 119.

states and states, which are tutored and protected by the United Nations? In both cases power is fictitious rather than factual.

Unlike the concept of legal personality in national law, the international law concept of legal personality has always been closely linked to capacity of law-making. In accordance with the notion that international legal personality comes in varieties, depending on the status and/or capacity of the actor in question, the law-making capacity could equally be perceived as one that is functional and fluid. In order to differentiate between various forms of law-making, however, we must (1) engage different theoretical and conceptual perceptions of law-making and (2) differentiate between the process of law-making, that is to say, the political process of influencing the legislative procedure and its statutory outcomes and the procedure of law-making, that is to say, the formal role that non-state actors may perform in procedures leading to the determination of the law.

In its traditional form, the international legal system does neither theoretically nor conceptually include non-state actors in its law-making procedures. Adhering to this formal determination, must logically lead to the conclusion that 'it is on the process of *influencing* state policy and state practice, and the agendas of intergovernmental organizations, in relation to corporate interests that the law-making function of firms is to be seen' as Peter Muchlinski argues. [12] The question than raises, according to Cedric Ryngaert whether 'the accountability, transparency and predictability of international law-making' is 'served' by this political process of influencing and its various forms of open and concealed lobbying and advocacy.[13] If law-making is taken as a process rather then a procedure, all those involved could be denominated as 'participants' rather than actors as argued by Math Noortmann in line with the New Haven School and work of Boyle and Chinkin.[14] The distinction between law-making as a process and law-making as a procedure, however, is a formal one, which does not necessarily contributes the a more legitimate transparent or predictable outcome. According to Cedric Ryngaert, it is at the same time 'premature and probably undesirable to lay down general principles' for the involvement of non-state actors in law-making processes and procedures, notwithstanding the normative desirability of non-state actor involvement. However, it is equally unwise according to the same author to 'resist the tide of democratization of international law-making.'[15]

One way of capturing that 'tide' is to perceive law-making at the global level as a institutional complexity, which incorporates both political processes as well as legal procedures. Law-making is generally understood to include both the debate on as well the passing of the law. Both debate and considerations concerning a specific international legislative text are neither confined to the final session of the conference, nor are debate and considerations captured by the final text.

12 p. 10.
13 p. 75.
14 p. 161 et. seq.
15 p. 81.

It is not without reason that we include the *travaux préparatoires*, context, and subsequent practice and opinions in our interpretative efforts. These elements of treaty interpretation, can be found within and across all levels of government, both below and above the state, including a variety of institutions both state as well as non-state. Crucial to any investigation on the role *and* position of non-state actors in international law is the – in many cases – rhetorical question whether we should or must translate this empirical fact into a legal fact. As pointed out repeatedly in this publication, the conversion of an empirical fact into a judicial fact, for example the conversion of a real person into a legal person, or the conversion of political practice and opinion into legal practice and opinion, requires more than mere observation; it requires the judicial confirmation of that observation. The question than is whether, to put it in the words of Peter Muchlinski, we can 'brush aside' the fact that MNEs, civil society groups and NGOs, and other non-governmental groups, are contesting the content of international legal agendas [...] as if the only element in the law-making process is inter-state diplomacy and state practice.' Indeed, it seems 'absurd as suggesting that we can understand national law just by reading statutes and cases. This is the scholarship of the past.'[16]

However, it is precisely that 'scholarship of the past' that determines the direction of the development of international law, both in socio-political as well as judicial terms. On the one hand we witness an ongoing expansion of international legislation (criminal, economic, environmental, humanitarian) that directly and indirectly impacts the lives and livelihoods of individuals and the movement of non-state entities, but on the other hand, we preserve a traditional system of international law-making, which excludes substantial and procedural involvement of others than (inter)governmental actors. We do so by implicitly adhering to the mainstream theoretical perception of international law, which is both state centred in terms of actor involvement and positivistic in terms of procedural formalities. The conversion of politically relevant actors into judicially relevant actors not only requires a combined reconsideration of our theoretical understanding of international law and our practices of international law.

While we might all observe and agree upon the growing involvement of non-state actors in the international realm in quantitative terms we also differ in the assessment of the (qualitative) consequences of that involvement. Cedric Ryngaert, for example maintains that from a 'Habermasian deliberative or discursive democracy theory, there is no such thing as 'original subjects' who have the prerogative of pulling the strings of participation in international law-making.'[17] To Leyla Davarnejad, however, 'States and IGOs are still the legitimate public authority and [...] and principle actor.'[18] Peter Muchlinski is not quite so sure. He concludes that 'MNEs act [...] as informal 'law-makers' in the system

16 p. 14.
17 p. 86.
18 p. 61.

of international investment law.'[19] Noemi Gal-Or as indicated above, concludes that 'in any event, the extent of ILP reached [by NSAs] will not parallel that of the state',[20] while Janne Nijman's 'capacity approach' suggests a theoretical possibility that states and non-state actors may acquire a similar for of international legal personality depending on their contextual socio-political and economic standing.[21]

The different conclusions do not only resemble the differences in empirical study and observation, but also our outlooks on the international legal system. Indeed, Jean d'Aspremont's question as to 'what international legal system' we are talking about is a crucial one.[22] Jean d'Aspremont and Math Noortmann answer this question differently. While d'Aspremont opines that scholarly perceptions and constructions of non-state actors are to 'a very large extent dependent upon their own understanding of international law as a whole', Noortmann argues the opposite in the sense that our understanding of international *as a whole* law depends on our perception and construction of the world as a whole and of the perception of role and status of non-state actors in particular. Only if we perceive international law and international law-making from the perspective of non-state actors can that legal system be understood and explained as a 'transnational' one or as 'a process of decision-making'. The perceptions of those who are looking out from the international legal system's inside or those who are looking in from the international legal system's outside is mainly differ as to the normative consequences for international law, that is to say, should international law formally recognize the new role that non-state actors have come to play in the international arena and the new statuses many of them have acquired. The question whether states and non-state actors are inherently different and should therefore be conceptually treated different continuous to permeate the NSA discourses, as is also reflected in some of the contributions to this publication. Since non-state actors 'promote particular interests' they 'might therefore be biased [and] their contribution should primarily be regarded as policymaking and not as law' argues Leyla Davarnejad. It is a popular argument among international legal students and difficult to overcome given the idea that states represent the public interests in the international legal arena. But the argument has its flaws (Noortmann 2006).

A question that has not been explicitly raised in this publication, but that perhaps should be raised as a basis for future research on non-state actors in international law is whether the formalization of the participation of non-state actors in international law-making and other international legal processes and procedures would enhance the quality of overall and specific processes and procedures of international decision making. Would a Convention on the Prohibition of the Use, Stockpiling, Production and Transfer of Anti-Personnel Mines and on their

19 p. 34.

20 p. 86.

21 Chapter 5.

22 p. 172.

Destruction be more successful if non-state users of land-mines would be Parties to the treaty? Would conventions on the transfer and proliferation of small arms and light weapons be more successful of small arms producers would be parties to the treaties? Would treaties in general be more effective if stakeholders and interested actors would have a formal vote on their final texts?

These questions are of course not limited to law-making, but would equally apply to other forms and instances of international decision-making, such as dispute settlement, fact-finding, implementation and enforcement.

A research-agenda (Noortmann 2002) that would increasingly differentiate between different actors, both state as well as non-state in terms of capacity or estimated socio-economic and political influence and that would investigate the role and position of particular actors in specific procedures and processes in different legal and political contexts is needed to overcome the traditional and formalized dichotomy between states and non-state actors. Like international legal personality, law-making and law-taking come in degrees of significance: full, limited, partial, specific and so forth and its is these different degrees of significance that we must capture and subject to more specific (case) studies.

There is increasingly little additional value in seeking to qualify or disqualify non-state actors as a whole in terms of international law. The indiscriminate category of 'non-state actors' is too diverse to gain significance in the complex normative processes of international law and politics. There is beyond any doubt a general non-state actor dynamic in international law. Does that means that all non-state actors have or should be endowed with a form of international legal personality or law-making capacity? Of course not. Does that mean that we have to consider an enhancement of legal personality for some non-state actors and more clearly differentiate between forms of legal personality based on capacity rather then status? Or does that mean that we have to discuss and perhaps reconceptualize the relationship between law-making processes and law-making procedures, *that is to say*, between the politics and the practices of international law? Of course!

In presenting seven different approaches and opinions on the question whether non-state actors in international law are changing from law-takers to law-makers, this edited volume reflects the dynamics of the discourse on non-state actors inn international law and the general dynamics in the normative complexity of the world community. All authors agreed on a common interdisciplinary understanding that 'non-state actors do matter' (Arts 2003, Noortmann, Arts and Reinalda 2001, Pietilä and Vickers 1994), but were at variance as to the degree and consequences of the 'mattering'. The question as to whether non-state actors matter in international law-making should be more refined: who matters when, where and how in international law-making? Answering that question we would probably validate some non-state actors as law-makers, but unmask a great many others as not being law-makers, both in the political as well as legal terms.

References

Arts, B. 2003. *Non-State Actors in Global Governance, Three Faces of Power.* Bonn: Max Planck Gesellschaft.

Charney, J.I. 1983. Transnational Corporations and Developing Public International Law. *Duke Law Journal*, 1983, 748–788.

Hymer, S. 1976. *The International Operations of National Firms: A Study of Direct Foreign Investment.* Cambridge, Mass.: MIT Press.

Kokkini-Iatridou, D. and Waart de, P.J.I.M. 1983. Foreign Investments in Developing Countries; Legal personality of Multinationals in International Law, *Netherlands Yearbook of International Law,* 14, 87–131.

Noortmann, M. 2002. Globalisation, Global Governance and Non-State Actors: Researching Beyond the State. *International Law FORUM du droit international*, 4(1), 5.

Noortmann, M., Arts, B. and Reinalda, B. 2001. Non-State Actors in International Relations: Do They Matter?, in *Non-State Actors in International Relations*, edited by B. Arts, M. Noortmann and B. Reinalda. Aldershot: Ashgate.

Pietilä, H. and Vickers, J. 1994. *Making Women Matter: The Role of the United Nations*. London: Zed Books.

Roever de, A. 2002. *Jacht op Sandelhout.* Zutphen: Walburg Pers.

Van Ittersum, M.J. 2006. *Profit and Principle: Hugo Grotius, Natural Rights Theories and the Rise of Dutch Power in the East Indies, 1595–1615.* Leiden and Boston: Brill.

Index